CURLEW MOON

MARY COLWELL

CURLEW
MOON

ILLUSTRATED BY JESSICA HOLM

WILLIAM
COLLINS

William Collins
An imprint of HarperCollins*Publishers*
1 London Bridge Street
London SE1 9GF
WilliamCollinsBooks.com

First published in the United Kingdom by William Collins in 2018

23 22 21 20 19 18
11 10 9 8 7 6 5 4 3 2 1

Printed and bound in Great Britain by
CPI Group (UK) Ltd, Croydon

MIX
Paper from
responsible sources
FSC™ C007454

Curlew Moon is dedicated to my two sons, Dom and Greg, who were bemused by the idea of walking 500 miles for curlews, but actually think it's quite cool.

Contents

Contents

Chapter 1

WHAT IS A CURLEW?

There is a wildlife spectacle that can transport the soul to a place of yearning and beauty, to an experience that has inspired generations of thinkers and dreamers. Imagine, if you will, a blustery cold day in December. Bitterly cold. A bird stands alone on the edge of a mudflat, some distance from where you are standing. Its silhouette is unmistakable. A plump body sits atop stilty legs. The long neck arcs into a small head, which tapers further into an extended, curved bill. The smooth, convex outlines of this curlew are alluring. They touch some ancestral attraction we all have for shapes that are round and sleek. The curved curlew's outline is anomalous in this planar landscape, but its colour blends well. The mud is gunmetal grey, the bird brown and the water murky. The sky is dull with a hint of drab. The air is tangy with the smells of decay.

Occasionally the bird wanders a short distance and probes the mud with its beak, sometimes digging it in and twisting it around a little. Every now and then it pulls something clear of the surface, throws back its head and swallows. It is most likely a worm or shellfish, which is consumed without a fight. There is no showiness or drama, no prey is torn apart with dagger-like talons or razor beaks, it is just take a step, probe, suck; take a step, probe, eat – and repeat. It is absorbing to watch in its rhythmic motions. Icy gusts tease the bird's feathers; at times, the curlew looks like it might be blown off its thin legs, but walk on it does, interrogating the mud beneath its feet.

Observing this self-reliant being in the distance can feel like an act of endurance. The wind is coming straight off the sea, cold and peevish. It finds every buttonhole and cuff, intent on extracting warmth. On this raw day, standing still is not pleasant. It is tempting to move closer, but despite all our inventiveness we have nothing that negotiates deep, cloying mud. Certainly not boots. Besides, curlews are nervous. If you cross an invisible line a few hundred metres away they will take off, crying in alarm. Best to stay in one spot, pressed to the binoculars, and tough it out. In the distance, the water stretches away and merges with the sky – grey into grey. The curlew is safe from unwanted encroachments in this shifting, liminal world.

Besides the admiration that you feel that something so insubstantial can withstand the rigours of this unforgiving landscape, you may not be particularly awe-inspired. You might decide it is time to get back in the car and go home, but stay with it – something magical is about to happen.

Alan McClure, in the first verse of 'Schrödinger's Curlew', asks the same question. Why keep on watching the curlew visible through his window?

> On the face of it, there isn't much about this bird
> To stop me in my tracks.
> Brown, oblivious, busy with the ground
> It totters along on stilted legs
> Probing among the frozen fields.[1]

He does keep watching, though, and so will we. There is no sound, apart from the wind over mudflats. Wilderness has its own quality of silence, an ancient, unchanging quiet. And suddenly, for no obvious reason, the curlew takes flight. Its long legs and pointed wings launch it into the air. It soars along the horizon. Its outline resembles a miniature Concorde, purposeful and strong. But it is not the sight that is astonishing, it is the sound. The air is cleaved by a piercing, soul-aching cry – 'curlee, curlee' – that spreads over land and water. It is at once sweet and painful to hear, following Norman MacCaig's description in his poem, 'Curlew':

> Music as desolate, as beautiful
> as your loved places,
> mountainy marshes and glistening mudflats
> by the stealthy sea.[2]

The pauses between the calls are as poignant as the cries themselves; they define the silence and fill it with expectation and emotion. Given a religious turn of mind, you could almost describe it as a benediction. It is as though the winterscape has been blessed.

'Schrödinger's Curlew' also ends with an epiphany:

> And then, untouched by my musings
> The bird spreads its wings and lifts,
> Naming itself, with a long, pure note
>
> And my heart, in two states,
> Leaps
> and breaks.[3]

If you haven't done so before, you have now met the bird named after a sliver of the moon and the taut curve of an archer's bow, *Numenius arquata*, an everyday sprite, otherwise known as the Eurasian Curlew. At once magical and down-to-earth, this bird is a mysterious prober of dung and earth, mud and meadow.

Both parts of its name – *Numenius* and *arquata* – refer to its most conspicuous, long curved bill. *Numenius* is the Latinised version of two Greek words, *neos* for new and *mene* for moon, that thin shaving of light that is full of potential. *Arquata* is Latin for the archer's bow; taut and stretched into a smooth arc. *Numenius arquata*, then, is the new-moon, bow-beaked bird.

Eurasian Curlews are Europe's largest wading bird. The body is about the size of a mallard duck, but with much longer legs to hold it clear of the water. The small head, supported by a stretchy neck, terminates in that astonishing sickle-shaped bill. They are predominantly brown and grey, but when in flight, the white rump and underside flash against the sky. Eurasian Curlews are found across the European continent, from the west of Ireland through to Siberia; there are thought to be around one million birds in all, but that is only a best guess. Many areas they occupy are remote and difficult to access, so we know surprisingly little about this common European bird.

In the winter, curlews are distributed widely along the coastlines of northwest Europe, the Mediterranean, Africa, the Middle East, India and Southeast Asia. They form large flocks that can be thousands strong, feeding and roosting together. In the UK, winter numbers of curlews swell to

150,000, boosted by the arrival of northern European birds, their own homes having become too frozen for these probers of mud. We are truly fortunate, one might say honoured, to have so many marvels around our shores to lift the winter months. They mingle with our own native birds that stay all year round. That figure is put at an overly optimistic 66,000 pairs. Curlews that breed in the north of England and Scotland tend to winter around northern estuaries like the Dee or Moray Firth. Southern-breeding birds go to The Wash in East Anglia, the Severn estuary and to the rocky shores and inlets of southwest England, Wales and Ireland. Some go further, to the warmth of southern Europe.

Come early spring, the coast empties as the European birds go back to the continent and the British and Irish ones head inland to breed on moors, peat bogs, rough pasture, damp, lowland flower-rich meadows and even silage fields. In simple scrapes on the ground, they lay three or four olive-green and brown mottled eggs, which the parents take turns to incubate. As Britain and Ireland are home to 25 per cent of breeding Eurasian Curlews, these islands are vitally important for their future.

Spending time watching curlews, whatever the season, is to observe a spectacle, but not in an arresting, adrenaline-pumping way. It is more of an inner experience, at the level of the soul, where the ordinary and everyday becomes extraordinary. And it is as much an experience of sound as of vision, of mind and heart.

That long bill is the most recognisable feature. It is unmissable. Three times the length of the head, up to 15 centimetres long in females, though slightly shorter in males, and curving gently downwards. It is both elegant and surprising. The pleasing arc removes from it any association with daggers and spikes; it is unthreatening, sculptural even. Psychologists tell us that roundness and smoothness trigger associations with health and youthfulness, like strong muscle against taut skin. A curlew's bill is something that you might like to hold and run your fingers over.

The curve is there for a reason. With this arcuate tool, curlews can probe deep into sediment and explore the complex tunnels and pathways made by buried worms and shellfish far more easily than a straight bill would allow. Straight-billed wading birds, like godwits and oystercatchers, rapidly jab into the sediment and take their prey by surprise. Curlews do it differently; they plunge deep and

use the bulbous, sensitive tip to feel around. The nerve-filled end of the bill opens independently, the tips acting like a pair of remote-controlled tweezers. This is made possible by joints in the skull which can push the upper bill forwards so that it can act alone. With its finger-tip sensitivity it is remarkably good at detecting deeply buried food. It is also ideal for poking around in the surface nooks and crannies of a rocky shore. The length allows access to food out of reach to those less endowed in the bill department.

Curves have their disadvantages, though. Structurally, they are weaker than straight bills and have to be strengthened by internal struts and thickenings. The reinforcements narrow the internal passage so that a curlew's tongue can't reach down to the tip to help extract and swallow buried food. It has to withdraw its bill and then move the food to the tongue by jerking its head. Big prey, such as crabs, are winkled from their hiding places and tossed around, often violently, before being swallowed. You can see curlews shaking them so hard their legs fall off (the crab's legs, not the curlew's) before they are moved to the top of the bill and down the gullet.

The prominence of the bill has, inevitably, set our imaginations whirring. In some areas, a local name for curlews is whaup, partly referring to the sound of one of its calls, but also because it evoked folk memories of those half-human, malevolent little people that plagued generations gone by. A whaup was an evil, long-nosed, thin-necked goblin that ran around the roofs of houses at night. They were notoriously mischievous and spread rumours and bad

luck. 'A whaup in the nest' refers to some brewing unpleas-
antness, or the hatching of evil plans. A Scottish
Highlander's prayer asks to be protected from 'witches,
warlocks and long-nebbed (nosed) things'. The curlew
became synonymous with these negative notions and in
some places it became a bird to be feared. A long bill, finely
tuned by evolution for feeding in muddy environments,
must also, it seems, give rise to unfortunate connections
with our complex, cultural world.

A curlew's bill may be the feature that catches our eye,
but when it opens and starts broadcasting, it is the sound
that captures our soul. The experience of hearing the call
of the curlew is, for me, akin to what C.S. Lewis described
as being 'surprised by joy'. For Lewis, joy is not merely
happiness, it is far deeper and unfathomable. He describes
it as an unexpected, centuries-old upwelling of longing and
desire that has somehow always been there but has
remained unnamed. It is usually fleeting, overwhelming,
always complicated, always layered. It has associations
with memories that we can never quite define. 'All Joy
reminds,' says Lewis. 'It is never a possession, always a
desire for something longer ago or further away or still
'about to be.'[4] The late Terry Pratchett, in *A Hat Full of Sky*,
had an earthier turn of phrase: 'Joy is to fun what the deep
sea is to a puddle. A feeling inside that can hardly be
contained.' This is the surprising joy evoked by the varied
calls of the curlew, whether it is the bubbling mating song
tumbling in cadences from a summer sky, or the simpler,
arrowed sound of its name, firing across the reaches of a
mudflat in winter. Pure, unmitigated joy.

Curlews are highly vocal and have something to say in most situations. Their calls range from harsh barking and yelping to growling and soft, low whistles – and much else in between. They have specific sounds to communicate with developing chicks inside the egg, to call their mate to warn of danger, to scare away predators and to mark their territory. The signature call, the one from which the bird gets its name, is *coorli* or *curlee*, which is often heard as the bird takes flight over moorland and estuary. 'Lancing their voices/through the skin of this light',[5] as Ted Hughes described this soul-aching cry that lingers in the air long after the bird has flown. If you imagine the shape of the call as a word, it is also curved. The ending of curlee rises in tone, similar to the pen-stroke flourish of a flamboyant scribe. Both the call of the curlew and its bill are curlicued.

But perhaps the most haunting song is a melody that can lighten even the most desolate of days – the bubbling call, most often heard in the breeding season. It is a gradually building trail of notes that rises up through the scale, sounding louder and ever more urgent as the bird flies skywards. As the call ends, the curlew then swoops through the air on stiffened wings. One anonymous poet described it as:

> A crescendo of
> sound bubbles
> bursting in cadences
> of liquid joy.

The cry bursts forth from the bird's lungs through its binary voice box – two tubes that work in harmony to produce a richness of tone that intertwines both the major and minor keys, confusing our emotions. The bubbling call is ecstatic, both full of life but with deeply melancholic undertones. 'Such trifling themes as life and death are kept in Curlew's calls ...' wrote A.W. Bullen in his poem 'Curlews'. 'If my voice could be anything like theirs ... if only ... I would swallow my share of lugworms to know their truths ...'

Lord Edward Grey, ornithologist and politician, found a sense of calm and hope in the music of the new moon bird:

> Of all bird songs or sounds known to me there is none
> that I would prefer than the spring notes of the
> Curlew ... The notes do not sound passionate, they
> suggest peace, rest, healing joy, an assurance of
> happiness past, present and to come. To listen to
> Curlews on a bright, clear April day, with the fullness
> of spring still in anticipation, is one of the best
> experiences that a lover of birds can have.[6]

For many, to hear a curlew is to listen to the wild. It is music that crystallises the range of emotions that well to the surface when standing on a lonely moor or walking through a spring meadow. Like adding seasoning to a dish, their calls add highlights or depth to the landscape. You might hear the 'sweet crystalline cry' recorded by W.B. Yeats, or perhaps the more melancholic 'lingering, threadbare cry' noted by another Irish poet, Thomas Kinsella.

Alfred, Lord Tennyson only heard bleakness and described calling curlews as 'Dreary gleams about the moorland flying over Locksley Hall.' You may, though, feel happiness and hear Ted Hughes' 'wobbling water-call' and smile.

Curlews are shape-shifting sprites that tease and tangle our emotions. Their evocative cries are aural keys that unlock our secret thoughts, and have inspired poets, artists, writers and musicians from time immemorial – and still do. This is perhaps all the more remarkable, given that their appearance is relatively unprepossessing. Looking past their beak, their colouring is less than striking. From a distance, they may even seem a little dowdy. But as with many works of art, the true beauty is discovered in the detail. At close quarters, the intricate patterning of brown, grey and cream feathers is exquisite, shimmering with the rippling tide or merging into the bright colours of a flower-filled meadow. Rain, cloud or sun bestow different characteristics. But to see the loveliness in curlews requires more than a passing glance.

G.K. Chesterton understood that what can appear dull on the surface often belies a shifting palette. When challenged about the drabness of grey as a colour, he asks us to consider an English village on a dull day. To some it may seem boring, but watch a while and it is a wealth of charm. 'Clouds and colours of every varied dawn and eve are perpetually touching it and turning it from clay to gold, or from gold to ivory … The little hamlets of the warm grey stone have a geniality which is not achieved by all the artistic scarlet of the suburbs.' This can only be seen by taking enough time to absorb the ever-changing delights. So too with curlews; to watch them in rain or sunshine, at dawn or dusk, is to see a restless beauty adorning a muddy marsh.

While many creative juices have flowed at the sight and sound of curlews, many gastric ones have, too. Being the UK's largest wading bird, they have provided flesh for the pot for centuries. It is illegal to hunt them now, but before they were protected by the Wildlife and Countryside Act of 1981, it was said that the best time of year to eat them was soon after the breeding season. Weeks of feeding on insects and berries was thought to make their flesh sweet. According to one old Cornish recipe, this was the ideal time to make curlew pie, which required mincing up two birds with onions. Eaten later in the year, warned the chef, their flesh would be rank with the flavour of mud and shellfish, and will need more herbs to disguise the taste.

Winston Graham, the writer of the *Poldark* series, also refers to curlew pie being served in a pub in his novel *The Loving Cup: A Novel of Cornwall 1813–1815*. A seven-teenth-century Lincolnshire proverb puts a price on them, and they weren't cheap: 'Be she lean or be she fat, a curlew has twelve pence on her back.' Some versions change lean and fat to white or black, as it was thought the plumage of curlews darkens in the summer, though I have never found other references to this.

In *Feast Day Cookbook*, written by Katherine Burton and Helmut Ripperger, published in 1951, a Christmas Day pie extravaganza is described from the days of old, but no exact date is specified:

It is said to have contained, besides the crust, the
following: four geese, three rabbits, four wild ducks,
two woodcocks, six snipe, four partridges, two curlews,
six pigeons, seven blackbirds; and it was served on a
cart built especially to hold it!

The narrator of the medieval narrative poem 'Piers
Plowman', written by William Langland at the end of the
fourteenth century, says of the curlew that it is 'a bird
whose flesh is the finest'. Curlews also put in an appearance in *The Forme of Cury*, one of the oldest-known manu-
scripts on the art of cooking in the English language. It is
believed to have been written in the late fourteenth
century by the head chefs of Richard II (1377–99). It is a
scroll made of calfskin containing 196 recipes. The word
'cury' is the Middle English word for 'cookery', and the
recipes are full of exotic spices, Mediterranean delicacies
and creatures we would not dream of serving today, such
as whales, seals, porpoises and cranes.

By the fifteenth century, public feasts had taken on
monstrous proportions, and curlews were part of the
steamed, roasted and boiled menagerie that were used to
display social standing. This is an account of the feast for
2,500 people made to celebrate the enthronement of
George Neville as Archbishop of York in 1465:

They consumed 4000 pigeons and 4000 crays, 2000
chickens, 204 cranes, 104 peacocks, 100 dozen quails,
400 swans, 400 herons, 113 oxen, 6 wild bulls, 608
pikes and bream, 12 porpoises and seals, 1000 sheep,

304 calves, 2000 pigs, 1000 capons, 400 plovers, 200 dozen of the birds called 'rees', 4000 mallards and teals, 204 kids, 204 bitterns, 200 pheasants, 500 partridges, 400 woodcocks, 100 curlews, 1000 egrets, over 500 stags, bucks and roes, 4000 cold and 1500 hot venison pies, 4000 dishes of jelly, 4000 baked tarts, 2000 hot custards with a proportionate quantity of bread, sugared delicacies and cakes. 300 tuns of ale were drunk, and 100 tuns of wine, a tun containing 252 gallons according to the usual reckoning.

According to *The Booke of Goode Cookry Very Necessary for all such As Delight Therein* (1584), the correct way to roast a curlew is to put its legs behind the body, cut off the wings and wind the neck so that the bill rests on the breast. Others suggest 'letting the heads hang over the pot for show'.

In the seventeenth century, curlews baked in a pie, and also roasted, were served to King James I, and a few decades later, at the end of the century, they appear in a cookbook by Hannah Woolley, instructing servants in the correct terminology for 'the curious art' of carving different birds.

In cutting up small birds it is proper to say thigh them, as thigh that Woodcock, thigh that Pigeon: but as to others say, mince that Plover, wing that Quail, and wing that Partridge, allay that Pheasant, untach that Curlew, unjoint that Bittern, disfigure that Peacock, display that Crane, dismember that Heron, unbrace that Mallard, frust that Chicken, spoil that Hen, sawce

that Capon, lift that Swan, reer that Goose, tire that
Egg.

It is a testament to their former abundance that many a
curlew will have come untached. In some areas, their eggs
were also collected and served alongside the meat up until
the middle of the twentieth century. Alas, that vision of a
plethora of new moon birds gracing the land from the tip
of Scotland to the moors of Cornwall, from Kerry to
Norfolk, is a distant memory.

Over the last thirty years, numbers of curlews have
declined on average by 20 per cent across the European
continent, but that figure is misleading for the UK and
Ireland, where losses are much higher. In their most western reaches in the Irish Republic there is nothing short of
a disaster unfolding before our eyes. In the 1980s there
were many thousands of pairs of nesting curlews, but today
only around 120 remain. The official population for the
UK is 66,000 breeding pairs, although my personal opinion
is that this is optimistic and the real figure is much lower,
maybe less than half that number. In Northern Ireland, for
example, there has been a decline from 5,000 to 250 pairs
since the 80s. The Welsh population has fallen by over 80
per cent and is now thought to be fewer than 400 breeding
pairs. England and Scotland have lost around 60 per cent
of breeding curlews in the last twenty years. So alarming
are the figures that curlews were made a species of highest
conservation concern in the UK in December 2015, and
put onto the red list of threatened species by the
International Union for Conservation of Nature (IUCN),

the worldwide union of conservation bodies that monitors the status of animals and plants throughout the globe. They are now in the same category as jaguars, 'near threatened', indicating that extinction is likely in the future.

The reasons for such dramatic declines across the board are many and varied. Farming methods, the spread of forestry, the drainage of uplands to create pasture for sheep and cows and predation of their eggs and chicks have all taken their toll, but despite the great losses not everyone has noticed they are disappearing. Curlews suffer from a problem specific to them: a distortion of our perception. The winter curlew population of 150,000, boosted by birds from Scandinavia and Finland, means that between September and February large congregations of curlews can be seen around the coast. The arrival of these continental birds gives the impression of curlew-abundance and that all is well. Come early spring, however, when the large flocks disperse, many fly back to northern Europe to breed, leaving our residents scattered increasingly thinly across Ireland and the UK.

There is no escaping the fact that curlews are failing to thrive and breed in the UK and Ireland. Year after year their numbers fall, and few of those that remain are managing to breed successfully in an increasingly hostile landscape. With precious few youngsters surviving to take the place of the older birds, the trajectory is resolutely downhill.

The transition of curlews to high conservation status in December 2015 was the trigger for me to follow them more closely. It was then that the idea of a 500-mile journey on foot began to crystallise and became a concrete plan. This would be no aimless wander but a pilgrimage, an inner and outer journey that has a goal. It would follow a definite line across the countries at the far western edge of the range of the Eurasian Curlew, a path that, as far as I could discern, was unique. Walking was by far the best way for me to track these increasingly elusive birds; it allows time to connect with the landscape and feel its character, something that cannot be achieved in a car. I would start in the early spring when birds were first arriving on their breeding grounds in the west of Ireland, then continue through the heart of Ireland to Dublin. I would then sail to Wales, arriving as incubation was well under way. After travelling through Wales I would arrive in England to coincide with the first hatching of chicks. Six weeks after setting out, I would finish on the East Anglian coast as the fledglings were beginning to try out their wings. Here I would mark the place where many curlews would come to spend the winter.

This would be a journey of many layers. A geographical one from west to east through the variety of landscapes that range across Ireland and the UK, places that are at once familiar and yet still mysterious. I wanted to see where the birds are surviving, but also experience their absence from the fields that no longer host their songs. It would be a walk through a year in the life of curlews. I would watch them displaying to their mates, soaring on fresh winds over fields just emerging from winter, and then I would search for their hidden nests in meadows and on moorland. If I was lucky, I would see their young, all feet and feathers and beady eyes. This would also be an artistic journey to explore the many connections that curlews have to poetry, literature, art and music, both in the past and today. But, most of all, I wanted to really understand what it is that is edging them closer to extinction, the environmental problems that are so huge that we are in real danger of losing them as a breeding bird across Ireland and the UK.

All this I decided at the start of 2016, when curlews were still on winter-cold estuaries and coasts. This is when they are easiest to see, gathered together for safety on mudflats, beaches or wet coastal grasslands. It would be a chance to think about the walk ahead, surrounded by the birds that mean so much to me. The nineteenth-century poet Helen Maria Williams wrote in her poem, 'To the Curlew':

> Soothed by the murmurs of the sea-beat shore,
> His dun-grey plumage floating to the gale,
> The Curlew blends his melancholy wail,
> With those hoarse sounds the rushing waters
>   pour.

And so I started the year where the walk would end – on the east coast of England.

Chapter 2

BEGINNING AT THE END

The rain barely stopped falling throughout the winter that saw a wet 2015 turn into a soaking 2016. That December was the warmest and wettest ever recorded for the UK. By early January, large swathes of northern England were underwater. Thousands of people were soaked in misery, made worse by the filibustering of politicians. Further south and east, Norfolk was, thankfully, not so badly affected, but it was still drizzly and the ground sodden. This area is famous for its water. Once a giant wetland, it was drained in the seventeenth century to turn large swathes of it into more productive farmland. Now, ramrod rows of poplar and Leylandii puncture the horizon, and deep, straight dykes define the edges of large fields. They seem to stretch as far as the eye can see. Much of the land is below sea level, in some places by nearly three metres. It can be disconcerting to contemplate that the low wall along the coast seems to be all that stops the North Sea piling in on top of you.

The north Norfolk coast is separated from southern Lincolnshire by The Wash, over 15 well-defined square miles of shallow sea and tidal mudflat. Four rivers – the Whitham, the Welland, the Nene and the Great Ouse – flow into the North Sea here, depositing tonnes of sediment. When the tide is out this vast expanse of worm-filled, shellfish-rich mud forms one of the most important feeding areas for waterbirds in Europe. In winter, it is filled with avian life from all over the continent – 350,000 birds at any one time, and as many as 9,000 curlews.

As soon as I arrive in Norfolk I head for one small section of The Wash, the RSPB nature reserve in Snettisham, on the coast. The whole day has been mild and damp, everything about it redolent of wet, musty sacks. By mid-afternoon, the light is already losing its sharpness, slipping into that unsettling, crepuscular zone between thin winter light and cold darkness. In mid-winter this comes so early in the day it feels like theft.

Through binoculars, shapes reveal themselves to be a 'herd' of around thirty curlews. Herd is one of the collective nouns, and is not a bad description, as winter flocks generally move together and take flight as a group. The other collective is a near homograph: a curfew of curlews, possibly relating to their gathering at dusk.

Like sewing machines stitching the sky to the Earth with invisible threads, the curlews prod the ground and generally move in the same direction. They form a fragile alliance. Though focused on finding food, their nervousness is palpable. Perhaps being watched stirs some ancestral memory of being legal quarry in England before 1981, when they were regularly shot on their wintering grounds. Birdwatchers say that they are noticeably more tense in areas where they were once hunted, and Norfolk is one such place. Some call softly, a whistling sound that floats over the damp air, soothing to the ear and a balm for the soul.

My small camera is balanced on a fence post to keep it steady at maximum zoom. The picture is boring, the birds are too far away, but the sound alone fills the screen. But as I press the ON button, right on cue, the throaty rumble of a microlight edges into the soundscape and rapidly becomes a roar. Within seconds it drowns out the music of the field. The giant petrol-powered set of wings takes an age to move along. If only the creators of the combustion engine could have made it sound like a wind harp or grand piano, maybe even a xylophone. Anything would be preferable to this grating, intrusive drone that fills the sky for what seems like hours.

In any case, the moment is lost. The curlews take flight, piping as they make their way towards the sea. And perhaps the microlight isn't entirely to blame; it is just as likely the birds can feel the shifting tide in every cell of their bodies and register the failing light as a signal to move on to a safer place for the night. I pack up and follow them.

Mud and ankle-deep puddles form the narrow path to the shingle ridge that overlooks the vast expanse of shimmering tidal flats. It offers up a strange and beautiful sight. Channels of water meander across the exposed mud, silvery sinews on a dark surface, at times taking on the sheen of mother of pearl. There seems no end to the mud; it stretches on and on towards the darkening horizon, rippled and ruffled by the water, strangely enticing and mysterious. Even the thousands of birds here are dwarfed by the vastness of the estuary. The air is filled with bird calls and a caustic, rich smell. The curlews are out there somewhere, a part of this mighty throng, big and small.

Bulky shelduck patrol the surface of the mud like avian minesweepers, their distinctive upturned bills swishing to and fro, scooping up tiny molluscs. Pink-footed geese stream in from feeding in fields: an airborne, honking choir. Neurotic redshanks strut and fuss, then take fright at the slightest disturbance, sailing into the air, emitting their high-pitched wails. The 'Sentinel of the Marshes' they are called, the first to warn of danger; red-legged bird versions of Lance Corporal Jack Jones in *Dad's Army* – 'Don't panic!'

The real star of The Wash winter show is the knot. Thousands of small brown and white waders seem to be held together by magnets. They rise as one, twisting and

spiralling through the sky, like a creature in agony. The display confounds predators and mesmerises humans.

The sea creeps closer, pushing the birds towards the shore. They bunch together like commuters on a constantly dwindling platform. On days when the tide is very high, they can run out of space completely and tens of thousands take to the air and stream inland. You can find yourself standing beneath an aerial river of birds. It is one of the greatest wildlife spectacles that Britain has to offer. But today there is only a middling tide, and the birds stay on the seaward side of the wall.

Just a handful of us birdwatchers are dotted along the shore, each alone with our own thoughts, bathed in evening light and surround sound of calling waterfowl. I am imagining how different this will all seem in six months' time, at the end of May. I will arrive on this eastern coast footsore and tired after six weeks on the road. There will be greenery and leafy trees, warm air and the hum of insects. The sun still high in the sky. There will also be far fewer birds. All being well, curlews should still be on their breeding grounds and guarding their growing families. If they manage to hatch young they will be kept busy until late summer. If not, if they fail to find a suitable nesting site, or if predators eat their eggs and chicks, they will already be gathering into small flocks, preparing for winter once more. The pattern of previous years doesn't bode well. For most curlews in large parts of Britain and Ireland, far too many will, yet again, gain the depressing title of 'failed breeders' and arrive back on the coast way ahead of time. They will have lost the chance to produce young once more. The world is an increasingly uncertain place for them, as it is for many other birds.

All over the Earth the great pendulum of bird life swings to and fro in time to the beat of the seasons. Some migrants are well studied, but others are only just revealing their secrets as different kinds of tracking devices are developed and become smaller, lighter and more reliable. Hopefully, we will learn more about curlews in the future. It is amazing how little we know about their lives, particularly considering they were once so numerous and widespread. The everyday rarely gets the attention it deserves, until, that is, it becomes increasingly hard to find.

Organic farmer, naturalist and former wildlife camera-woman, Rebecca Hosking, described to me on Facebook her experience of catching a glimpse of winter curlew in Devon:

The north winds blew a pair of curlew to the farm this morning. Their unmistakable calls rooted me to the spot, as I watched them spiral downward to feed in one of the lower meadows. To me, their cry is the essence of wildness, both haunting and beguiling. I was astonished at the level of emotion those bubbling trills invoked. Pure joy and excitement, for this was the first time I've ever heard them at Modbury. Yet that joy soon turned to sorrow and lament, knowing how drastic their decline has been. My knee-jerk reaction was to run and find Dad so he too could hear. As we stood in the garden listening, the pair lifted back to the sky, calling their plaintive, lonely 'cour-leees' as they circled overhead. I looked across at Dad to see his reaction; his eyes were beginning to well, 'I haven't heard that bird in this valley in over 40 years,' he said. We watched them slowly reel their way towards the coast, until they flew out of sight.

A fifth of Europe's curlews visit the coasts and estuaries of the UK and Ireland in the winter, a number that is steadily declining. It is an awesome responsibility to hold the fate of these world travellers in our hands. Although most of the birds are unstudied, there are some hotspots for

research, and The Wash Wader Ringing Group has been busy fitting identification rings onto the legs of curlews for decades. It has amassed some interesting results. Most of The Wash curlews breed in Scandinavia, France and Germany; only 25 per cent are British birds that stay all year round. Some visitors travel a long way. One curlew ringed in The Wash in September 2000 was shot in Russia the following May, over 2,000 miles away. It was fifteen years old. Surprisingly, this is only middle-aged. A bird caught in Lincolnshire in 2015 was twenty-nine, nearly matching the record for longevity which goes to one found dead in the Wirral in 2011 at the grand old age of thirty-two.

Thankfully, more projects are getting under way to understand the lives of these wonderful birds. In the weeks leading up to my walk I wanted to find out more about winter curlews, and so in early February I made my way to the northeast coast of Scotland, to the Moray Firth, where I had been told interesting things were happening.

I arrive to bright sunshine and a clear blue sky. A period of glorious winter weather is gracing eastern Scotland. After a few hours of searching, Bob Swann and I find curlews roosting on Bunchrew Bay, near Inverness, on the Beauly Firth. Bob is a retired teacher, wiry and strong, passionate about nature and with an encyclopaedic knowledge about sea birds in particular. He is a legend in the world of Scottish bird ringing, and along with others in the Highland Ringing Group, has contributed immeasurably to our understanding of bird life. I couldn't be in better company.

The Moray Firth is another important wintering site for many species of wading birds. Numbers in excess of 36,000 spend the winter in and around its many inlets and lochs. Dunlin, redshank, golden plover, lapwing, ringed plover, sanderling, purple sandpiper and knot join curlew here, many coming over from Scandinavia. The Highland Ringing Group has been monitoring numbers and fitting identification rings onto the legs of curlews for many years. The results show that all of the curlews wintering in the Moray Firth are either Scottish or Scandinavian birds. Overall, there are more males than females (58 per cent male to 42 per cent female), and some specific sites are predominantly male. Very few juveniles have been ringed, only 4 per cent, indicating that either they roost elsewhere or, far more worryingly, there are very few around to ring. Over the years birds have either been spotted or re-caught in the same places. The Scottish curlews – and it seems to be the same everywhere – are very much creatures of habit, returning year on year to the same places.

A simple identification ring fitted onto a bird's leg is one way of getting information about an individual, but as technology advances we are able to resolve mysteries about their lives – which was impossible before this digital, data-streaming age. For example, as tracking technology gets smaller and lighter, we can now vicariously tag along on the journeys they make throughout the year. On 31 March 2009 Bob was part of a team that caught a female curlew at Bunchrew Bay and fixed a satellite transmitter to feathers on her back. It is rather cumbersome-looking with a long antenna attached to a small black box (a couple of centimetres squared), but it is light and only in place for a few months since it falls off when the feathers moult in the autumn. As the bird was caught at the end of March, the suspicion was that this was a Scandinavian female. We know that curlews breeding in northern Europe remain on their Scottish wintering grounds longer than local birds, waiting for milder weather to melt the frozen northern lands. By the middle of March, British birds are already on the hills, preparing to nest.

Once she set off, the transmitter sent back data every few days over the spring and summer. Technology now allowed the Highland Ringing Group to track one bird's annual migration through data streamed to a computer screen.

The female left Scotland in mid-April and flew over the middle of Norway, passing through a gap in the mountains. After a few days' rest in Sweden, on the Gulf of Bothnia, the data then showed a flight across to Finland. For fifty-three days she was stationary, long enough to nest and raise young. The return trip to Scotland took a different route via the southern tip of Norway, before crossing over the North Sea to arrive north of Aberdeen by 1 July. Eventually, by 5 July, the female arrived back where she started, on the Beauly Firth.[1] Thus we have a circular migration, not a straight line back and forth, showing that curlews depend on vast areas to support them through the year and all these places are important for their survival. It's interesting that the satellite transmitter confirmed that this curlew was away from Scotland for no more than three months of the year, highlighting that the birds we call 'northern European' are actually spending three-quarters of their time in the UK. Protecting wintering areas around our shores is therefore just as important as safeguarding their nesting sites.

The project provided an insight into the year of just one curlew, so plans have been drawn up to expand the database. The next phase, which I was here to see, involved catching many more curlews and fixing smaller, cheaper devices, called geolocators, to the rings on their legs. These marvels of technology collect data and store it onboard the locator, rather than constantly streaming it back to a computer. Geolocators record light levels so that sunrise and sunset can be worked out and the birds' positions identified. Cheap and less cumbersome, for sure, but in order to retrieve the data the same birds have to be recaptured later in the year and the geolocator removed, although, as curlews are so site-faithful, that is not such a tall order as it sounds.

The first step involves catching lots of curlews. If you are not *au fait* with cannon netting, and just happen to come across it in action, you might think something heinous is going on. It involves laying explosives, creeping about in the dark, setting off very loud bangs and trapping frightened birds under nets, but it is all for a good cause.

The proposed curlew catch on Bunchrew Bay requires preparation. A long net, with two firing cannons attached to the ends, is buried in the beach where the curlews are known to roost overnight. The detonator is hidden in bushes and attached to the cannons by long cables. When the birds are standing peacefully, the explosives will be detonated and the net will shoot into the air and over their heads, trapping them underneath. They will then be put into holding pens and the geolocators attached.

After a few hours of lugging and digging, everything is set for the next morning.

I leave the guesthouse before dawn; a hard frost covers cars and pavements. Scotland glistens under the streetlights as I drive to meet Bob and his ringing colleagues by the beach. Most of the group, like Bob, are retired, field-fit, passionate bird lovers. The birds are exactly where we hoped they would be, so if all goes well, we'll have a large catch. Bob, with walky-talky and binoculars, creeps to the far side of the beach and into the bush with the detonator. The rest of us move quietly to the other side to hide in a small patch of woodland. As Bob sends updates about the birds' position, we sort out who can run the fastest. Once the cannons have been fired, speed will be essential. The quickest sprinters will leave the bags and equipment with the slower ones, then race ahead to retrieve the birds from under the net. The birds would be panicking, so getting them to the safety of the holding pens is vital. This is where I feel I can contribute. Having run a few half-marathons, and being a keen gym-goer and jogger, I confidently put myself forward to go with the advance party. After what seems like an age of whispering and walky-talky instructions, Bob counts down. Five, four, three, two, one – FIRE! An enormous bang shatters the early morning air, followed immediately by alarm-calling birds. RUN! I race off at full speed. My fellow sprinters streak ahead so fast Mo Farah would struggle to keep up. I arrive only just ahead of the 'slower' group, who have had to transport all the bags. But there is no time to soothe my bruised ego ...

Retrieving the trapped birds is fast and efficient. This well-oiled machine of seasoned bird ringers has been through this routine many times. The birds settle quickly. In all, over a hundred have been caught. The list reads: one wigeon, four teal, one oystercatcher, eight curlew, two dunlin, seventy-four redshank, thirteen black-headed and three common gulls. All are weighed, aged, measured, ringed and released. The curlews also have their geolocators fitted, and, for the first time, I get to hold a curlew in my hands.

Not surprisingly for wild creatures, some species of bird will peck and struggle when held. The more pointed the talons, or sharp the bill, the greater the caution needed. They glare fiercely at their captor with rage or terror. Some are notoriously vicious, like the sea-cliff-dwelling razorbills (the clue is in the name). Curlews, however, don't do histrionics. Despite having a bill that could take your eye out, they simply sink into your hands and have a look around. They are gentle captives and exude a Buddha-like calm. It is as though being cradled in our hands takes away the pressure for survival for a short while. I am sure this is far from the truth, but the impression they give is one of serenity, not panic.

It is a special, life-giving moment to be so close to birds that I have loved and admired for so long. As I cradle them one at a time, I feel their hearts beat fast but steady. Under their soft feathers, they are warm and surprisingly fragile. We look each other in the eye and I fancy there is a connection. I stop short of giving each one a soft kiss on the head – that is way too infra dig in front of the Highland Ringing Group.

By mid-morning each bird has been released into the bright sunshine and the cold, fresh air. As they fly away I wish them well and hope they come back in the autumn so that the geolocators can be retrieved and reveal their secrets. The curlews call out their characteristic 'curlee' as they wheel down the beach. I worry that the exploding net and human handling might have traumatised them, but, reassuringly, after some indignant shaking, each one starts feeding. By the time we have packed up, the beach is once again calm, as though nothing has happened. Months of waiting now lie ahead before the birds return in the autumn and the cannon nets are laid out again.

Cannon netting might seem dramatic but it is a useful tool for birds like curlews that are hard to catch in any other way; and its use is spreading. Two weeks later, at the end of February, I find myself once again stumbling through woodland in semi-darkness. This time it was to find out more about a new inland cannon netting project in the Yorkshire Dales.

It is late afternoon and I am following (or trying to follow) a silent, stealthy, ex-army officer who barely cracks a twig as he moves through the shadows with ease. His training with the Irish Guards, and a Military Cross for bravery in Iraq, are obviously useful for birding. He floats over the ground and uses the tree trunks as cover. I, on the other hand, fall over every root, get snared on brambles and catch my rucksack on most overhead branches. I can barely see a thing.

Tom Orde-Powlett is in his late thirties, and retired from the army to help run the family business, which happens to involve the upkeep of a medieval castle and a 6000-acre grouse moor. For six centuries his ancestors have owned and managed Bolton Castle Estate. He also has four small children, so life is busy. Tom, though, is fired with a passion for birds and is involved in all kinds of ringing and monitoring projects around the area. I will return to the grouse moor later in the year, but this visit is to see the large number of curlews that winter in the fields along the River Ure, which tumbles through the valley below the castle. Most curlews in the UK winter on the coast, but some come inland to places like this in quite large numbers. A few hundred birds are known to spend the winter in Wensleydale, making the most of the rough, wet fields below the hills. This is a stunningly beautiful part of England. On this wintry day, the elongated, smooth moors are dusted with snow and produce stark, white wedges against a pale blue sky. England is a crowded country, but the Yorkshire Dales feel wide open and sparse. There is space to breathe.

The light is fading fast. The fourteenth-century fortress that once hosted the fugitive Mary Queen of Scots looms above us, dark and brooding. Tom leads the way through the small shelterbelt of conifers to the edge of the field where a hundred or so curlews often roost overnight. There is no cannon netting tonight; this is a reconnaissance trip to check their location. We settle on a log, telescopes ready, and chat quietly. Little is known about these Yorkshire birds. Do they breed on local hills or have they come from far away? Are they a mixture of sexes and ages? One theory suggests curlews that winter inland may be predominantly males, as their shorter bills are more suited to reaching food in wet, soft soil. The females, with their longer bills, are more adept at extracting food from sandy, muddy shores and rocky coasts. No one knows for sure, and so Tom, with the help of local nature groups, is trying to find out. In January, over forty birds had been caught using cannon nets and each bird was given a unique set of coloured bands for identification. While the rings were being fitted the birds were also weighed and measured. The majority were found to be male, supporting the theory that the sexes may separate to some extent in winter. More cannon netting is being planned, but in the meantime it is important to keep a lookout for birds already ringed. Once spring arrives it might be possible to see where they nest, or to hope for reported sightings if they are breeding elsewhere.

There is something tinglingly magical about woodlands, even small patches like this, in the half-light of a winter evening. They are steadfast and full of expectation; there is a sense of a change of shift from day to night, from the known, visible world to the realm of covert creatures that move in shadows. After the wet, warm winter the rotting leaves and rich soil give off a primeval, earthy smell. As a cold wind buffets the valley, the trees provide a sense of calm. I feel I am wrapped in a woody blanket.

A lacework of bare hedges defines the large field ahead. The ground is sodden and an area of standing water in the middle reflects the grey and pink sky. After a short time, the calls of curlews drift in from the distance. They sail overhead, landing by the water, touching down like fighter planes. Their long, pointed wings tilt to kill the lift and slow momentum. Their heads and necks stretch out and downwards, and their long legs, with pointed toes, dangle below. They delicately touch the earth. At first just a few arrive, then they are joined by more and more. They whistle and call to each other and begin to feed in a herd of about eighty birds, moving first one way, then turning and walking back. A brown hare appears in the background, sniffs the cold wind and lopes away. Occasionally, one curlew rises into the air and sings a succession of ascending notes before floating back to the group. They are trying out their mating displays, and seem restless. Something is stirring in the February air; the approaching spring seems to be awakening their instincts.

Despite the cold, short days, winter is coming to an end. The world is on the cusp of change. Birdsong becomes louder and more musical, more earnest. Buds bulge and green shoots have more vigour. The curlews feel it. Their migration to their summer grounds is about to begin. It will be a staged journey, not a direct flight. Very soon this group in Wensleydale will split up and head to the same breeding grounds they have always gone to. These are birds of routine and faithfulness. They will stop for a few days in the same fields, in fact the same spot in the same fields, calling and displaying, searching each other out, always heading closer to their final nesting place.

Most of the Wensleydale curlews might not have far to go. It is likely they spread out over the surrounding moors and upland farms. Others, though, could travel hundreds of miles. Previous studies suggest some birds may head to Teesdale before heading out to Scandinavia. This new ringing project will help fill in some of the gaps, and I left Tom with plans to return when the birds are nesting and the valleys and moors are burgeoning with life. I drove back to Bristol with a mind full of wintery new moon birds singing in a grey, flooded field.

As the seasons shift, so too do the winds around the Earth and the currents in the sea. Movements in air and water bring a fresh energy to a winter-weary world. That energy can bring new life and new generations – but it can also be lethal. Gales, fog, heavy rain and storms can hit just when the birds are on the wing.

On an unusually foggy, cold night, on 9 March 1911, there was 'a tremendous night of Curlew cries over Dublin'.[2] Thousands of birds of different species – including curlews, thrushes, starlings, robins and skylarks – were 'streaming over the south and east coasts of Ireland, heading north. They were exhausted and disorientated.' One man near Waterford recorded, 'The whole bird creation was astir and the people of the town were kept awake by the shriek of the Curlew, Duck and Snipe hovering over the town.' A ship's captain reported 'millions of birds' alighting on his ship. 'Amongst them was a number of curlews.' Lighthouse keepers told of birds crying and wheeling around the lanterns in the dead of night. A certain Mr Fanning was awoken from his sleep and wrote, 'Curlew were heard calling continuously over the town of Lismore … the air was full of them. The nights were dark and foggy, and the birds kept hovering over towns where gas-lamps were lighted.' And in Carlow, 'the sky was almost obscured by vast numbers of Curlew and Starling … The streets were practically littered in the morning with the bodies of dead birds.' Another report describes a man out walking at midnight and finding curlews, 'walking up and down the flat bank at the side of the river, screaming piteously.' It must have been a tragic and disturbing sight.

Returning to their breeding grounds from wintering in southern Europe, these poor creatures seem to have been caught out by extreme and unusual weather. Having been

held back for longer than normal by intense cold across the continent, the temperature across France suddenly rose, accompanied by a change in wind direction. The birds took their chance and left en masse, but what the birds didn't know was that Britain and Ireland were still in the grip of a deep freeze. As warm continental air hit the cold air over the North Sea, a bank of fog extended 30 miles from the coast and conditions were made worse by a waning moon, providing very little light. Cold, exhausted and disorientated, the birds made for any light source they could find, hence their landing on ships and lighthouses. Thousands died.

Bad weather during migration is not uncommon, but extreme events like this are, thankfully, rare. However, migration is always dangerous. Hunting and lack of food at stop-over sites make a hazardous journey far worse. Yet, still, the urge to fly to far away lands full of insects and good nesting areas is strong; it is an instinct that is impossible to resist.

The shift from winter to early spring was making me restless, too. The date set for the start of my long walk, 21 April, was just a few weeks away. It was time to plan my own, hopefully far less perilous, journey to Ireland.

Chapter 3

ARRIVING IN IRELAND

On a day when the curlew returns,
Its cry circling the moor,
Suddenly, to the man
In love with time, the whole land
Is the poem he will never write,
Birth cry, love song, threnody
Woven in voices of the living
And voices of the dead.[1]

I travelled to Ireland on 17 April, a few days earlier than
the start date of my walk, for two reasons. I wanted to visit
County Antrim to see an RSPB project working to restore
curlews to the uplands, which now host just a remnant
population. The other reason was personal. I spent many
childhood holidays in Northern Ireland, as my mother was
born into a large Catholic family in Enniskillen. Her death

in April 2015, just a year before, gave the start of the walk added poignancy. I would begin my odyssey in a place she had loved, and I wanted time to say goodbye.

My mother lived in England all her married life. As the only one of six siblings to leave Ireland, she held tight to her roots. The religious division and social injustice that blighted the lives of so many in Northern Ireland erupted into thirty years of war in The Troubles. On frequent visits during the 1970s and 80s, it seemed that every street corner was festooned with either the Union Jack or the Irish tricolour, flapping defiantly in the rain-soaked wind. My mother had a life-long loathing of national flags. To her unending credit, even in the darkest days of The Troubles, she never tolerated any taking of sides. She was steadfast in her view that evil was evil no matter who perpetrated it, even though those years of horror profoundly affected her own family. She understood what drove people to extremes. She recognised the inner strength of the 'ordinary' people of Northern Ireland, both Protestant and Catholic, and the rich cultures that shaped their experiences.

For my own part, life with a fiery Irish Catholic mother and a quiet, intellectual father, a Church of England doctor whose soul was rooted in the hard work and grit of the industrial Midlands, made for an interesting background to family life. My mother's Irish-Catholic view of the world, full of compassion and ritual, complexity and contradiction, merged with my father's gentle, measured Anglican stance. It was an unusual combination. And then, strangely, curlews appear in the middle of it all. As is often the case, separate strands of life can suddenly and unexpectedly weave together. Grief for my mother and hope for the future of a bird gave an emotional depth to the start of the New Moon Walk.

It is a cold, still dawn as the ferry draws closer to Belfast. Over one thousand years earlier, an Anglo-Saxon seafarer had written a poem about the hazards of crossing northern seas in an open boat. Storms swept over the deck, sleet and snow chilled his bones, and his ship:

> Hung about with icicles,
> Hail flew in showers.
> There I heard nothing
> but the roaring sea,
> the ice cold wave.[2]

The prosaic truth about my crossing, however, is that my Liverpool to Belfast sailing was more like crossing a mill pond, and far from my feet being, 'bound by frosts in cold clasps', the boat was overly warm and the bar a little too noisy. 'I take my gladness in the ... sound of the curlew instead of the laughter of men,' the ancient sailor had written, feeling lonely and uncertain on his gale-ridden sea. I did share that in common with him. I have ears only for the call of curlews, a curlew earworm, overriding the muzak and the chatter in the restaurant. Mind you, had the ferry been more akin to an Anglo-Saxon ship I might have been more prepared for the wintry blasts that strip the skin from your body in County Antrim.

Stretching north from Belfast is an area of high plateau cut through by valleys, or glens as they are more commonly called. Even today, many of the higher reaches of Antrim are remote. Glenwherry, in the heart of upland Antrim, is my first stop before heading out to Enniskillen. Sitting at around 400 metres, this is a landscape of bog and rough pasture dominated by an extinct volcano – Slemish Mountain – a giant Celtic beast crouched on bogland.

Glenwherry gets its fair share of rain – lots and lots of rain – and on the day of my visit this is mixed with sleet. It is easy to imagine how glaciers up to a mile high bore down on this land 30,000 years ago, their icy fingers prising open every crack in the rocks and tearing out boulders like flesh off a bone. When the climate began to warm and the glaciers retreated about 12,000 years ago, the land that reappeared from beneath the ice had been stripped of life and was scarred, bare and exhausted. But, slowly, vegetation and wildlife returned.

Over the millennia that followed, Ireland was colonised by hunter-gatherers and then farmers, expanding westwards from mainland Britain and Europe. The great forests were cut down as agriculture spread. The climate continued to change, and after long periods of warmth and low rainfall it became increasingly colder and wetter. Upland soils were leached of their nutrients and became acidic. From 4,500 years ago, bogs began to form across Ireland. In many places farming was abandoned until iron tools allowed these sodden, poor soils to be worked again. The hopes and beliefs of these early Irish people are writ large across the landscape in the form of tombs, dolmens and standing stones. As Christianity spread, these made way for churches as the modern spiritual expression of local communities.

In 1832 Lieutenant Robert Botler noted that the last wolf in Ireland was seen in Glenwherry in the seventeenth century. No doubt it cut a lonely figure, stressed and hungry in a hostile land. Standing here today, I could be on a film set for Sherlock Holmes' *The Hound of the Baskervilles*. Through the grey, low cloud I can easily visualise a slinking form circling a stone sheep enclosure, providing scant protection from a beast ravaged by hunger. The wolf record is given added credence by an adjacent area of peat land called Wolf Bog, now home to five wind turbines.

In 1836 James Boyle wrote in his memoirs that the people who lived here were kind, shrewd, hard-working descendants of Scottish Presbyterians and Calvinists. They were livestock farmers, and their occupation is carried on to this day. In a land where rain and gales sweep in from the west for much of the year, it is the only practical option; growing crops is well nigh impossible. While Boyle admired the upright grittiness of the people, he was somewhat less inspired by the landscape:

> The valley of Glenwherry is wild and mountainous, presenting no variety of scenery, either in its natural or artificial state, destitute of planting or hedgerows, its steep but smooth sides mountainous but presenting nothing bold or striking in their forms, being in fact, except along the banks of the river, one unvaried and uncultivated waste. At the western end of the parish the scenery is not so wild and there is more cultivation, but proceeding towards the eastern end of the glen the scenery becomes wild, dreary and uninteresting.[3]

Glenwherry was, and still is, a tough place to live.

Place names can tell us much about the past character and wildlife of an area. In England, former animal denizens are recorded as Buckfast and Wolford, for example. Others are more obscure, such as Birkenhead, meaning the headland where birch trees grow. In Northern Ireland, *Doire*, or Derry, means oak grove, and *Cúil Raithin*, the town of Coleraine, is a place of many ferns. *Laios na n Gealbhán*, or Lisnaglevin, means 'fort of the sparrows'. Cranfield, in County Antrim, is the anglicised version of *Creamhchoill*, or wild-garlic wood. All of life, whether sought after for food or fuel, grand or humble, is to be found in place names. In County Tyrone the townland of Pollnameeltogue means 'hollow of the midges', and Knockiniller is the 'hill of the eagle'. A journey through the towns of Ireland is a glimpse into an abundant past natural history, where people named their homes in terms of the life around them.

Glenwherry has the quaintly named Whappstown Road. Whapp or whaup is an onomatopoeic Celtic name, reproducing the sound of one of the curlew's barking calls. It also gives its name to Whaup Hill in County Antrim and Whaup Island in County Down. When an old musician from the Sperrin Mountains was asked to sing a song, he said, 'I whaups a bit on the flute as well, ye know,' and 'What's thou waap-whaupin aboot?' was a rebuke to a crying child in the northeast of England.

Whappstown Road is a hint that curlews were once common here in Antrim. Maybe their calls over the hills as they returned to breed in early spring lifted the hearts of those past generations of tough farmers. Neal Warnock, the RSPB Conservation Advisor for Glenwherry, told me how much he looked forward to their arrival in March. 'For me, being up in the hills all year round, there's quite a few months when you're faced with silence, and the more I work up here the more the anticipation grows of hearing the first curlew of the spring return. It's fantastic to hear them call across the valley and the farmers look forward to them coming back, too. They hold an important place in the hearts and minds of the people that live in this area.'

It seems they always have. In the late nineteenth century, James McKowen, a worker in a bleach factory near Belfast, led a double life as a poet and songwriter. He used the pen name 'Curlew', or sometimes 'Kitty Connor', and wrote lyrics for ballads. Though his hands helped turn the wheels of industry, his heart was alone on the bogs with curlews in spring. His collection of poems appeared in *The Harp of Erin*, in 1869, and his song 'The Curlew' relives his boyhood joy of wandering through the glens of Antrim, listening to that soulful cry of the wilderness, alongside those of the golden eagle and the turtle dove.

The Curlew

By the marge of the sea has thy foot ever strayed,
When eve shed its deep mellow tinge?

Hast thou lingered to hear the sweet music that's
    made
By the ocean-waves' whispering fringe?

Tis then you may hear the wild barnacle's call
The scream of the sea-coving mew,

And that deep thrilling note that is wilder than
    all
The voice of the wailing curlew.

The song of the linnet is sweet from the spray
The blackbird's comes rich from the thorn;

And clear is the lark's when he's soaring away
To herald the birth of the morn.

The note of the eagle is piercing and loud,
The turtle's, as soft as it's true;

But give me, oh! give me, that song from the
    cloud
The voice of the wailing curlew.

Sky minstrel! How often I've paused as a child,
As I've roamed in my own native vale,

To listen thy music so fitful and wild,
Born far on the wings of a gale.

And still, as I rest by the door of my cot,
Thy voice can youth's feelings renew;

And strangely I'm tempted to envy thy lot,
Thou wild-noted, wailing curlew.[4]

Glenwherry is an anglicised version of the original Irish name *Gleannfaire*, translated as 'valley of the watching'. The original reason for this name is lost in time, but it is apt once again thanks to the RSPB project based here to closely observe the area's breeding curlews as part of its Curlew Recovery Programme, led by Sarah Sanders. They recorded forty-four pairs in 2016, and by today's standards that makes Glenwherry a hotspot for curlews in Northern Ireland.

A key part of the Curlew Recovery Programme is the snappily named Trial Management Project (TMP). Despite the corporate terminology, the TMP is a practical, five-year project concentrating on six upland areas (of which Glenwherry is one) spread throughout northern England, Scotland, North Wales and Northern Ireland. Each site consists of two roughly 10 square-kilometre plots situated close to each other. One plot will see all the action – habitat management, predator control, special grazing regimes and so on – whereas on the other site it will be business as usual with no special measures. In the active site, in Glenwherry, the RSPB is working with farmers to thin out rushes and create better feeding and nesting areas by targeted grazing of cattle. Some shrubs and trees are also being removed so that predators such as hooded crows can't use them as lookout posts to spot eggs and chicks. Foxes and crows will also be controlled in the active plot, but not in the control site. At the end of the five-year period, hopefully, a clearer idea will have emerged about what kind of management is needed to stabilise or even reverse the decline of upland curlews.

When I visited Glenwherry in April 2016 it was only year two of the TMP, so too early for any results, but the project hasn't come a day too soon. The last thirty years have been catastrophic for Northern Irish curlews, and many other farmland birds. Back in 1986 a survey found 5,000 pairs of breeding curlews throughout the province. By 2015 their numbers had crashed to fewer than 500 pairs, and probably closer to 250. That is a decline of over 90 per cent. The cause? Changes in farming. Agriculture dominates Northern Ireland, three-quarters of the land is farmed. It is the country of toil and soil. Prior to the 1970s, small mixed farms, with both arable farming and livestock, were widespread. They were family-run affairs that were, to use the jargon, 'extensive' in character. Extensive (as opposed to 'intensive') means low chemical input in terms of fertiliser and pesticides, low stocking density and lower yield per acre. A seven-year rotation system was used for crops such as oats, potatoes, and pasture for hay. Over the decades that followed, these smaller farms have been amal-gamated into larger, specialised, intensive businesses, centred mainly on livestock. There are now 1.7 million cows in Northern Ireland providing both milk and meat, compared to a million in 1965, and over the same time frame land given over to crops declined by two-thirds. Fields that once grew food for people are now laid to grass for livestock.

In 1965 cows were fed through the winter months on hay, 90 per cent of which was cut in August. By 1995 hay was replaced by silage – a method of growing food for cows by frequently cutting grass and storing it anaerobi-cally under large sheets of black plastic. If they can produce enough grass, farmers can now feed cows throughout the year. Soil is 'enhanced' by the addition of fertiliser and the grass is sprayed with pesticides. By using super-productive varieties such as rye grass, larger quantities can be grown and then cut as often as every three weeks from April onwards and stored in silos. The dairy sector is particualry important. In 1965 there were 196,000 dairy cows in Northern Ireland; today, 312,000 cows produce milk and cheese, two-thirds of which is exported. The dairy industry is vital to the economy of Northern Ireland – and it depends on silage.

Patrick G. McBride was a farmer in the Glens of Antrim for much of the twentieth century. His memoir, *Where the Curlew Flies*, describes the old ways of doing things. He celebrates the daily joys of working on the land, as well as being realistic about the hard labour of farming with hand tools and horses. Hay was made with rakes and forks, and 'meadow hay' on wet ground was always cut with a scythe. In his lifetime, slow-paced, hands-on farming was replaced by fast-paced machines that could harvest multiple cuts every year. He experienced directly the seismic shift in agriculture. Reflecting upon it, he concludes, 'I think that no other generation will ever see as many changes in farming as my generation has lived through.'

Agriculture dominates Northern Ireland. Farms have been passed down through generations and land is integral to Irish identity. When farming was extensive, it was good for curlews and lots of other wildlife. When it changed from manual to mechanised, organic to chemical, hay to silage, it spelled disaster. Ground-nesting birds such as the corncrake and curlew were eradicated in large areas. Farming machinery destroys eggs and chicks indiscriminately. Faced with danger, curlew chicks will sink down into the grass and freeze, where they are killed instantly by the rotating blades. Nests full of eggs are flattened. Those birds that do manage to survive the machines will often fall prey to foxes and crows, two species that do well in intensive farmland.

The border county of Tyrone was once a curlew stronghold. Like County Antrim, this too was a land of rugged
bogs and farms, but it underwent a dramatic transformation in the 1980s. Many of the peat bogs were stripped for
turf and the floodplains of rivers such as the Blackwater
were drained. The River Blackwater itself was dredged,
deepened and widened, removing valuable wetland habitat
for all kinds of wildlife. Some of the more marginal farmland was abandoned. Because curlews were once so numerous there, the RSPB set up a curlew recovery project, but
sometime in the early 2000s they disappeared from the
landscape and the project was abandoned. It took less than
a generation to see curlews eradicated from a large area
where they used to be common. Snipe, lapwing and
redshank have all but gone, too. It was a stark example of
how quickly birds can vanish. Now the only places that are
safe for waders are where agriculture remains extensive or
protected as nature reserves, such as cold, wet, upland
Glenwherry and the islands in the middle of Lough Erne,
County Fermanagh. The rest of Northern Ireland is now
curlew-free. But even Glenwherry, which largely escaped
the intensification of the lowlands, is under threat.

Neal and I sit in the car for a while in a layby to let the
worst of a squall pass. Through the misting windows he
points out the patchwork appearance of the view in front
of us. Sections of bog are being turned into bright green rye
grass fields or planted with conifers, both activities encouraged by subsidies. 'We need to help farmers to keep some
areas rough and unimproved for the curlews,' he says.
Keeping forestry at bay on land that is deemed

unproductive in terms of farming is a big challenge. The Northern Ireland government has a target to increase tree cover by 50 per cent by 2056. Curlews, like many other ground-nesting birds, avoid nesting within 500 metres of the edge of forest, nervous of predators like foxes, badgers and crows. Far more land is therefore taken out of nesting habitat than just the area that is planted. Wind and solar farm applications are now commonplace in marginal land, bringing their own dangers for flying birds and disturbance on the ground. Glenwherry is currently considering proposals for a 250-acre solar farm, and wind farms can be seen all around the area. Slowly the upland bog is being transformed into a tamed, multi-use landscape. Somehow, in all of this complexity of human needs and endeavour, curlews must try to survive in their dwindling niche.

As the sleet tests the mettle of my new waterproof jacket, Neal and I wander along a puddle-strewn track between fields in the active Trial Management Project area, hoping to see a pair of curlews that had been spotted nearby. They have not long arrived back for the breeding season and their behaviour suggests they are staking out their territory and strengthening their pair bond, prior to laying eggs. Kerry Darbishire describes early-arriving curlews in her poem, 'Messengers of Spring':

> In pairs they returned
> from winter marsh like ghosts
> to sink their new moon beaks
> deep into turf soft as rain.

Mike Smart, an ornithologist friend who monitors curlews throughout the year in the west of England, describes their typical courtship behaviour when they first arrive on their territory:

> They seem to adopt very characteristic behaviour; they are generally in twos, stalking round in a rather proprietorial sort of way, a little way apart, feeding quietly, and not getting very close together. Sometimes, however, they move quite close and start courtship display, in a moderate way, running around quite quickly together, sometimes in parallel, sometimes one ahead of the other, often picking up bits of grass or vegetation as they go, and throwing it down again; this can last for ten minutes. Occasionally, the male opens his wings slightly and does a couple of flaps, and seems to hold his tail up, rather like a Snipe. Sometimes the male displays by swooping and calling to a female on the ground and then they carry on feeding together in the surrounding grasslands.

Under normal circumstances, there would be many pairs of curlews with males sometimes fighting each other to define the edges of their territory. In March and April, uplands like Glenwherry should come alive with the sounds of calling curlews. In his book, *Waders, their Breeding, Haunts and Watchers*, Desmond Nethersole-Thompson describes how, 'On a still morning, the moor soon rings with the marvellous bubbling songs and the air dances of different cocks.'[5] Males and females would dance

and sing to each other, chasing around and seeing off intruders from dawn to dusk. Angry males would rip up grass and throw it about, displaying their white undersides, psychologically bullying any male that tried to muscle in. Sometimes clashes would involve exchanging blows with their wings, but rarely with their delicate and easily damaged bills. Eventually, hierarchy and territories would be established, and nests would be built at least 100 metres apart, often more. The birds would be spread over the landscape, the best areas taken by the dominant pairs. But there is no such vying for territory today, and these cannot be described as normal circumstances. Neal and I have to search for quite a while to find even a single pair. The air is not full of wonderful bubbling and trilling; it is largely silent.

I envy Neal his wellies in this waterlogged world. 'Stick your boots in the turf of this island and they fill up with the bog water,' wrote blogger Alen McFadzean about walking the hills of Antrim. Maybe he had been along this footpath, too. Suddenly, out of the silence, comes a fluty call – half mournful, half laughing. In the distance, a curlew and its mate fly low and land further away from us. They had spied us and we had spooked them. I am amazed we can provoke this reaction from such a distance, but curlews are always nervous, and in this seemingly empty landscape we stand out. But this is proof they have made it back again, this pair and a few others we hear over the course of the morning, pouring intermittent music over a bleak, frozen moor. Ted Hughes heard curlews on a winter's morning, carving sound out of frosty air. 'I listened in emptiness on the moor-ridge/The curlew's tear turned its edge on the silence.'[6]

No one knows for sure if curlews re-pair with the same partner each year, but it's generally believed that they do. Through binoculars, I can just make them out as they land in rushes and creep away like soldiers in combat. Brown birds in a brown field – a tantalising glimpse of life that melts into the bog all too soon. Northern Ireland seems to be full of things half-seen. Religion and myth intertwine here. The ghosts of ancient kings, fairies and giants hang like mists over the land, and the remnants of the havoc they caused by their battles and magical spells are the boulders, loughs, depressions, cliffs and mountains. That potent symbol of Ulster, the Red Hand, is founded on a boat race over the sea where mythical kings raced each other to the shore. Whoever touched the land first could proclaim ownership. One king was so desperate to win he cut off his own hand and threw it onto the beach, declaring his sovereignty with blood.

It seems almost every feature of the landscape tells a fantastical tale of good and evil or love and hate. Large glacial boulders are the stones thrown by petulant giants. The Giant's Causeway – that astonishing area of black, columnar basalt on the Antrim coast – is supposedly the remnant of a walkway built by a giant called Finn McCool. He made it so that he could walk over the sea to fight his enormous Scottish enemy, the giant Benandonner. After some trickery and deception, the Scottish giant ran away and Finn tore up a clod of earth to hurl after him. The hole left behind filled with water to form Lough Neagh (the largest freshwater lake in the UK and Ireland, just to the southwest of Glenwherry). The lump of earth that landed in the sea is said to be the Isle of Man. Finn then destroyed the causeway. The ragged remnants are now a World Heritage Site, attracting tourists from all over the world, keen to learn more about the bad behaviour of these ill-tempered ancients. Ireland was the stage for wild gods to act upon, or, as Austin Clarke in his novel *The Singing Men at Cashel* wrote, 'There was no hill or wood in all the land which has not been remembered in poetry. Had not those great teachers of the past taught that matter was as holy as the mind, that hill and wood were an external manifestation of immortal regions?'[7]

Wherever you look in Celtic Britain there are stories like these; folk tales that have been told and retold. Jeremy

Mynott, author, classicist and naturalist distils perfectly how these stories take on a modern resonance. 'These are myths that have become snowballs, gathering size and picking up bits and pieces from other folklores as they roll through the ages. No one can stop them to construct them more neatly or make them internally consistent, as we would scientific theories. But they also flare brightly in our imaginations, like a comet streaking across the sky in a blaze, trailing its comet's tail of vaguer associations, memories and intimations.' Perhaps their real value is in connecting us to what W.B. Yeats called the 'brooding memory and dangerous hope'[8] of our ancestors. And behind all this intensity, the once-common call of the curlew provided the mood music for these flights of imagination.

As we walk back to the car, leaving the curlews to their moorland peace, the looming form of Slemish Mountain is emerging from under a blanket of cloud. This vast monument to Christian fortitude is another place shrouded in half-truths and legends. It was supposedly the site of the

enslavement of Ireland's most famous saint. St Patrick was himself a figure of misconception and contradiction. This most Irish of saints was probably born in Wales and has never been canonised by a pope, but he became a saint by popular acclaim. One famous story tells us how Patrick drove all the snakes out of Ireland – not that there have ever been any snakes on the island. It is most likely a metaphor for eradicating paganism.

St Patrick lived in the fifth century, when Christianity was taking hold of Europe but paganism was still widespread in the West. Paganism, a complex and varied system of beliefs based on the worship of many gods, is deeply related to the natural world. The veil that divides the spiritual realm from nature and humanity is thin and insubstantial. In ancient Ireland, the gods were feisty and flighty, as quick to rage as to bestow blessings, making the natural world an unpredictable place. Nature took on dual characteristics. The eagle was the earthly embodiment of kingship and power, the swan represented the spirits of love and purity. The owl was linked to the shadowy goddess of moonlight and mourning, and Morrigan, the goddess of battle, took the form of the crow. The curlew, with its haunting cry, was associated with the mysterious god Dalua, who calls people to ponder their place on Earth amidst the beauty of lonely places. The cry that embodies both sorrow and grief gave voice to inexpressible fears. This meshing of gods, human beings and the Earth dominated the stories of ancient pagan Europe.

This was the world of St Patrick: two belief systems living uneasily side by side and often in conflict. Patrick was raised in a Christian household. When he was a teenager it is thought he was kidnapped by Irish slave traders and forced to work as a shepherd for the pagan chief, Milchu, in what is now County Antrim. On the windswept and rain-soaked Slemish Mountain, he increasingly turned to the faith of his father. After six years he escaped back to his homeland and trained to be a priest. Thirty years later he returned to Ireland to convert his captors. Some believe St Patrick used the famous Celtic cross as a means to connect with the pagan inhabitants of Ireland. The traditional crucifix with the circle of life binding the arms is the iconic symbol of Celtic Christianity, combining the Christian meaning of the crucifix with the pagan symbolism of the life-giving sun. Paganism, with its stress on the sacredness of life, lived on in a new form in this early Christian era.

Some legends about St Patrick echo the strong pagan relationship between the spiritual and natural worlds. One Irish folktale has Patrick trying to cross the sea to the Isle of Man, but a dense mist prevented him seeing the shore. He was in mortal danger until the clear call of a curlew directed him towards land, and hence to safety. He was grateful and blessed the curlew, decreeing that these birds should be protected from harm and that their nests must always be difficult to find. Celtic Irish folktales also have curlews warning Jesus of the approach of enemies, either by calling loudly to wake him from sleep, or by covering over his footprints in the sand. These tales intricately bind curlews (and many other creatures) to God and human salvation. Nature is seen as an active player in the Christian story, where selfless acts of sacrifice and compassion are freely given.

St Patrick's captivity on Slemish Mountain is a treasured story in Northern Ireland, and on his feast day, 17 March, large crowds make a pilgrimage to the summit. On the same day, say local farmers, curlews return to breed, and from the break of dawn their calls ring from the hillsides. St Patrick would have heard them, heralding warmer days and the prospect of new life, as he prayed in the cold solitude of the mountain. The curlew and St Patrick are intertwined in the minds and hearts of generations of farmers in Antrim. To lose the last remaining curlews from this land would be to lose a part of the soul of Northern Ireland.

Neal and I retreat to a farm owned by Sam and Wilma Bonnar, a family who have farmed Glenwherry for generations. They are friendly, hard-working people and their warm and comfortable farmhouse is a thoroughly modern bungalow, like many rural buildings in Ireland today. A large picture window looks out over the fields and distant bog, giving an airy feel in an open landscape. On a clear day I am sure you can see for miles. As it is, I can barely make out the field right next to the house where a lone lapwing calls plaintively to unseen companions. It's a sad sound, as rain beats against the panes. We chat about the weather and the hardships of farming through the winter, while their two-year-old grandson runs around the room. There is a real sense that this is a family that is deeply rooted in the land and values the wildlife they host. They work with the RSPB to keep the Trial Management Project on target, and without them, and other like-minded volunteers,

Neal's job would be nigh impossible. Apart from helping
with the physical work of management, Sam knows what's
around, telling Neal where he has seen birds and whether
numbers are up or down compared to previous years. I ask
about the subsidies available for combining farming with
wildlife conservation; is enough money being made available? Sam's answer is a first warning shot across the bow,
and I will hear many like it over the coming weeks. Wildlife
is good to have, but it has to pay its way. Without help
from agri-environment schemes, farmers wouldn't be able
to prioritise curlews, lapwings, or anything else that
requires taking land out of intensive production. There is
too much pressure to increase yields and too many costs to
meet. Curlews are not seen as a pest species, they are not
unwelcome, but their needs cannot be met without financial help. In other words, wildlife has to pay rent on land
that is no longer theirs.

It is time to move on; the official start date of the walk
is just days away. I leave Antrim and head east towards
Enniskillen as the sun breaks through the clouds. The land
softens as mountains give way to low-lying green meadows
and the watery basin of the River Erne in County
Fermanagh. There is already much to think about.

Chapter 4

THE LAND
OF LAKES

Sunlight on water is always beautiful; when sparkling ripples spread into the distance, the air shimmers with dancing sunbeams. My sister Sarah and I stand on the shore of Lower Lough Erne, 300 square miles of freshwater, waving reeds and tranquillity. We place a lock of my mother's hair onto the surface and hold hands, watching as this little piece of her is carried off on the waves. Enniskillen, built on an island between Upper and Lower Lough Erne, was her home town. Dementia took her a year ago to this day. Even though the disease systematically destroyed her faculties, right up until the end she would smile at the mention of Fermanagh and Lough Erne.

Our family home was in Stoke-on Trent, as unlike County Fermanagh as you can get, and one of the things my mother and her family often reminisced about was the sound of summer fields, with vocals provided by corn-crakes. Their grating croaks filled the warm night air from April until September. They are consummate callers; one bird can deliver 20,000 rasps a night, which can be heard a mile away. Their Latin name, *Crex crex*, gives a good idea of the sound; a piece of hard plastic scraping a cheese grater. The mythical poet, warrior and seer of ancient Ireland, Finn, called corncrakes 'strenuous bards'.

In the early twentieth century there were tens of thou-sands of corncrakes breeding throughout Britain and Ireland, flying in from southern Africa in the early spring. The lush fields shaped by traditional agriculture provided them with perfect habitat for nesting. Their numbers were legion, but that alone is no guarantee of safety. The swift changes in farming practices and the switch to silage wiped them out in a generation. By 1994 not a single corncrake was recorded breeding in Northern Ireland. They simply disappeared from a landscape where they had been a part of agricultural life for centuries. Occasionally a solo male will still arrive and emit a lonely call from a field in Tyrone or on Rathlin Island, hoping to attract a mate, but so far his song has gone unheeded. Today their rarity has turned them into celebrities. If one is heard calling, crowds gather alongside TV, radio and newspaper reporters. So keen are people to hear that wheeze once more and reconnect with the sound of their yesterdays, they are willing to travel from miles around. Many listen in tears.

Northern Ireland is not alone in losing corncrakes. The early nineteenth-century English poet John Clare was familiar with the feathered croaker as he laboured in the fields of Northamptonshire. Back then, they were literally everywhere in the spring and summer months, but it was almost impossible to find them – they could disappear without a trace, all the while still calling loudly. Corncrakes are accomplished ventriloquists, throwing their croaks around the meadow. Just when you think you've got one cornered, it is sneakily creeping through the grass on the other side of the field. A trick John Clare was familiar with:

> And yet tis heard in every vale
> An undiscovered song
> And makes a pleasant wonder tale
> For all the summer long.[1]

Yet by the middle of the twentieth century the corncrake had gone from England and Wales as well as most of Scotland. Today it still breeds in the Western Isles, where concerted conservation efforts over many years have restored their numbers to around 1,000 calling males. Could there be a starker example of how we can eradicate wildlife from our lives? Corncrakes were once a widespread breeding bird in the UK, and now they are barely a memory. What happened to the corncrake is happening to the curlew throughout much of its range, which makes conservation projects like the one on the islands of Lough Erne all the more important.

Lough Erne is one of the largest lakes in the UK. It is divided into Upper and Lower Lough Erne, separated by a pinch point upon which sits the city of Enniskillen. There are around 154 islands dotted throughout these great lakes. As with so many places in Ireland, Lough Erne abounds in myth. According to legend, it was named after Erne, a Lady in Waiting to the warrior Queen Meabh, who fled from a fearsome monster emerging from a cave. She was drowned in the lough, and as her body dissolved in the water she infused it with life-giving powers that nourish the surrounding land. There is often a moral to these tales of tragedy: where life springs from death, and fear and destruction make way for renewal.

Northern Ireland saw more than its fair share of destruction in the closing thirty years of the twentieth century. In a war between two sides defined largely by their Christian denomination – Protestant or Catholic – the violence had little to do with doctrine and everything to do with social justice and the distribution of power. The Troubles tore Northern Ireland apart; 3,600 people lost their lives and thousands more were injured. In 1987 Enniskillen saw one of the worst attacks. Twelve people died and sixty-three were injured when a bomb exploded in the city on Remembrance Sunday. I spoke to my mother on the phone that day and remember hearing the despair in her voice for a country where there seemed to be so much religion and so little Christianity.

Those years of misery not only blighted lives but also took their toll on the economy of the North. 'There is a sense of wanting to catch up after the decades of low investment during The Troubles,' says Brad Robson, the RSPB's Conservation Manager for County Fermanagh. 'Conservation isn't really a priority. It's not that people don't care about nature, the land is in their blood, but they want the country to make up for lost years.' Since the end of The Troubles, Northern Ireland's economy has grown at twice the rate of the rest of the UK. In the midst of all this rebuilding, the loss of breeding waders might have been considered as little more than collateral damage.

There are forty-three islands in the RSPB reserve on Lower Lough Erne. Twelve of them are managed for breeding waders, intensively so for the last few years. There have been successes, not just for curlews but for other species like redshank, too. An auspicious place, I think, to begin a walk for curlews. The day before I begin, I meet Brad at dawn in a layby on the side of the road that follows the western edge of Lower Lough Erne. Paddles in hand, we walk down through the trees that fringe the shore to a hidden Canadian canoe and push off into cold, calm, grey water.

Islands, particularly uninhabited ones, always hold an air of mystery. Gazing at them from afar, they tantalise the imagination. Landing on their shores is an exciting step into a different world, even though the one we are headed for is very well trodden by conservationists. As we paddle towards Muckinish Island the rhythmic splashing of the oars adds to the sense of early morning peace. I experience pangs of grief at the thought of my mother's hair floating somewhere on the surface. There are no cars on the roads, no planes overhead, just the lapping of water and a cold breeze. I am half hoping to catch a glimpse of the fabled Lady of the Lake; a beautiful woman dressed in white, who, so the story goes, walks from island to island carrying garlands of wildflowers. She is said to step lightly over the surface of the water, barely visible through the morning mists. To see her, so they say, is an omen for good times ahead. But there is no drifting mist or floaty lady scattering blooms, just an increasing amount of noise as we get closer to the island.

The honking of Canada geese can really get under your skin. In the still morning air they sound like an unruly orchestra of home-made instruments. There are other calls, too, if you could but hear them through the geese. The lovely whistle of sandpipers occasionally cuts through, as does the urgent, panicky piping of the redshank, the sentry of these watery worlds. And then, as our canoe moves closer, the thrilling sound of two curlews calling and bubbling above us, slicing through the anserine cacophony. They are flying high and scythe through the air above the leafless trees that fringe the island, before swooping low and disappearing behind the canopy.

Muckinish Island is small. We walk around it in twenty minutes, accompanied by the sounds of indignant Canada geese strutting around their huge nests. Brad gets a text message to say a curlew has been found dead at another location, probably the victim of a peregrine attack. The air reeks of guano and the ground is rough underfoot. To me, this island seems overworked; it has the feel of a place that has had a lot expected of it for many years. Generations of farmers brought their sheep and cows here to graze, crops were grown in small fields, and now it is a carefully managed bird reserve. Most of the trees and scrub have been recently cleared, leaving mossy stumps, easily tripped over. It's had invasions, too. A few years ago, some badgers managed to swim the 250 metres that separates Muckinish from the mainland. They established a sett and swiftly set about eating the eggs and chicks of nesting waders. A shiny electric fence now stretches across one side, separating remnant woodland where the badgers live from wader habitat. It is obvious how much effort has gone into just this one island, and there are many more to work on.

We see five curlews in all on Muckinish, displaying and calling. They have flown in from farms on the mainland where they have been feeding and roosting overnight. The softer soils of the mainland have worms and insects that can be extracted more easily than tackling the thin shingle covering the islands. But the birds can't nest on the farms. Danger lies in every direction; too many grass-cutting machines, trampling hooves, people with dogs and hungry predators. We survey the fertilised, emerald grassy squares from the rough shoreline of the island. Sheep graze peacefully. 'It shows how important a mixed countryside is,' says Brad. 'Curlews don't just need safe nesting areas in long grass, they have to be able to feed in shorter vegetation when they have chicks. And in the winter, they go to the coast and mudflats. To protect curlews we have to think

big.' The curlew is a bird that spreads its wings. It flies over
the whole country. It needs land that is wet and dry, green
and brown, long grass and short, mud and marsh, high
ground and lowland. Curlews live in the whole landscape,
not just in one place. It is a bird that binds together many
different places, and to look after them we must consider
everywhere from the coast to the mountains. The work
under way on the islands of Lough Erne is just one piece
of a very large jigsaw.

When Brad arrived to take up the job in 1997, waders
of all species were declining rapidly. In 1998 the area that
is now the reserve had sixty pairs of curlews. By 2009 that
had declined further to thirty-four pairs. Even those that
did breed only occasionally managed to fledge chicks. In
the worst case, on one large island, fledglings survived in
only two out of fourteen years. 'Curlews were in a really
desperate situation,' says Brad. 'Like corncrakes, they did
very well in hay meadows that were cut late, it gave the
birds a chance to raise their young before the grass was cut.
Given the changing weather we have these days, it isn't a
surprise people cut for silage as often as they can, but early
cutting isn't compatible with ground-nesting birds.' The
silage machines did for the curlews in the mainland fields,
but even on the islands, where they should have been safe,
numbers continued to fall. Many of the islands had been
farmed for generations, but things were changing. In some
places farming had been all but abandoned and the land
scrubbed over. Water levels of the lake were artificially
varied, affecting the foreshore where many birds nested.
Forests were planted, providing perfect lookouts for

predators like hooded crows. Foxes are good swimmers and increasing numbers on the mainland meant they were becoming more of a problem offshore. Slowly but surely even these island havens of tranquillity were becoming less suitable for ground-nesting birds.

From the late 1990s onwards, small-scale targeted management on the RSPB reserve started to turn things around. Continued removal of trees, scrub and predators and improved grazing management meant that by 2014 the curlew population had increased to forty-seven pairs. Two-thirds of their nests hatched young. And it was not just the curlew that benefited; all of the wader populations responded. From the low point of 104 pairs of waders in 2000, there was an increase to 219 pairs in 2014. 'We have demonstrated that curlews will respond to management,' says Brad. 'The next step is to roll this out into the wider countryside.' It is a big ask. Everything about the direction of travel is away from making land wildlife-friendly and more towards using every inch of it to make money. Curlew, snipe, redshank, lapwing and oystercatchers are not money-spinners, and though they are well liked and part of our culture and heritage, they are not a priority.

None of this habitat management comes cheap. Electric fencing is expensive and keeping the island curlew-friendly requires strategic planning, physical work, and liaison and negotiation with local communities. Curlews not only have to pay their way on farmland through subsidies, they also have to rely on the donations received by charities to survive in nature reserves. You could say that curlews everywhere have to sing for their supper in a world where money rules. It seems there is no place for them just to be. The Antrim and Fermanagh new moon birds are lucky to have the spending power of the RSPB behind them.

We sit in the canoe and chat for a while about the future of Northern Ireland's curlews. Antrim and Fermanagh hold well over 90 per cent of the Northern Ireland population. Both Brad Robson and Neal Warnock know that without the cooperation of farmers, and the general public giving to wildlife charities, it will be very difficult to reverse the downward trend seen throughout Europe, and most especially in Ireland. There is some hope to be derived from the fact that the people of the North are still closely connected to the land. There is a blurring of lines between town and country, with many people still having strong links to a farming way of life, either directly or through close relatives. And this is a small country where the rural and urban sit closely together; where farmers' fields end by the garden fence.

Tapping into this public connection with the environment, and the Irish love of all things lyrical, in 2010 the RSPB asked the Northern Irish Nobel Prize-winning poet, Seamus Heaney, to write the foreword to the conservation plan for Lough Beg, the place where he grew up in County Antrim. The un-poetically named Lough Beg Management Plan was thus given poetry through Heaney's appeal to reconnect with what he called 'the country of the mind', the place where memory and feeling come to life through the past. The names and places highlighted in the Management Plan, he said:

'... belong first and foremost in memory and imagination. They evoke a dream land that was once the real land, a shore at evening, quiet water, wind in the grass, the calls of birds, maybe a man or woman out in a back field just standing looking, counting cattle, listening. The Lough Beg Management Plan intends to make that country of the mind a reality once again. It wants to bring back a landscape where the peewit and the curlew and the whirring snipe are as common as they used to be on those 1940s evenings when I'd go with my father to check on our cattle on the strand.'[2]

This very human appeal to emotion and memory engages people on a different level to the language of science, strategy and directive. Inviting Heaney's contribution was a stroke of genius. A 'country of the mind', beautifully drawn out in the poet's gentle phrases, is a place we hold dear, where past landscapes energise our plans for the future. Perhaps all conservation literature should be written by poets, employing the power of meaningful words to galvanise the hearts and minds of a wide range of people. Mario Cuomo, the American Democratic politician, famously believed, 'You campaign in poetry, you govern in prose.'

In many ways, the span of Seamus Heaney's life (1939–2013) captured the dramatic changes that engulfed Northern Ireland. His poetry in *Death of a Naturalist* conveys the quiet, rural simplicity of his childhood, when lighting was by gas lamps and turf was cut by hand. His final words, sent to his wife by text message just minutes before he died, were *'Noli timere'*, Latin for 'do not be afraid'. Huge changes and an uncertain future were about to engulf his family, and from his mobile phone he used an ancient language and a phrase found frequently in the Bible to comfort them. He was born into a time when life was slow and rooted in the soil, he died when his beloved country was brightly lit and mechanised, with high-speed communications moving fast through the ether. Heaney embraced the old and the new, but he never lost his great love of the visceral, beautiful land of his childhood.

The night before I set off, 20 April, is clear. I stand outside my bed and breakfast and look up at the sky; a full moon hangs peacefully in the blackness. Is this a good omen? A full moon has ancient associations with lunacy, from the Latin *luna*, for moon. This silver disc was thought to exercise a powerful influence over our emotions, tugging them as it does the waters of the seas. Lunatics were thus at the mercy of the waxing and waning of the moon. Standing in the cool breeze on this calm, starry night, I can't help but think that the task ahead is in many ways a

lunatic scheme. The journey feels enormous, and nothing feels solid. I have never met most of the people I will be staying with; the only contact we have had so far has been on social media. Nor have I ever travelled down most of the roads I have marked out on my maps. In my mind they appear as insubstantial as threads of cotton, snaking their way towards an unknown horizon. Five hundred miles of twisting roads – a lunatic walk for a new moon bird.

The following morning dawns bright and sunny. The date of my departure has not been picked at random. I had a number of reasons for setting out on 21 April. From a biological point of view, I wanted to begin when the birds were just starting to nest. The main laying season for curlews in northern Europe begins around now; the walk will end when the first chicks are fledging. But there were other reasons; 21 April is the feast day of a little-known saint, who could well be the first recorded curlew conservationist.

St Beuno (pronounced Bayno) was a sixth-century Welsh abbot who lived in west Wales, on the Llyn Peninsula. He is best known for establishing Christianity throughout North Wales and for his inspiring preaching, travelling widely over land and sea. He was also a dab hand at bringing people back to life, especially if they had had their heads cut off. He famously replaced his chaste cousin St Winifred's head, which was removed when she rejected an amorous suitor wielding an axe. There is another story about St Beuno, though, which makes me smile, as he had a special relationship with a curlew. Legend has it that one day he was sailing between Anglesey and the Llyn when he dropped his book of sermons into the water. Immediately a curlew flew down, picked up the book and took it to the shore to dry. In an ending to the story remarkably similar to the tale told about St Patrick, St Beuno was so grateful he blessed the bird and said it should always be protected. So maybe we have St Beuno to blame for the fact that a curlew's scrape in the ground is infuriatingly hard to spot unless you happen almost to stand on it. You could say that St Beuno's blessing has protected curlews for well over a thousand years, though. On his feast day in 2016 I reckoned the poor, beleaguered curlews could well do with a renewal of his benediction.

And last, but not least, it is also the birthday of my personal conservation hero, John Muir. Born in 1838 in Dunbar, in southeast Scotland, he was taken to America by his father to work on a frontier farm. After an early life of drudgery and severe Christianity, Muir went on to travel throughout America and eventually began the process of establishing National Parks from Alaska to the southern deserts, protecting wildlife and landscapes for generations to come. He is most closely associated with the awe-inspiring Yosemite Valley, nestled high in California's Sierra Nevada mountains, which Muir called the 'Range of Light'. He loved the natural world with a passion that was impossible to contain. It flowed out from his heart and through his pen into articles and books that held America in thrall. He urged a money-hungry, landscape-ravaging nation to cherish their country and sincerely believed that the wildlife and magnificent landscapes of America were gifts for all of humanity and should be protected in perpetuity, as 'places to pray in and play in.' And he also deeply cherished the more humble life on Earth, the dowdy and the overlooked, he treasured an ant as much as a mountain. 'As long as I live, I'll hear waterfalls and birds and winds sing,' wrote Muir. There can be no other choice, therefore, for day one of the Curlew Walk than 21 April.

In the early morning, I hear that the first curlew eggs have been found on the Lough Erne reserve. At a small family gathering in a leisure-centre car park in the middle of Enniskillen, we say our goodbyes, and I set off. It feels good to be on my way, a relief after so much planning. I have a mile-long walk along a busy highway before turning off to a quieter road to Swanlinbar, in the Republic. After just a short while my mobile rings. The caller asks if we can meet. Minutes later, Giles Knight arrives in a 4x4 with Ulster Wildlife Trust written on the side, pulling into a side street as lorries thunder past. Giles works on restoring wildflower meadows, 97 per cent of which have disappeared from Northern Ireland over the last fifty years. It was his father, Gordon Knight, who had inspired his love of wild places. 'Without his influence I wouldn't be doing this,' Giles says. 'He taught me to love wildlife.' Gordon had died suddenly in 1999 and it is clear how much Giles still misses him. 'He had a particular soft spot for curlews. He wrote a poem about them, and I'd like you to have it,' says Giles, pulling a piece of paper from his pocket and handing it to me. 'Perhaps it will bring you luck.'

I am so moved; it is a truly touching and memorable moment, and it proves once again that curlews have the power to inspire. Giles and his family had no idea about the poem until after Gordon's death. It tells of the birds' seasonal swings between estuaries and the hills, and it celebrates the fact that their wild lives are governed by different rules to the ones that humanity now chooses to obey.

For Whom the Curlews Call

Twice daily calls the tide
Up valleys where the sea clouds ride
To where high meadows touch the sky
And wild curlews cry.

No thoughts of day or night
Nor if the bubbling shore's in sight
Disturb the ebbing, distant sea
Or emptying estuary.

Yet the curlews always hear,
Be it windy, wet, dull or clear,
Perhaps by some aquatic sigh
When muds emerging dry.

Then to the air they spring
And off to sea they eager wing,
Sweet soul-sounds of the gathering sky
That down the darkness fly.

No weaving journey here,
No anxious aims inspired by fear,
But just obedience to the tide
That sun and moon provide.

So why does man invent
The everlastingly lament
The plastics and the trash galore
Which litter every shore?

Or sickly twisted tales
Whose squalid, booming bookstall sales
Confirm he heeds no tide
Nor longer seeks his Guide?

But the curlews calling flight
Crossing estuaries through the night
Recalls to haunted man
The shores from which he ran.

For the spirit of winds and tides
Whose face the Earth mists hides
Shall one day restore all
To whom the curlews call.

It is a powerful message to ponder as I leave the main road and begin to absorb the peace of a country road. The surrounding fields are mainly small and well-kept and fringed by mature trees just coming into leaf. Receiving the poem is a boost, melting away the insecurities of the night before. This is not just a walk for curlews but also for the people who love them like I do, for those who care enough to drive to meet me and give me a poem, or who donate money to curlew projects; for the people who send me encouraging messages, or who offer me food and accommodation when they have never met me. It is for all those people who spend time caring about the planet and the creatures that live alongside us. This is a walk for curlews as well as for the good, kind, compassionate people who strive to make the world a better place for all of us.

The hedgerow birds sing clear and strong and the scurrying white clouds cast light and shade over distant mountains. The undulating road takes me through a watercolour landscape; sublime in its layering of subtle colour. After a couple of hours I sit down for a rest on a polished stone bench by an old bridge over the Arney River. It is little more than a stream at this point, barely a few metres wide, but tumbling and joyful; the surface sparkles as it races under the seventeenth-century arches. Around the sides of the polished limestone seat is carved, in beautiful script, a verse from a poem written by the renowned Enniskillen poet and artist, T.P. Flanagan, who loved this spot. Historically, it was a place where locals met on an evening to chat over the day and courting couples huddled together on the banks and made plans for their future lives together. Flanagan was a friend of Seamus Heaney, who described him as one of Ireland's greatest landscape artists. Heaney greatly admired his paintings for their delicate, light-filled scenes of Fermanagh and the adjacent County Sligo. His watercolours have a translucent quality; they perfectly capture both the physical world and the parallel ethereal mist of legend. They are poetry in paint, and Flanagan obviously had poetry in his soul, too. 'On Arney Bridge' was written about this very spot in 1945 when Flanagan was only sixteen, and he captures in words the teasing mischief of those, both real and imagined, who assembled here many moons ago:

> On Arney Bridge, so some men say
> On Arney Bridge, where the winds are sweet,
> There's noise of maidens' dancing feet;
> There's tossing arms and flying hair
> Flashing eyes and faces fair
> There's moon-fire in the water
> And haunting girlish laughter;
> And sylph-like forms bend and sway,
> Like reeds in the bud-tossing winds of May.
> On Arney Bridge, so some men say.[3]

The bench, designed by the stonemason Michael Hoy, had only recently been installed and is a work of art in its own right – art inspired by art. The curved, graceful script is as playful as the poem and as flowing as the river. Poetry, rock and river, merging into one.

An hour further on I meet a Fermanagh man with such shining eyes that he could have been a character in that poem. Joe McLoughlin lives close to the border between Northern and Southern Ireland, and he and his wife Ann invite me in for a bite to eat. I think they noticed my increasingly obvious limp from the first blisters, and my flagging disposition. Ann disappears to do chores while Joe and I chat on their lawn in the sunshine, as their two lovely dogs, both rescued from cruelty and starvation, sit by my feet and stare at my sandwich. Joe has that quintessential Irish twinkle, and, like Giles, emanates kindness. He used to work at the post office, but now spends his days just enjoying life. Did he know about curlews? Not really, but he had heard me talking on the radio just that morning and thought they must be worth saving. The tea and sandwich are their contribution to the cause. I ask him how far I have to go to get to the Irish border. 'There is no border,' he says with a broad smile and tapping the side of his head, 'just the one in people's minds.' He advises me to take a minor road that had been used during The Troubles for running guns from the South. Eventually the army barricaded it and blew up the surface. I tear myself away from the comfortable sun lounger and the congenial company and carry on, cheered by their hospitality. The road is narrow and shaded by trees, with no trace of any past horrors.

Twenty minutes later a car draws up beside me and Joe leans out of the window and hands me an ice cream and a can of Coke. 'Thought you might be hot,' he says, with his twinkling smile. For the third time that day the road ahead is made easier by the simple goodness of ordinary people. Swanlinbar, the small town literally just across the border in the Republic, is now just a couple of miles away.

Although the hedgerows are alive with bird music, the call of the curlew is conspicuously absent from the fields. I often stop to listen, but there is nothing. The farmland is a curlew desert. It will be increasingly hard to persuade governments and farmers to implement compassionate farming if the sweet soul-sounds of curlews are heard no more. Why change a farming routine, and perhaps even take a financial hit, for a bird no one knows? But then, as I come to the border, I hear it. Over in the distance, still just inside Northern Ireland, a curlew calls from a field on a hill. I wonder if I have imagined it, but no, there it is again – 'curlee, curlee'. I make a note of the location and quicken my pace to Swanlinbar, where I am to meet Michael Bell from BirdWatch Ireland. We could come back to this spot and search together. It is a wonderful, cheering moment. In 'The Fairy Lough' Irish poet Moira O'Neill is uplifted by the disembodied voice of a curlew:

> When the hills are dark
> An 'airy
> 'Tis a curlew whistles sweet![4]

She was right. It is such a sweet, clear sound. Half an hour later I am back in the same spot with Michael, trying to find the singer of the song. It is a perfect start to my trek through Southern Ireland. It might seem fanciful, but it feels a little like the curlew is calling me on my way into the South.

Chapter 5

ENTERING EIRE

You don't know that you've crossed the border into the Republic of Ireland – there is no sign, no fence. The border that caused so much bloodshed registers as nothing more than a slight change in atmosphere. Perhaps a little more laid-back? It's hard to define. For a short distance prices are displayed in both euros and pounds, but when I ask a girl if I am still in the North, she shrugs and says, 'no idea'.

County Cavan is the land of drumlins and lakes, 365 lakes in fact, one for each day of the year. It is a corrugated landscape shaped by ancient glaciers into low, smooth hills and hollows, in-filled with watery bogs and forest; it has a closed-in feel. One claim to fame for Cavan is that in medieval times it was home to a wealthy family called O'Reilly, who built castles and bolstered the economy. It appears they liked a good time, hence the phrase 'the life of Reilly'. The county's sturdy motto is 'Manliness and Truth'.

Swanlinbar lies just inside the County Cavan border with Fermanagh and is a small, attractive village with a solid feel. The houses are thickset and pleasingly proportioned, hinting at past wealth. In its heyday in the eighteenth and nineteenth centuries this was a spa town where mineral-rich waters, bubbling up through limestone, enticed wealthy city dwellers to bathe away their urban maladies. One illustrious visitor was the Methodist preacher John Wesley. In his *Journal* he described the people of Swanlinbar 'as simple and artless as if they had lived upon the Welsh mountains'. He also decided to see if he could convert them.

'Thursday 4th May 1769 – About six I preached at the town's end, the very Papists appearing as attentive as the Protestants; and I doubt not thousands of these would soon be zealous Christians, were it not for their wretched Priests, who will not enter into the kingdom of God themselves, and diligently hinder those that would.'[1]

Religious rivalry is nothing new in this land.

The eighteenth century saw another grand guest, the Anglo-Irish writer, essayist and cleric Jonathan Swift. The original Irish name for Swanlinbar means iron foundry, as a small iron industry flourished here for a while. Its products did not impress Mr Swift. In his 1728 essay entitled 'On Barbarous Denominations in Ireland', he declared that Swanlinbar is 'where the worst iron in the kingdom is made.' Perhaps iron ore extracted from mountains rich in myth is imbued with different qualities to ore from more pedestrian places. The source of the ore was Cuilcagh Mountain, which rises to 666 metres, but somehow it seems larger and more important than its measurements suggest. It is the largest mountain in the area and lies a few miles to the west of Swanlinbar. From the summit the ridges of drumlins, boggy plains and sparkling loughs spread out like a carpet. Parts of the surrounding land were once cloaked in ancient oak forests, which provided the charcoal for the furnaces. The night sky must have glowed red until all the trees were chopped down by the mid-nineteenth century and the iron industry folded.

Cuilcagh Mountain is also the source for the Shannon, the longest river in Ireland. This great waterway springs from a small pool on its slopes called the Shannon Pot. Long ago, so they say, the pool was surrounded by the wonderfully named Nine Hazel Trees of Knowledge, which produced fruits, flowers and seeds all at the same time. When the nuts fell into the water, the also wonderfully named Salmon of Knowledge, which lived in the pool, ate them and thus gained great wisdom. Only the king was allowed to visit this magical pool, but Sionann, a young goddess with searing ambition, wanted to eat the salmon and become the most knowledgeable of all Earth's creatures. With echoes of Eve eating a forbidden apple from the Tree of Knowledge of Good and Evil in the Garden of Eden, this proved to be a bad idea. The waters of the pool rose and swept the hapless goddess out to sea, where she drowned. The river of retribution bears her name, the River Sionann or Shannon.

My mother's connection with Swanlinbar came to light only after her death. As children in Enniskillen, she and her siblings were sent on their bikes over the border to buy contraband butter, where it was cheaper than in the North. 'Swaddie', as they called Swanlinbar, was 12 miles away, just a little too far to carry butter tucked into a jumper, as one of my aunts discovered on a particularly warm day when trying to avoid the attention of the border police.

Large areas of blanket bog remain around the mountains and drumlin fields, albeit altered and 'improved'. Breeding curlews were once numerous here. *The Historical Atlas of Breeding Birds in Britain and Ireland, 1875–1900*, states, 'The curlew bred extensively in Ireland, chiefly on the flat bogs and mountain moors.' The area surrounding Swanlinbar must have been perfect, but not a single pair breeds there now. When trying to find out more about curlews in Cavan I came into contact with Heather Bothwell, a BirdWatch Ireland supporter. Heather is originally from County Antrim, in Northern Ireland, but moved to Cavan in 1987 when she married a local farmer. She surveys birds for BirdWatch and took part in the curlew surveys of 2015 and 2016. Writing to me, she described the curlew situation in Cavan:

> My husband Desmond remembers finding one big spotty egg in 1980, in a field that had never had much fertiliser. He was bringing in the cows and he remembers there was a curlew calling overhead. The field was ploughed and reseeded in 1984, and cut for silage for many years after that. He never had breeding curlew since on the farm. I have found no curlew in Cavan. This part of Cavan had many small areas of bogs and 'bottoms' (low peaty fields) in between the ribbed moraines and drumlins; however, they are small and many have been drained and altered. Old rough grazing was ploughed up and changed in the 1970s. This farm changed from carrying 12 cows and a horse in the 1950s to 32 cows and their followers in the late 70s. Everybody else, of course, was at the same work, bit by bit, and the rest was planted.

Intensification, silage cutting, drainage, forestry and stocking density – the same story is replicated across the island of Ireland.

Michael Bell also surveys for BirdWatch Ireland in County Sligo and is waiting for me in the main street of Swanlinbar. Michael is one of the stars I meet on my walk, one of those stand-out individuals who have a passion for the world around them, which directs their lives and infuses everything they do. They swim against the tide of what appears to be so much indifference towards nature.

Michael is as excited as I am about the lone voice from the hill nearby, and we drive back to the spot where I had heard the calls – by a crossroads and bus shelter on a busy road on the border. As soon as we step out of the car, there it is again, a plaintive lament from a distant field. The nearest farmhouse is set back from the road and we meet the farmer's wife in the backyard, where she is playing with her two small children. She is astonished to find that the person she had heard on the radio in the morning, talking about a bird she had never heard of, is now standing at her door asking for permission to find it in her fields. 'Yes of course, go and look. What was the name of it again?' 'Curlews, they used to be very common around here,' I explain. She looks perplexed. 'Don't know them, but we'll look them up on the computer while you're gone, won't we?' Her two children nod eagerly.

Michael and I search everywhere, through damp fields and grazed meadows. We walk down tracks and scan the

horizon through binoculars. We sit quietly beside a wall
and listen, willing the bird to make just one more call, but
like an Irish sprite it has simply vanished into thin air. After
forty minutes of blister-aggravating hunting we give up and
go back to the farmhouse to say thank you. 'I couldn't find
anything on the internet,' says the farmer's wife. 'You do
spell it c u r l y?'

That evening I give a talk in the city of Sligo about the
plight of curlews throughout Britain and Ireland, and I am
greeted with great warmth as well as consternation. Many
of the older people have treasured memories, particularly
of hearing the call when working on the bogs or in the
fields, and they find it hard to fathom that something that
was once part of everyday life is now on the edge of
collapse. They are shocked they haven't noticed. I, too, am
surprised at how few people know the trouble the birds
are in. A decline from many thousands of pairs in the 1980s
to 130 today is dramatic, and you would think the silence
from the fields would be deafening. But as with so much
wildlife, the familiar can edge away into the shadows with
no fuss or fight. While we focus on the immediate and the
obvious, creatures that occupy the margins can gradually
fade from our consciousness until one day – gone. Then
perhaps, at some point, a soundtrack on a film or a picture
in a book jolts the memory. But despite a desire to hear
that call again, it is too late. Someone in the audience
points out that the same scenario happened to the corncrake and now Ireland is allowing it to happen again –
letting the beloved curlew slip away like water through
their fingers. Can it really be happening twice in one

lifetime? What is being done to stop it? There is a palpable sense of frustration laced with sadness. A wildlife ranger despairs at the lack of official action; a group huddles round him and they talk earnestly amongst themselves.

Sligo is a salutary place to give a curlew talk, the great Irish poet William Butler Yeats often holidayed here as a child. Just down the road is Lough Gill, with its uninhabited island, Innisfree, the setting for Yeats's famous poem, 'The Lake Isle of Innisfree', a heartfelt yearning for a life surrounded by nature. It evokes a place where 'peace comes dropping slow', and where the evening is 'full of the linnet's wings.' It was written in London, where a small fountain in a shop window seems to have jolted Yeats back to the place of his childhood. The sight of the bubbling water produced a flood of memories of mountain streams tumbling through bog. He yearned to get away from the pavements, with their crowds and noise. Through the beauty of words, Yeats expresses a longing to live on Innisfree, where the gentle drone of bees and the lapping of waves provide a quiet underscore to a life surrounded by the natural world. I have no doubt curlews were part of that scene, shaping his inner life, as they often appear in his work, '… a curlew cried and in the luminous wind/A curlew answered', he wrote in 'Paudeen'.

The idea for 'The Lake Isle of Innisfree' may have taken some of its inspiration from a classic book on life in the wilds, 'Walden' by Henry David Thoreau, written half a century earlier. Yeats greatly admired this book, which documents the two years in which Thoreau lived alone in a home-made cabin in the woods by Walden Pond, in

Massachusetts. In his autobiography, Yeats fantasised about doing the same thing; leaving the crowds for a harmonious life with nature. His feelings of exile were offset by daydreaming.

> Sometimes I told myself very adventurous love-stories with myself for hero, and at other times I planned out a life of lonely austerity, and at other times mixed the ideals and planned a life of lonely austerity mitigated by periodical lapses. I had still the ambition, formed in Sligo in my teens, of living in imitation of Thoreau on Innisfree, a little island in Lough Gill, and when walking through Fleet Street very homesick I heard a little tinkle of water and saw a fountain in a shop-window which balanced a little ball upon its jet, and began to remember lake water. From the sudden remembrance came my poem 'Innisfree', my first lyric with anything in its rhythm of my own music.[2]

The people at my talk want to reconnect with nature, too, and they express feelings of nostalgia for a time when wildlife was rich and abundant, and there was time to savour it. Everyone agrees that there is something about the call of the curlew that captures these sentiments; it brings to the surface a remembrance of a lost connection; to a time when life was very different in County Sligo.

When Yeats was here at the end of the nineteenth century, the town had a population of around 10,000. By the end of the twentieth century, this had grown to 18,000, a modest increase, but traditionally nothing happens very quickly on the northwestern edges of Europe. But what happened next shattered any notions of Old Ireland. The 90s heralded a period of unprecedented economic and social change, commonly referred to as the Celtic Tiger. Sligo, along with the rest of Ireland, experienced a wild, unrestrained, headlong rush into development, progress and economic growth. Today, the population of Sligo and its adjacent new commuter towns is 30,000.

Between the mid-1990s and 2008 Ireland went from being one of the poorest countries in the European Union to one of the wealthiest. Its economy was pumped and primed by foreign investment taking advantage of the low Corporation Tax, by state-driven developments and by membership of the European Union. Since joining the EU in 1973, Ireland has received over €58 billion, much of which went to expanding and improving its infrastructure and supporting businesses. Sligo now has fast links to Northern Ireland, Dublin, the northwest and the south-west coasts. Throughout the island, bog lands were drained, methods of farming updated and fields improved. In just a few short decades, Ireland was transformed from an economic backwater to a full player in a modern, forward-looking European Union.

Naturally, people welcomed this new world and the increased standard of living that it provides. Suddenly, the once remote west of Ireland was a key part of a high-tech, integrated continent. Emigration slowed as opportunities at home burgeoned, reversing a long and dispiriting trend. The population of Ireland as a whole increased by almost 15 per cent between 1996 and 2005. In one year alone

(July 2004–June 2005), employment increased by 5 per cent. Ireland became a land of opportunity for many workers from the ten newest European Union member states. Ancient whitewashed cottages were left to decay, and showy, modern houses, many looking as though they had been transported in from Florida, sprang up alongside. Second homes appeared everywhere on scenic roads, coastal areas and bogs. Ninety thousand new homes were built in Ireland in 2006, the highest figure recorded, and one-third of Ireland's houses standing today were built since the 90s. Out-of-town shopping malls, industrial areas and civic amenities sprang up along the new highways. In my visits to Ireland over the last few decades I watched with amazement at how towns like Letterkenny in County Donegal and Swords in County Dublin were transformed beyond all recognition. The Ireland of the old has been washed away by a tsunami of development.

And curlews, what of them in this land of burgeoning opportunity? Darwinian theory says that only the most adaptable to change will survive – in other words, adapt or die.

Curlews, along with many other farmland birds, were particularly badly affected by this rapid alteration of the landscape – corncrake, skylark, stock dove, mistle thrush, grey partridge and kestrel all severely declined in the Tiger years. It takes generations of evolution to hone a species to its surroundings, but it takes a blink of the eye – in evolutionary terms – for us to completely transform the land and change the parameters. A brown, rushy wet field can be drained in weeks. Fast-growing Sitka spruce plantations can cover an area of bog in a handful of years. Chemicals can quickly turn peat land into lush grazing. It seems to be a universal truth that when money talks, the birds go silent. It was certainly the case in Ireland.

> O curlew cry no more to the air,
> Or only to the water in the West;
> Because your crying brings to my mind
> Passion-dimmed eyes and long heavy hair
> That was shaken out over my breast.
> There is enough evil in the crying of the wind.

No one knows how many pairs of breeding curlews there were in County Sligo when Yeats wrote his poem of love, loss and dying passion, 'He Reproves the Curlew', in 1899, because no one was counting, but there must have been many hundreds of pairs of breeding birds spread over the 2,000 square kilometres of mountains, bogs and small fields of this rugged county. There is no doubt Yeats would have heard their fluting call in the spring, their 'sweet crystalline cry' as they nested in the fields and bogs. But how things change. In 2016 there were just two confirmed pairs that nested successfully in the whole of the county, probably producing three chicks, but whether those chicks fledged is unknown. A couple of other sightings were reported but they couldn't be verified, and nothing is known about whether their attempts at breeding were successful – if indeed they nested at all. The devastating truth is that curlews have almost gone as a breeding bird in County Sligo. Michael Bell wrote to me a few months after my walk to tell me that he and his teenage daughter, Molly, had seen a curlew over a bog near their home. 'It was a wonderful moment but the wonder was tempered by the worry that she may not get to see breeding curlew in Ireland as an adult.'

After my curlew talk in Sligo town, I am taken to where I will spend my first night on the road, a beautiful eighteenth-century farmhouse that stands on a bluff above the shores of Lough Allen. My host is farmer Tommy Earley, another wildlife hero. Tommy manages his land organically and is working to encourage the return of a whole raft of wildlife, including curlews (they haven't appeared yet), and working with other farmers in the area to do the same. It is after midnight by the time we say goodnight. The night is cold and clear. My room is in an annexe of the main farmhouse, so before going to bed I stand alone outside and breathe in the inky blackness. It has been a long day, but for me now, too, peace comes dropping slow. There is not a sound, just the stars and a cool wind. I could be a million miles away from home. I walk around a little and feel on the edge of something I can't define. It is strange to arrive in a place after dark and have no idea what it looks like. The blackness is so intense that all I can see is the outline of a couple of trees and the solid form of the farmhouse against the stars. There seems to be nothing else out there. I awake next morning around six o'clock to what sounds like a loud cuckoo clock, but it is in fact the real thing, just outside my window.

Southern Ireland now stretches before me. Much of the rest of my walk will follow the great River Shannon, pouring out of the slopes of Cuilcagh Mountain. At 360 kilometres long, the river cuts a significant natural boundary, separating the rugged west from the more populous eastern counties. Many tributaries flow into the main river, creating a lacework of watery threads that meander, coalesce and part again, giving central Ireland the feeling of a place that has as much water as land, especially when it rains. At one time this wetland provided nesting places for thousands of curlews in the herb-rich, damp meadows, bogs and fluvial islands.

While walking, I try to imagine the days when tarmac roads were dirt tracks and pilgrim pathways. I ponder on the religious communities that left their traces in carvings on old churches, wells and remote stone cells; mysterious holy souls living quiet lives of prayer and austerity. The tarmac of today cannot efface those ancient ways that once carried seekers of truth and mystery across a meaningful land, where it seems almost every bird and flower had a message to convey. The tension between the quest for transcendence and the everyday reality of hunger and toil produced poetry and prayers of great beauty. Such yearnings can't be so easily covered over, and they live on in stories and long-held traditions by those who follow their footsteps as modern pilgrims. They too use walking to express outwardly the inner experiences they feel most intensely.

Many of the sayings and blessings are anonymous, such as this one, perhaps written one stormy night when the wind and rain kept one seeker awake: 'The curlew cannot sleep at all/His voice is shrill above the deep/Reverberations of the storm;/Between the streams he will not sleep.' The cry of the Storm Bird must have provided a melancholic backdrop to an earnest and hard life. The association of curlews with storms and rain is well documented through time, and many Irish tales feature the call of the curlew, especially if heard at night, as a warning of rain-laden gales sweeping in from the sea. Ancient stories have fishermen turning their boats back for land if they hear a curlew call overhead. In Ireland, the new moon bird is also a storm bird.

No rain falls on me on my second day in Southern Ireland, but I meet two more wildlife stars in County Leitrim. In the small town of Ballinamore, which sits on a river connecting Lough Erne with the Shannon, I had arranged to meet Kay Maguire, who had contacted me by email a few weeks earlier. Kay is a human dynamo, the kind of person you could consider yourself blessed to have standing next to you in a crisis; warm-hearted and wonderfully efficient. Within minutes, I am collected, photographed, given a 'Keep Ballinamore Tidy' thermal mug and driven to a school. It is a little way off my route, taking me east, not south, but Kay has arranged for me to take a class of 17–18-year-old boys and girls who are studying for their final exams in Agriculture and the Environment.

Being faced with a room full of teenagers who have no interest in you, and don't try to disguise the fact, is like the nightmare job interview where you know the panel have dismissed you in the first five seconds. There is no option but to plough on with a fixed smile. I begin by showing the class a picture of a curlew. Anyone know what this bird is?

Silence. Okay, they are more often heard than seen, so I play recordings of the common calls. Anyone recognise these sounds; they are a farmland bird after all? No one, not one in a room of young people studying agriculture had heard of, or seen or heard a curlew. The teacher had heard of curlews but didn't know anything about them. This is profoundly worrying: these young people are the future of Irish farming and this class was being taught in a rural part of the country. Since no agricultural colleges in Ireland teach their students about wildlife, it is unlikely that these youngsters will ever know what they are losing. To be fair, one young man does seem a little interested and is the only one to ask a question at the end of the lesson. Why not breed them in captivity, to be released? A good point. I don't know if anyone has ever tried, but if it does come to that, I suggest to him, it would be tantamount to an admission of total failure on our part. Surely, I urge the class, we can do something before that is necessary? In fact, I was unaware that it was already being trialled in Poland and plans were being considered in England – a recognition of how serious the situation has become.

I finish by telling them that they are the first generation in Ireland never to hear a corncrake in the spring, and probably the last to hear the calls of breeding curlew. What do they think about that, as future custodians of the land? There is an awkward silence. The bell goes and the room empties. It is time for me to get back on track and head south.

I wasn't expecting to hear a Stoke-on-Trent accent in the middle of County Leitrim, and it is both welcome and disconcerting. Neil Foulkes provides me with a lift back to the planned route; he is one of those people who can live for years in a country and never pick up even a hint of the local accent. His Stoke roots were advertised loud and clear in that unmistakable twang that is a cross between the pronounced inflexions of Birmingham and Manchester. Only a few days after making an offering to Lough Erne in memory of my mum, I am now being spoken to in the accent of my home town, and it brings memories of my beloved dad sharply into focus. He died in 2013, and not a day goes by when I don't talk to him and ask his opinion. He would have liked Neil, and so do I.

Neil Foulkes came to Ireland in his twenties and is now Mr Hedgerow. He loves the tangled corridors of rose, hawthorn and ivy – the buzzing, singing colourful divisions that parcel up the land. Some date back a thousand years, and as Ireland has very little native woodland, the hedgerows take on the role of woodland edges. They are vibrant places that do a vital job all year round, providing nesting, food and shelter for birds such as yellowhammers and linnets, mammals like bats and hedgehogs, and a multitude of insects. It is currently illegal to cut hedges between the beginning of March and the end of August, but there is always pressure to allow hedge-cutting a month earlier, in July, when yellowhammers may still be nesting. Farmers want the flexibility of cutting early to control wildfires, to give them more time to prepare for the winter weather, and help them make the land eligible for various grants. The controversy rages on while Neil is doing what he can to protect the hedgerows.

Over the last forty years, many thousands of kilometres of hedgerow in Ireland have been ripped out for the new developments, much as they have in England, but there are no official statistics. Neil wants Irish hedges to be loved again; to be replenished and treasured. He runs workshops on the ancient skills of hedge-laying, which maximises the intricate lattice work of stems and branches. He believes hedgerows are as much a part of Ireland's heritage as the old castles and rich folklore. He tells me that 40 kilometres of hedgerow are to be removed to accommodate a new runway at Dublin airport, but wholesale removal isn't his biggest worry. 'Of greater concern than direct removal, because it is more insidious, is the degradation and loss due to poor management, or complete lack of management.' It is this misunderstanding of the nature of hedges that he is trying to put right. I can only wish him well. When I arrived on the island of Ireland I noticed how many hedges in both the North and the South had recently been thrashed. Sharp, jagged green spears stuck out into the road; they looked like lines of weapons. The torn wood was white and fresh and the splinters raw. It seems a violent way to treat a complex, living entity. But time is money and this is the most efficient way to cut back miles of vegetation.

The effect of hearing Neil's Stoke accent, delivered with great kindness, makes saying goodbye difficult. I want to sit in his van and just listen to him talk. Through the flat vowels and distinctive lilt I am transported back to my childhood in the Staffordshire Peaks with my dad, looking for fossils in the stone walls, hearing the curlews call overhead. If I could fashion my father out of the air, back into a living form even for a few moments, I would hold his hand one more time and thank him for everything. But as it is, I watch Neil's van disappear down the road and I find it hard to hold back tears. Suddenly the world feels unstable again and the road ahead utterly unknowable.

In the late afternoon I arrive at Lough Rynn, a small lake in the southern part of County Leitrim which is part of the complex of waterways feeding into and fed by the Shannon. Bed-and-breakfast owner Martina Fox has offered to put me up for the night in one of her holiday homes, a small modern house on an estate close to the water's edge. All of the surrounding land used to belong to a grand stately home, Lough Rynn Castle, that stands at the end of the road, just a few hundred metres away. It is now a luxury hotel. In the nineteenth century, this impressive house belonged to one of the most hated English landlords in all of Ireland, the 3rd Earl of Leitrim, William Sydney Clements, described as 'evil at its worst'. By all accounts, Clements was a truly unpleasant man. Even other English gentry, not themselves given to conspicuous displays of kindness and compassion, thought he took things too far. He famously evicted wholesale his tenants on another of his estates in Donegal, people already desperately poor and starving from the effects of the famine. Mean, ruthless, cruel, given to violence and misogyny, he was eventually murdered by his own farm workers. Like many a stately home, the grandeur of Lough Rynn Castle belies the unpleasant truths of histories of exploitation and appropriation.

On the road that leads down to the hotel entrance I meet a farmer pulling out of a field on his tractor. He stops for a chat and we talk about the estate with its once vast 90,000 acres of farmland, ruled over by Clements. Had I noticed that none of the old workers' cottages had any back doors or windows? To be honest no, I hadn't. 'They don't,' he says, with that Irish twinkle in his eyes, leaning forwards on the steering wheel. 'They were built like that to stop the tenants escaping out the back when the land-lord wanted his rent.' How true this is I don't know, but it paints a good picture. He tells another story about the infa-mous Mr Clements that pretty much sums him up. One elderly tenant farmer was summoned to the estate office and was left waiting outside all day in pouring rain. The old man was made to stand from morning until evening with no shelter and only his winter coat for protection. When Clements eventually turned up that night, he marvelled at the quality of the coat's wool and how well it had faired against the rain. 'If you can afford a coat like that,' he snarled, 'you are too well off!' And immediately doubled the farmer's rent. A story told with a smile, but which delivers a sting – very much the stuff of Irish humour – and I feel conscious of my English accent. I ask him if he knows of any curlews nesting around here. 'They used to,' he said, 'lots of them. Haven't seen one in years.'

The sun begins to slip behind the trees fringing the lough and there is a real sense of peace. The water looks beautiful. As day fades into evening, it is hard to believe there could be anything wrong with the world. I sit down with a mug of tea and a packet of biscuits in the clean, modern kitchen of the holiday home and begin to write notes. It is very quiet and it feels strange to have a whole house to myself, but good to have some time alone to think. Then, straight away, my mobile rings. John Matthews, the National Parks and Wildlife Service (NPWS) ranger who had been at my talk in Sligo, asks if I want to see some curlews. South Leitrim is under his jurisdiction and he knows the locations. Despite longing for a night alone, it is too good an offer to miss. 'I'll be there in a few minutes!' he says. And thus began one of the most magical curlew evenings of my six weeks of walking.

John arrives in a whirlwind of energy. Originally from Dublin, he learned about wildlife in the fields that once surrounded the city. Curlews had even once nested near the town that I was familiar with, Swords, just to the north of Dublin airport – something that is impossible to imagine now. I offer him tea and biscuits ('Ah go on! I will now – the Divils at me elbow!') and he tells me how he is engaged in one long battle to protect the bogs from forestry and turf-cutting. There are curlews nesting near to where we are now, though, and the evening is a good time to see them.

South Leitrim, roughly the area between Tommy Earley's farm on the southern shores of Lough Allen, to just below Lough Rynn, used to be a curlew hotspot. There is so much prime habitat in this watery wonderland, but this part of Ireland is where serious peat-cutting begins. The extensive blanket bogs that have built up in this low-lying area over thousands of years are used as fuel, both for small-scale home burning and for Ireland's three large peat-burning power stations. Cutting peat is big business and provides jobs in a region that has always suffered from high unemployment. Left unexploited, these areas are perfect grounds for the curlew – generally speaking, where there is peat, there are usually curlews.

John has a licence to play curlew calls loudly through a speaker, a technique that helps monitor bird numbers. By playing the call of the bird, real birds in the area will often call back or come and investigate. They don't want a rival settling on their patch. Done properly, it's a good tool, but it has to be used with care, and a licence from the National Parks and Wildlife Service is essential. We drive to a green lane, a boreen in Irish, which leads from the roadside to a stretch of bog. The narrow track is bordered by ancient hedgerows and prettily dotted with primroses.

It seems quiet in the lazy evening sunlight; life is shutting up shop and changing shifts. John plays the bubbling curlew call and we scan the horizon for a response. Within seconds a bird flies up from a patch of bog in the valley and calls back. It flies straight towards us and circles round. 'Good to see it's still there,' says John. Only one pair, but one is better than none. I watch its dark shape, the long bill unmistakable, against the sky, and savour the song, loud, sweet and clear. We move on to another boreen by another bog, this time with a peat extractor sitting by a large pile of cut turf. This bog is de-listed, meaning it is no longer protected, and can be exploited for fuel or for plantations.

Again, John plays the call and again a bird responds, calling loud from the air behind us. Eventually it lands on top of the pile of turf, a strange sight with its beak silhouetted against the sky and its long legs planted firmly on the stacked black slabs. 'Good, that pair are still here, too,' says John, ticking them off. 'I think they are nesting in the fields some ways off.' Their voices carry through the reddening sky. The poet John Masefield once wrote of 'the curlew calling time of Irish dusk', and, witnessing this at first hand now, the bog somehow seems complete. We see another bird a little further on and watch it flying over its fragile domain – its home. A calm April evening, a beautiful sunset and the call of curlews scattering their haunting notes across the land. Isn't this how it should be?

You cannot replicate real contact with nature. No wildlife film or piece of writing can replace the emotion and the thrill of seeing a wild creature in its natural

surroundings. Joy can only be experienced in the moment, and then it is gone. The memory may remain as an after-glow, but the intensity cannot be caught and pinned down by words or pixels. And if the moment is shared, there is no need to talk. John lets fall his characteristic banter, and stands silently with me as we watch the calling curlews disappear back into their secret lives. How long will anyone be able to do this? How many years before experiences like this become a thing of the past, known only through thoughts scribbled in notebooks and written in books or blogs? The sinister-looking silhouette of the peat extractor sits on the horizon, surrounded by piles of cut turf – a solid, cold reminder that the odds are stacked against future encounters like this.

I would have loved to have found a nest, to lie low on the wet bog and watch a curlew sitting alert on the eggs, dedicated and single-minded, but they are notoriously difficult to find, often taking hours to track down to the exact spot. And anyway, these birds need peace and it is getting late. I am content to know that they are out there. It is almost dark when John packs up his recorder.

We find a fast-food shop and sit at a red plastic table eating bags of chips under harsh fluorescent lights. 'If you compare curlew conservation in Ireland with the last 150 pairs of white rhino in Africa,' muses John, 'there would be protection for its habitat and platoons of armed guards carrying out round-the-clock patrols. But these are only curlews and this is only poor, "developing" Ireland. People and profits are far more important than curlews and conserving habitats and bogs.' His despair is well founded. Out of seven pairs that attempted to breed in the area in 2015, not one is known to have successfully produced any chicks. In every case there were either too many predators or too much disturbance. In 2016, out of five nesting attempts in County Leitrim, not one chick was recorded.

As we drive back to my bed and breakfast, John tells me of the many evenings he has spent looking through planning applications, trying to identify new proposals for forestry on the bogs, so that he can oppose them before the diggers arrive. 'Trees are money, curlews aren't. Some I win, some I lose, and I don't get to see the planning applications in time – it's shocking there isn't more transparency. There are too many officials with too many relatives with farming interests. There's a saying in this land of

Saints and Scholars, "you can't throw a stone around here without hitting someone's cousin." Well, that's true. Where is the famous "gra" ("love" in Gaelic) for the land, that we Irish are supposed to have? I'll tell you – there is no more gra for the land, only gra for money and development. But hey, feck it! None of us can lift up the world, but little by little it will turn around.' The night ends with laughter, and memories of the curlews flying home against a blood-red sky.

I go to sleep grateful for my meetings with John, Kay, Neil, Tommy, Michael and the other stars whose paths I have crossed so far in Southern Ireland. No doubt there are many others out there, and over the coming days I will meet a few more of them along the route. This beautiful country would feel bleak without them, left to plough ahead with its seemingly unstoppable transformation of the land. And the next day I would walk deeper into peat-extraction territory.

Chapter 6

INTO THE BOGS

The café is cold and the waitress unfriendly. She wants me to leave, it is closing time and there is only me, eking out a cold cup of tea, and someone in the corner with a paper. I want to stay, though; this is my meeting place for my overnight accommodation, but no one has arrived. I check my watch. Pat and Liam should have been here twenty minutes ago. Pat had written to me via Facebook saying they would be delighted to put me up for a night. As a keen birdwatcher she loves curlews and wants to help. I begin to wonder if I have got the dates confused and if there is a hotel nearby. Suddenly the man in the corner stands up, folds his newspaper and walks over. 'I was watching you to make sure you were alright,' he says, with no smile. 'The car is outside.'

I try to chat politely as we drive down increasingly remote and minor roads. It is like getting the proverbial blood out of a stone. Liam stares ahead and says nothing.

He is perhaps in his fifties, thin, and he exudes pent-up anger. The car is full of oiled paper, straw, old blankets and discarded coffee cups – the stuff of farming. Eventually we arrive at large iron gates in the middle of high hedges. They are black and imposing. He unlocks them, we drive through and as he turns to lock them again, I ask if Pat is at home. He spits out, 'She left me.' He locks the gates.

There is a long drive down to the detached old farm-house and all I can think of is that my blisters are so sore I can't run. Inside is gloomy and Liam points to a room at the top of the stairs and says I can sleep in there. It is fusty and cold. The sheets are threadbare and the single pillow is flat. I am not sure what to do – I don't want to go down-stairs but feel it is rude to stay put. Eventually, I find the kitchen. There is a plate of cold potatoes and cheese, some bread and a glass of water put out on a table that is covered in bills, old newspapers and unwashed glasses. Liam is nowhere to be seen but I can hear vague sounds from behind a door. I eat and go back upstairs and try to call home, but there is no signal.

By ten o'clock I venture out to the bathroom. I can't find the hall light switch so I take my torch. I have heard nothing since supper. Liam seems to have disappeared. The bathroom is at the end of the corridor and as I reach it a door opens. He is framed against weak light coming from the room. There is no friendliness or warmth in his demeanour and I feel ridiculously frightened. 'We will leave at eight in the morning,' he says and shuts the door. Back in my room I put every piece of furniture that I can move against the door.

By five the next morning I am sitting on the edge of the bed, packed and ready to go. As we drive back to my route I stare out at peat bog, torn apart and desolate by turf-cutting. There are burnt scrubby trees and rubbish dumped in ditches. Discarded plastic sheeting flaps in the wind. This is not land that is respected. Somehow, the pain in the car is mirrored in the vista outside the window. A land torn apart, a life in tatters. As the landscape that has lost its heart whizzes past the window, I wonder what a curlew feels when it arrives back to breed and its territory is no more. Does it, too, feel distressed and disorientated, in a world that no longer makes sense? Do curlews experience solastalgia? I try to catch a glimpse of one; after all, this should be their heartland. But the bog is too churned up, too damaged to support singers of beautiful songs. Eventually the car stops and our goodbyes are polite and restrained. I feel ashamed about my reactions the day before. Despite the sudden turmoil in his life, Liam

stood by his commitment to me, for which I am very grateful. Kindness is not always sugar-coated.

As I carry on walking towards the county town of Longford, I try to remember when I first fell in love with curlews. I have a strong image in my mind of standing alone by a loch on the mainland of Orkney. It was a late spring afternoon and a gentle wind was blowing. Peace comes easy in these northern isles, where energetic winds blow away the cobwebs of a busy life in a southern city, at least for a while. Suddenly, the air quivered as a curlew took flight and soared over the water. I can't explain why this moment in particular was my curlew epiphany. After all, I grew up in the Staffordshire moorlands where curlews were often heard over the rough crags of millstone grit moors. Perhaps my senses were heightened, my mood poetical after walking around an enigmatic stone circle, the Ring of Brodgar. These elegant sandstone slabs seem to pen in time and hint at ancient rituals and ways of thinking lost to us a long time ago. When building this monument to their hopes and fears, those ancients would have heard curlews fly overhead, too.

I recall being transfixed by the combination of scenery and sound. The purity of the bubbling notes, the freshness of the air, the crystalline appearance of the water, all sharpened the moment, making it more than the sum of its parts. The landscape was speaking in a language that is not human. The curlew call over that peaceful loch seemed to bind the past to the present to the future. In his poem 'What the Curlew Said', the sound evokes a powerful response from Irish author John Moriarty:

What an unearthly aria that call was.
Sometimes I would sit and think, it isn't a call at
    all.
But if it isn't, what is it?
Is it a spontaneity of eternity that has somehow
    come through into time?[1]

From then on, I was aware of the birds wherever I went. It really was a little bit like falling in love.

Perhaps love is not exactly the right word. I don't know that I *love* curlews. If I said to my husband that I loved him as much as a curlew, he might raise an eyebrow. I think *cherish* is more accurate. Cherish is used for special-ness, in people or treasures. The root of the word is from the French *cher*, meaning dear, inferring a combination of respect and affection, not intimate love. Going back further, the Indo-European root for cherish is *ka*, meaning to serve or help. It is the basis for the Latin *caritas*, or charity, where the true meaning of charity is an overwhelming affection for life, combined with a desire to nurture. Cherish therefore encompasses compassion, fondness, truthful relationship, kindness, direct action and love of life. David Attenborough's recommendation is, 'Cherish the natural world, because you are part of it and depend on it.' Even though it is hard to pin down all the nuances of meaning contained in the word, we all know what cherish means. I don't so much love curlews as cherish them.

So does Noel Kiernan. He has a sign at the entrance of his farm-come-nature reserve on the shores of Lough Ree, which shows a line drawing of a curlew standing in water.

Next to it is printed the phrase, 'Cherishing wildlife before it's gone.' He chose the word cherish specifically because of its associations.

I meet Noel in a café in the county town of Longford after a long day's walk through curlew-free bog and farm-land. 'Hello,' he says, 'I am the Little Red Hen of County Longford.' A somewhat surprising introduction.

The Little Red Hen is a traditional children's folktale, probably originating in Russia. It features a kindly, hard-working hen who finds some wheat seeds and asks her farm friends to help her plant them. Unfortunately, no one ever seems to have the time or the inclination.

'Not I,' barked the lazy dog.
'Not I,' purred the sleepy cat.
'Not I,' quacked the noisy yellow duck.
'Then I will do it myself,' said the little red hen.

And so it goes on. At every step in the process of turning the wheat into bread – the ripening, harvesting, threshing, grinding and baking, the little red hen asks for their help but each time they are too tired, too busy or too lazy to oblige. But eventually, when the hen emerges from the kitchen carrying a richly smelling, freshly baked loaf and asks, 'Who will help me eat the bread?', there is suddenly no shortage of volunteers. Of course, the moral of the story is 'if any would not work, then neither should they eat', and so the Little Red Hen rebuffs the lazy animals and she and her chicks sit down to a feast on their own, leaving not one crumb. I wasn't sure why Noel thought this charming moral tale applied to him, but I was about to find out.

As we drive to the farmhouse, in a remote part of southern County Longford, I look out onto what superficially appear to be vast, brown, ploughed fields, but they are obviously not fields. I ask Noel what on earth this landscape is, this huge area of ridged brown earth, black plastic, drainage ditches full of water and very large machines. 'It's a Bord na Móna company bog, where they get the peat for the local power station.' I ask him to stop the car, then I get out and stare in disbelief. As far as I can see, on both sides of the road, raised bog, thousands of years old, is being scooped up by huge diggers, loaded into railway trucks and taken to Lough Ree Power Station.

Lough Ree came on stream in 2004 and is the smallest of the three peat-fired stations in the Republic of Ireland, the others being in West Offaly and in Edenderry, further south. It burns 92 tonnes of peat in one hour, producing 100MW of energy, which is a relatively small return; an average coal-fired plant produces around 600MW. Between them, the three stations consume 3.8 million tonnes of peat per year. That's an awful lot of wildlife habitat going up in flames.

A potted history of peat as a fuel may be useful here. The bogs of Ireland have been used for over a thousand years, but it wasn't until the late eighteenth century that the systematic exploitation of the vast inland bogs really began in earnest. Two main objectives were identified: to transform bogs into farmland, and to increase the use of peat for fuel. Both could boost the economy of central

Ireland, where poverty and low standards of living were rife. If the economic potential of the bogs could be tapped into, they could become the means to lift the 'miserable and half-starved spectres who inhabit this dreary waste'[2] out of their penury.

By the 1930s plans were made to scale up peat extraction, to establish a standardisation code for the turf produced, and to organise its distribution around Ireland. In 1934 the Turf Development Board was formed to develop and drain the bogs.

The Second World War further boosted the development of turf, as coal became increasingly difficult to import. By the end of the war, the Turf Development Board became the company Bord na Móna. Plans were drawn up for 'two turf-powered power stations and the development of 24 bogs to produce over one million tonnes of sod peat per annum, the building of a moss peat litter factory (for horticultural peat) and the establishment of a peat research station'.[3] Between 1814 and 1946 half of Ireland's raised bogs were destroyed at a rate of 800,000 tonnes per year.

As the twentieth century progressed, oil was also being imported, but both the supply and the price were volatile. The mechanisation of peat extraction grew apace, allowing ever greater quantities of peat to be removed. In 1957 renewed investment saw turf-fired power stations built along Ireland's west coast, which provided jobs for local people and helped ride out fluctuations in the availability of oil. All of these are no longer in service. Now, just three modern power plants remain in Ireland, with a total capacity of 370MW. Lough Ree and West Offaly are owned by the government and subsidised, while Edenderry is run privately by Bord na Móna. Between them, they employ around 1,000 people, including everyone involved in harvesting, processing and burning the peat.

Peat is also used in homes and gardens. Right across Ireland, mountain and lowland bogs provide fuel for domestic use. Traditionally, it was cut by hand, but today this job is mechanised. The surface layer of a peat bog has moisture-loving plants such as mosses and bryophytes, called moss peat. It makes poor fuel, but is a perfect raw material for horticulture. Bord na Móna, and other companies, sell 2.6 million cubic metres of moss peat every year, producing an annual turnover of €48 million. Peat, as a fuel and for gardening, is big business in Ireland.

The jobs and opportunities offered by this burgeoning industry heralded a bright future for central Ireland. Todd Andrews was Bord na Móna's first Managing Director and 'took the company from small beginnings when turf was hand-won, to a modern company, which he had mainly developed from a collection of wildernesses'.[4] This was Ireland's industrial revolution, and Andrews was seen as a visionary who had led the way. There was little public resistance; bogs were widely regarded as nothing more than unproductive, sodden, disorientating wastelands. As Todd Andrews wrote, 'the bog itself in the Irish mind was a symbol of barrenness'. To turn these deserts into money was progress, a step into a better future.

For over 300 years, therefore, developing peat bogs was a way of killing many birds with one stone (excuse the pun). It relieved Ireland from ties to England for coal, it helped the country to cope with the uncertainties of oil supply, it boosted local economies in areas that badly needed jobs, and it helped erase the bad memories of central Ireland as a place of poverty. What was there not to like? Unless, of course, you were bog-dwelling wildlife.

The self-styled 'Little Red Hen of County Longford', Noel Kiernan, has a farmhouse surrounded by a Bord na Móna bog. Long strips of slashed turf end at the boundary of his land. Huge tractor-like machines plough up and down all day, visible from the windows. The sound of the machines dominates one side of the fence, the singing of birds can be heard on the other. The farm is an island of connection to nature in a sea of industrial extraction. There are areas for orchid-rich grasslands, a bird hide, a linnet plot, groves of native trees, a site for marsh fritillaries and sections that are used for organic, extensive farming. It is a defiant outpost for wildlife.

For seven years Noel has volunteered as a curlew surveyor in his patch of southern County Longford, walking the fields and driving for miles to find them. He has mostly worked alone with no outside help. He had witnessed the rapid disappearance of the corncrake, and recognised that curlews were going the same way. 'Twenty years ago, you would have said they were common, but now they have nearly gone, even from areas you'd think were still suitable. I wonder if they get depressed and lose heart after so much failure, and so few of them around. I swear they are quieter than they used to be.' Most of the farmland and stripped bogs have lost the birds, but, as with Lough Erne, curlews are finding small havens in the islands in the middle of the magnificent and wild Lough Ree.

Lough Ree is an exciting body of water. This 'Lake of the Kings' is situated in the geographical centre of Ireland, and is the second-largest lake on the Shannon after Lough Derg. It stretches for 30 kilometres from the town of Lanesborough on its northern shore to Athlone in the south. Dotted throughout are islands rich in legend. In the centre, the Island of Inchcleraun (Clothra's Island) is where the great warrior Queen Maeve is said to have been slain by a piece of cheese. Her nephew fired a lump from a slingshot while she was bathing, in revenge for the murder of his mother, which his warrior aunt had ordered. It was an inglorious end for a feisty queen who ruled the province of Connaught for sixty years and whose name means 'she who intoxicates'. Her tomb is thought to be in a mound in

County Sligo, where she is said to be buried standing upright, defiantly facing her enemies in Ulster.

The seven Black Isles are situated in the northern part of the Lough, and this is where we are headed. Surprisingly large, white-capped waves slap the shore as we wait for the boat. The lough is acting up, behaving like an ocean. A sharp wind tugs and pushes, bending the heads of the reeds into the water. Gulls screech as they fly overhead, and their harsh calls are blown across the lough. Our coats flap in the wind. I feel I have slipped through a veil into an ancient fable. 'The three oldest cries in the world are the wind cry, the water cry and the curlew cry,' wrote Yeats.[5]

A tune by the Irish band The Fureys, 'The Lonesome Boatman', keeps playing in my head. Its combination of melancholic tin whistle riding over a fast strumming guitar fits the scene perfectly; pathos and dynamism. 'People have drowned here,' says Noel, looking out over the frothing water; 'they underestimate it, it's capricious. You can suddenly be overwhelmed by wind and waves. More like being out at sea than on a lake.' I look at the small metal skiff being tossed around by the jetty, make my peace with the Almighty, and get in.

At the helm is Mark Craven, a Predator Control Officer for the National Parks and Wildlife Service. For the last eight years he has been coming out in all weathers, and he exudes a sense of calm control as the boat bounces over the water, showering us in icy-cold spray. Everything is energised. The sunlight is intense and the water, trees and birds all seemed whipped up into a frenzied motion. It's exciting to be out on the water, zipping away from the mainland, but a relief to land twenty minutes later on Nut Island and let the trees take the punishment of the wind for a while. These islands are far wilder than the ones in Lough Erne, less tamed and understood, more hidden from view.

It is a calmer walk through the old woodland. A herd of feral goats grazes over the remains of ancient walls, probably built by monks. They watch us with interest and then scatter. As trees give way to open, flat ground the twittering of chaffinches and tits fades into the harsher sounds of waterbirds, and the air carries the distinctive, sharp smell of guano. The water levels are dropping again after the winter floods, and the newly exposed shores are crowded with black-headed gulls, their nests so close together they almost touch. Egg laying is in full swing. Redshanks, oyster-catchers, shovellers, mallards, long-tailed ducks and even the increasingly rare common scoters are all vying for good places to nest. Curlews flute somewhere in the distance, and flocks of whimbrel stream overhead, their sights set further north. The ground, though, is already littered with broken eggshells, taken from the early nests of mallards. These common ducks, so familiar yet still so wild, crouch on their nests amongst the heather and trees. We pick up some fragments of eggshell. 'Grey crows,' says Mark. 'You just can't keep on top of them. I'd say they were the main problem now. Mink, too. I've removed one from this island already this year.'

Mink can cross water with ease. Once established, they can do untold damage, as Mark has seen. 'In the late 2000s the black-headed gull colony failed to breed on the King's

Island just over the water, and the whole colony moved off site. The following year I removed seven mink from four of the Black Islands and the gulls came back and they've bred successfully since then. The birds will tell you if there is something wrong.'

Nut and King's Islands are the largest of the Black Islands, around twenty and fourteen acres in size respectively. Twenty years ago, many curlews would have nested in both places. 'The islands are the last havens,' says Mark. 'Only two pairs on Nut Island now, at most, that's all I've seen.' Last year he and Noel saw five pairs displaying on one of the smaller islands up in the northern area of the lough, but only three stayed to breed. They also found the body of a juvenile, which had been dead for a couple of weeks. It showed no sign of predation and most likely died of illness or starvation.

We reach an expanse of shore and birds fly around in alarm. Mark and Noel stay back in the trees and point to an area of shingle where a pair of curlews has just laid eggs. I walk out into the fierce wind and the screeching of the birds. I am nervous. I could quite easily step on camouflaged eggs. I try to scan the ground quickly, increasingly concerned about the disturbance, but I see no curlews, no clutch of greeny-brown eggs – they really are well hidden. It's frustrating, but I retreat. The birds have enough problems without their precious eggs being trampled underfoot.

Lough Ree is just one small part of Mark's patch, which covers various wader-rich locations along the Shannon to as far away as the flooded fields of the Shannon Callows,

60 kilometres away. Trying to keep numbers of mink, foxes and crows at a level where ground-nesting birds can stand any chance of breeding successfully is a Herculean task for just one man. He has to rely on the assistance of the local gun clubs. Hunting is a traditional pastime, and there are 926 clubs with 28,000 members throughout the country. Many of these clubs are at the heart of their communities, and background predator control would simply not be possible without their help. It is not always easy to persuade hunters who prefer waterfowl or game birds to take on the humdrum business of controlling crows and foxes. A competition was set up between local clubs to reduce grey crow numbers around curlew breeding sites, something similar to the one set up for corncrake with the coveted Corncrake Cup Trophy. 'The whole idea worked very well,' says Mark. 'It allowed us to meet with gun clubs and go through trapping methods and humane disposal, as well as giving guidance on the wildlife, and after the first breeding season there was a remarkable difference in crow numbers. There is still a large background population constantly infilling the gaps, but at least the curlews have some respite for a few weeks at a vital time of year.'

Although it is a less sensitive subject in Ireland than in England, predator control is still difficult to discuss. Red fox and grey crow are as much a part of Irish fauna as redshank and curlew, but until the habitat for ground-nesting birds is restored and the natural balance between predator and prey regained, which will take time, there seems to be no alternative but to keep predator numbers down in the breeding season. Foxes and crows are certainly not endangered, grey crow numbers have dramatically increased, by as much as 100 per cent since the 1990s, but many waders are on the edge of survival. Curlews are on the very brink of collapse.

Interestingly, curlews themselves were on the Irish quarry list for the month of September until as late as 2012. By then it was abundantly clear that their numbers were in free fall, down by 95 per cent. Anecdotal reports suggest that, irrespective of their desperate situation, some are still shot by a minority of irresponsible hunters in the autumn.

A visit to the larger King's Island doesn't reveal any curlews either, but it does have an intriguing row of traditional whitewashed cottages, complete with beds, tables and chairs. At its peak, around twenty-five people from three families lived on the Black Islands, but the last residents moved out in the mid-1980s, leaving their homes as though they might return any day. It is an eerie sight and it feels intrusive to walk around their gardens and fields, peering in through windows at bright plastic tablecloths and carefully made beds. By one back door, four old milk bottles have been carefully placed upside down in a white tin bucket, and nearby a discarded metal teapot and saucepan are half hidden by the long grass. A mallard duck sits comfortably on her nest in a fireplace in a tumbledown outbuilding.

Life here must have been isolated and basic. The small fields grew potatoes, cabbage and corn. Protein came mainly from fish, but sheep and goats also provided meat and milk. Supplies could come over from the mainland, but if the lough was in a tempestuous mood, the islands could be cut off for days on end.

It wasn't all hard work, though, if the large pile of discarded brown beer bottles in one backyard is anything to go by. One of the cottages doubled as a shebeen, and traditional storytellers or shanachies gathered to entertain. Oh, to have been a fly on the wall on one of the party nights in the middle of Lough Ree – even better to have joined in. No doubt the tales got taller and taller as the night progressed. I stand alone in the middle of a field and close my eyes. I can imagine oats rustling in the wind. I can hear the bleating of goats and almost smell the sweet, homely aroma of wood fires. The distant cries of gulls could just as well be the ghostly peals of laughter of many merry islanders, egging on the shanachies to ever greater flights of fancy, and everyone well oiled with a local brew. King's Island is other-worldly and utterly enchanting; it's a privilege to be here.

When I find Mark and Noel again they are looking through telescopes at a large flock of black-tailed godwits roosting on a beach. These exquisite waders flutter up and down, changing position, floating on the wind, piping and calling to each other. Their orangey feathers glow in the bright sunlight; a breathtaking sight against the backdrop of blue and white water.

The next day, Lough Ree is in a sulk. It is shrouded in mist and hunkered down. There is barely a breath of wind and the islands have disappeared from view. Noel and I walk around the still, winter-flooded fields of the mainland, hoping to catch sight of curlews waiting for the water to retreat enough so they can begin nesting. In days gone by there would have been many. Grey crows are now perched in the twisted trees. 'Those need to come down,' says Noel. 'They are hunting.' We wade through a magical, Avalon world of water-drenched air, water-filled fields and half-submerged land. Willow and hawthorn stand tall out of the water. Reeds and rushes sway gently, hiding noisy duck and geese. A flock of whimbrels flies overhead and lands on sodden ground nearby, piping and whistling. 'The Whimbrel, grallotor with bill arch'd and long/Was also seen lifting his head midst the throng'. So wrote James Jennings in 1828.[6] He went on to say that this bird 'has all the manners of a curlew', except that it is distinctly smaller, has a shorter bill and an obvious dark stripe on its crown. It is easy to confuse the two, especially at a distance, but their calls are certainly different. In 'Curlew', Norman MacCaig wrote:

Yesterday, I saw a cousin of yours,
a whimbrel,
that, when close to, looks like yourself,
seen at a distance.

But who could mistake its tittery call,
For yours, brown bird, as you fly,
Trailing bubbles of music
Over the squelchy hillside?

There are no curlews in this watery, transitory world on the edge of Lough Ree, but there is a carcass of a swan, ripped apart outside a fox's den. Not much is left apart from the wings and ribcage, a trail of feathers leads back to the waterline, where it must have been taken unawares.

I was beginning to believe that looking for curlews in central Ireland was like searching for the proverbial needle in a haystack. There are gaps in the curlew map of Ireland – huge, gaping, curlew-shaped holes – but this is where our story is moving, into those gaps. It is a story of societal shift, cultural change, landscape-scale modifications and a re-framing of the connection between land and spirit. Through curlew eyes Ireland must look increasingly hostile year on year. Just a handful of pairs are dotted around here and there, trying to breed, but thwarted at every turn. But there are good people trying to help, and that at least is heartening.

It is time to move on from the wild, poetic, Lough Ree to another soft, dripping, watery world of an entirely different nature, the Shannon Callows.

On the long trek south, I meet an old man who had grown up on a farm but now lives in town. We chat for a while on a bench in the middle of a small town. I ask him if he knows about curlews; yes, but he hasn't seen one for a long time. They used to be very common around his family farm. Does he remember the sound? He looks unsure, so I play him the bubbling call on my iPad. Immediately his expression changes and he stares past the shop windows to some wild lands beyond the streets, to his own 'country of the mind'. His eyes fill with tears. 'You've taken me right back to my childhood,' he says with emotion in his voice. 'I can't believe I've forgotten that call – it must be years … please, turn it off.' He puts his hands over his ears and the tears fall. It's a moving demonstration of the power of the curlew to touch inner feelings. In 'Love and Revolution', Alastair McIntosh wrote:

> Have you heard the cry of the curlew?
> I tell you –
> I would rather we lost
> The entire contents
> Of every art gallery
> In the whole world
> Than lose
> Forever
> The cry of the curlew.

The Shannon Callows is fresh and green, an uplifting vision after the brooding darkness of stripped bogs. It is an area of around 30 square kilometres of flat meadowland bordering the Shannon between Lough Ree and Lough Derg. The topography of Ireland has often been described as saucer-like – raised around the edges and flat in the middle. The river here seems to relax and spread out, taking a breather from its race to the sea. The soft lapping of the water, the serenading of songbirds and the lowing of cattle bring to mind the Irish traditional blessing, 'May the rain fall softly upon your fields.' In some ways, the Shannon is the Irish equivalent of the Nile, the river as the ever-giving source of life. The yearly winter floods spread nutrients over the

fields so that summer pastures are alive with insects feeding off wildflowers and herbs, providing food for all manner
of wildlife. This is where my uncle Hugh's family had a
farm. When he died, in 2014, his sister Monica Foran wrote
a poem to his memory, the first verse of which reads:

> The West in boyhood times he loved,
> The land, the bog, the trees.
> The curlew, snipe and wild goose,
> When winter floods appeared.

Because of the flooding, the Callows has escaped the worst
of intensification experienced elsewhere. The lush grasslands make this rich dairy and beef country. It was once
rich curlew country, too. In *Birds of Ireland*, written in 1954
by the Dickensian-sounding Kennedy, Ruttledge and
Scroope, the authors record that 'the great Curlew breeding ground of South Connaught is the wastes and callows
between Banagher and Lough Derg … the nests are so
close as almost to rank as a colony.'

Shocking then that in 2017, in this land of soft sediment
and water, the official count revealed only ten pairs of
curlews. Thirty years ago they would have been jostling for
space. The Callows' air should resound to the bubbling of
the curlew, filling it with lyrical vibrations. Yet over the
couple of days I spend here I don't hear a single call. I see
just one bird flying low and cowed over the river, heading
for the riverine island of Inishee, but it is only a fleeting
glimpse. Hopefully it was returning to a nest that has
evaded the attention of predators. In the days when there

were many, they would rise together and mob any crow, fox, or human that came too near, but now they are loners.

BirdWatch Ireland is trying to help curlews, and the other waders, that should be so common in the Callows. Brian Caffrey, from the BirdWatch Midlands division, rows me out to Inishee Island, where much of their wader work is focused. Inishee sits in the middle of a wide, languid section of the Shannon. We make the crossing in a wooden rowing boat in just a few minutes. It is a warm, overcast day. The sky is heavy, the atmosphere feels oppressive. Inishee is not mysterious like the previous islands I have visited; it is flat, open and treeless, a bald hump in the centre of the river, about 30 hectares in area. In the winter it is submerged, but as the waters recede in the spring, perfect habitat emerges for lapwing, snipe, curlew and corncrake. To foxes, badgers or pine martens swimming over from the mainland, the island represents rich pickings. Ground-nesting birds are there for the taking, and take them they did until 2009, when an electric fence was erected right round the island.

Inishee was always a key breeding site in the Callows, holding the highest density of birds. BirdWatch Ireland used it as a research site between 2006 and 2008 when investigating why the whole of the Callows' wader population was in decline. Although initially things looked good and lots of nests were found, it soon became obvious that no young were being produced. Both nest and chick survival was well below that required to keep the populations stable. By the time the electric fence went up there was only a total of twenty-two pairs of breeding birds left;

lapwing had gone and there were just eight pairs of snipe, twelve redshank and two pairs of curlews. For some of the species the fence had worked wonders. Just five years later, ninety-seven pairs of birds were nesting successfully. The biggest beneficiaries were lapwing (thirteen pairs) and redshank (a staggering eighty-one pairs). Curlew and snipe continued to suffer, though, with just two pairs of snipe and one pair of curlew. It seems the fence was not enough.

Brian and I look out across the island. Lapwings are noisily mobbing a crow in the distance on one side, while on the other the silhouette of a curlew appears then disappears over the horizon. At least one pair is still here and, according to birdwatchers, successfully raised chicks in 2016. But one pair is woeful, considering they were seen as almost colonial nesting birds in the past.

Electricity is keeping any predators that swim over from the mainland from feasting on wader eggs and chicks, but it is no defence against another major problem: flooding. Farmers in the area are used to dealing with flooding during the winter months, and also in around one out of every five or six summers, but since 2000 the Callows have flooded badly in the summer every year, after constantly heavy rainfall.

It was in the rich meadows of the Callows that corncrakes were hanging on, even slowly increasing in number, benefiting from unimproved fields, and sensitive cutting of hay. However, these annual summer floods eroded their numbers each year from sixty pairs in 2000 to just one pair in 2014. Another huge flood in the late summer of 2015 sealed their fate, and they were heard no more. The river drowned out hope that corncrakes could make a comeback. Is it the same for curlews? Whether this is the result of climate change is open to debate, but in Ireland the Met Office has recorded an increase in rainfall of 15 per cent since the 1970s. More rain, combined with large-scale changes in land use, and the drainage of the water-absorbing peat bogs, can only make things worse.

I am coming to the end of the Irish leg of my journey. There is now just the last section heading east through to Dublin, a walk through what was once the largest raised bog in Ireland, the Bog of Allen. This once vast area stretched from the outskirts of Dublin to the Shannon, a flat, virtually unbroken stretch of peatland. Over the centuries the bog was partially converted to farmland and exploited for turf, parcelling it into many smaller bogs. Bord na Móna used it to provide peat for the two other power stations in central Ireland, Edenderry and West Offaly. Given the vast area it covered, I am looking forward to seeing the last remnants of this once mysterious and rich landscape.

The route was along the Grand Canal, built in the nineteenth century to take hand-cut turf to Dublin. The *Scenery and Antiquities of Ireland* by J. Stirling Coyne and N.P. Willis, written in 1841, describes the Bog of Allen as:

> This immense bog, or rather series of bogs … formerly contained 1,000,000 of acres, but by means of cultivation and drainage it is now diminished to 300,000 acres, and it is extremely probable that in a

few years these immense and dreary tracts will be entirely reclaimed.

Although the bogs of Ireland in their natural state are unprofitable to the agriculturist, they are not without their advantages to the poor peasantry, who derive from them all their fuel; and those dingy and barren wastes, covered with patches of coarse grass and brown heath, which suggest to the mind only feelings of desolation, contain within their dark bosoms the cheerful peat that bestows warmth and light to the cotter's humble hearth. Great quantities of this peat or turf are transported from the Bog of Allen to Dublin by means of long, flat-bottomed boats, which ply on the canal. The condition of the poor people, whose employment it is to cut and prepare this turf for sale, is miserable in the extreme. Their dwellings, which are mere hovels constructed of sods, are scattered along the banks of the canal, and present a melancholy picture to the eye of the traveller unaccustomed to the scenes of abject wretchedness which are too frequently to be found amongst the poor of Ireland.

I don't see any miserable hovels, but I do see vast areas of stripped and sliced peat. Large tracts of scraped brown earth are removed to feed the power stations, but there were also many smaller bogs that were being cut for home use.

The ancient tradition of burning peat for domestic use is a subject that arouses passion, especially if there is any suggestion of banning it on environmental grounds. The right to a turf fire is seen as inalienable and any threat as an attack on the very core of local and national pride. Turbary Rights, the rights of a family to cut turf, have been handed down through generations. In 'Digging', Seamus Heaney wrote:

> My grandfather cut more turf in a day
> Than any other man on Toner's bog.
> Once I carried him milk in a bottle
> Corked sloppily with paper. He straightened up
> To drink it, then fell to right away
> Nicking and slicing neatly, heaving sods
> Over his shoulder, going down and down
> For the good turf. Digging.

Barely any turf is dug by hand today; it is heavy machines that noisily and efficiently strip the sod. They take away the back-breaking work, but are vastly more destructive – to the bog itself and to the wildlife that depends on it. Paddy Sherridan, a local birdwatcher and conservationist, wrote to me about a curlew survey for BirdWatch Ireland in 2015. One pair of birds was trying to nest on a bog which was being cut, legally, for home use:

> On Sunday May 15 at about 5.15am, two of our members arrived at the bog to hopefully see or hear the pair of curlew that they were monitoring since first locating them on April 27. There was no sight nor sound of the curlew; instead they were greeted by five big hi-mac machines spread at various intervals over

roughly six to eight hundred metres apart. The very last one of these was already in operation even at this early stage of nesting.

Needless to say, the curlews were gone. Some bogs have been protected by law for their wildlife value, and the turf-cutters compensated for the loss of turf. Unfortunately, illegal cutting still takes place, even on bogs designated as an SAC, Site Area of Conservation. Paddy Sheridan wrote:

> I visited one SAC seven times last year (2015) and on the second-last visit I could not get to within 300 metres of the bog as I had two curlews constantly mobbing me. I hadn't the heart to look for the chicks and distress them any more, so I left them alone. To me it is an amazing feeling and sight to see this spectacle right above your head. Sadly, when I went back six days later, illegal turf-cutting had taken place, a portion of the bog was burnt and the birds were gone. We lost red grouse and grey partridge in the late 1990s and the curlew is rapidly getting there.

The breeding curlew figures for County Kildare speak for themselves. In 1849 William Thompson, in his *Natural History of Ireland*, wrote, 'The curlew bred in considerable numbers on the bog of Allen.' From *The Birds of Ireland* (1900), by Richard Ussher and Robert Warren, it was mentioned that the curlew were 'resident and numerous'. In 1954 Kennedy, Ruttledge and Scroope in their *Birds of Ireland*, noted, 'the curlew was abundant and widespread'.

From the 1960s onwards, however, numbers steadily declined as peat extraction accelerated. By 2015, through-out the whole of County Kildare, only five pairs of curlews were found attempting to breed, none successfully.

There is a growing awareness that inland raised bogs are a rare habitat and are of international importance, and something must be done before all of it is destroyed. But after 300 years of devastation any restoration projects, however welcome, can only scratch the surface. The Fourth National Report to the Convention on Biological Diversity in Ireland, published in 2010, stated, 'It is estimated that there has been a 99 per cent loss of the original area of actively growing raised bog in Ireland, and one-third of the remaining 1 per cent has been lost in the last 10 years.' Out of the 130 breeding pairs of curlews left in Southern Ireland, 70 per cent nest on raised bogs.

Whether burning for the home hearth or in power stations, against today's backdrop of climate change and environmental concern peat seems an outdated fuel. Emissions of CO_2 are high, both when the peat is burned and when the bogs are drained and degraded – burning peat releases twice as much carbon dioxide as natural gas.

Extracting the peat is damaging, too. A report by the United Nations Environment Programme and Wetlands International found that peat bogs store more carbon per hectare than any other land-based ecosystem, including rainforest. When degraded, they release the gas into the atmosphere, exacerbating the problem caused, in the first instance, by burning fossil fuels. It is also expensive. Peat is a highly inefficient fuel, and the Irish government subsidises peat power to the tune of €440 million per year, which is paid for from taxes. All in all, peat does not stand up as a viable option for twenty-first century energy. It will eventually be phased out. Bord na Móna's strapline is 'naturally driven'. Its website explains that the company is transitioning to a new age of energy production: 'Our land is a huge asset and we will continue to produce energy but it will be through biomass, solar, landfill gas, wind, and waste to energy.' Their commitment is to stop burning turf by 2030 and to not exploit any new bogs. Those that have been stripped will go to forestry, solar or wind farms, or be turned into community amenities. Some are being used, successfully, for wildlife and restoration projects. The Edenderry power station will continue its transition to co-burning with biofuels, one-third at present to be increased to half biofuels over the next decade. The battle to stop home cutting of turf, though, looks set to continue, although some good initiatives are under way as turf cutters and conservationists begin to work together.

The loss of peat bogs is also a human tragedy. If bogs were characters in a novel, they would be complex, doggedly independent, and antisocial but with a good, just heart. They refuse to bow down to the persistent pressure of colonising trees, repelling anything that cannot tolerate wet, acidic soil. Yet they are truly magnificent places too, full of contrast. Their horizons are wide, some would say intimidating, and their colours soft and muted. In the winter, they offer no shelter from wind and rain, yet in the spring and summer sun they can be transformed into bright, singing landscapes. Like giant speakers pointing to the sky, they broadcast the trills and pipings of skylarks, lapwings, meadow pipits, curlews and snipe. They hide many secrets in their surface folds and fissures; miniature worlds of mosses, shiny beetles and soft, wet amphibians, which tuck themselves away and live their ground-level lives away from human eyes. Dig a little deeper, into the stuff of the bog itself, and you enter a stranger, darker world. Right across the bogs of Europe, ancient, gaunt, mysterious bodies lie buried and forgotten. Seventeen bog bodies have been unearthed in Ireland. Some were ritually sacrificed to unknown gods, others were executed and their bodies thrown away, pinned to the ground with sticks. Some show signs of brutality before death, others had been fed and well cared for. There are women with babies, children and teenagers, men in their prime who may have been kings; all of them have found their final resting place in acid darkness. Their faces are clear, their expressions calm. Some have ligatures and blindfolds still in place. The bog takes them all and treats them the same. And above the burial pits is the cry of the curlew, which gives voice to the voiceless in the peat.

The vast peatlands of the world are undoubtedly strange and unknowable. Dr John Feehan, an Irish biologist and environmental historian, places them in deep time, inhabiting our ancestral memory.

The bogs are great, open expanses with distant horizons. You feel drawn to them as though they awakened an echo deep within us of the open savannah landscapes in which our human kind had its origins several million years ago.

They are also special for those who need to find solace in the silence of the wild. A place to be alone. One old parish priest from central Ireland, now in a home, told me he was sad to hear that the bogs were almost gone. 'They were the only places I could walk out into and scream.'

I know the feeling. Sometimes I too want to scream at the lack of appreciation for the natural world, the lack of a true awareness about the state of wildlife in central Ireland. There are undeniably wonderful people striving against the tide of destruction, but they are mainly isolated stars in a dark sky. In Dublin, I meet two such people who helped me draw up some plans for a 'Curlews in Crisis Workshop', to be held at the end of the year: Barry O'Donoghue, from the National Parks and Wildlife Service, and Barry McMahon, from University College Dublin. They will become valued collaborators. Between ourselves and Anita Donaghy from BirdWatch Ireland, we would try to bring curlews back from the brink – a last-ditch attempt to get everyone together and come up with solutions to help them. As I board the ferry to Wales, it seems to me that this is at least a glimmer of hope for the beleaguered birds of the Emerald Isle.

Chapter 7

INTO WALES

A museum drawer filled with carefully arranged curlew eggs is a strange sight. They are placed in sets of (usually) four, like a floret, mimicking how they would have been found in the wild. The more pointed ends meet in the centre, the broader ends face outwards. Rows of egg-flowers lie cushioned with cotton wool and covered by a glass lid. They are labelled with care. These valuable scientific specimens were collected in the nineteenth and early twentieth centuries, when egg collecting was legal. They hold a wealth of information on the diversity of shape and colour of eggs, the location where they were laid, and the date and time of collection. If the collector kept good notes, we are also told the type of vegetation where the nest was found, the stage of incubation, and how the parent bird reacted when it was disturbed. Today, technology allows us to study ever more detail, such as the molecular structure of the shells and their chemical composition. It is even possible to extract DNA from the membranes that line the inner surface of the eggshell. As science advances, perhaps more will be revealed about birds through the wonder that is an egg.

These historical collections are treasure troves, telling us about the past, but also helping to inform decisions for the future. The thinning of the egg shells of birds of prey following the widespread use of DDT in the 1950s, for example, alerted Rachel Carson to the insidious effects of pesticides on the ability of birds to produce viable eggs. The result was her ground-breaking book, *Silent Spring*, which launched a new wave of environmental action and awareness.

There is no doubt that egg collections can be a valuable resource, but still, there is something unsettling about museum eggs; they are as disconcerting as trays of butter-flies. Both are beautiful and a little sad. Once, they were capsules of life and full of potential, developing in a wild place – 'a brood of nature's minstrels', to borrow John Clare's description. They were warmed by the summer sun and soaked by gentle rain, tended carefully by adults who would take great risks to protect them from danger. Now they sit in a drawer, transformed into empty, musty objects of curiosity, trapped in darkness. They look fragile, as though just touching them would crush them and leave nothing but fragments and dust.

Out in the wild, though, curlew eggs are not delicate. They can withstand the weight of an adult, which can be over a kilo. They are also large, up to seven centimetres

long and four centimetres wide. A full clutch of three to
five eggs can weigh as much as 40 per cent of the female's
body weight. This is a demanding load and the female has
to be in good condition by the spring to make this size of
clutch. Positioning them in a floret allows the incubating
bird to cover the maximum surface area of each egg. If ever
they are left exposed, which happens for short periods,
their muted colours act as camouflage in heather and rushy
pasture. Brown-green eggs, streaked with black or russet
spots and smears, meld perfectly into the background. I can
vouch for that, having searched for many with little success.
The nest is a simple scrape in the earth; there is no lining
of down or soft moss – just a rough, shallow depression
with bits of grass.

Curlews won't give away their nest location easily. To find one requires time to watch and listen, being aware of nuances of behaviour. The sitting bird lies low, sometimes flattened against the ground. When it is time to change over incubating duties, the pair call to each other. Sometimes it is a low curlee, at other times a loud and urgent bubbling call. The incoming bird lands a distance away and walks in slowly, often pretending to feed. But there is something different about its movement compared to a bird that really is just feeding. It is secretive, a little tense; it is on a mission. Even the way it holds its head and the length of its stride sets it apart as a bird with a nest. You would imagine that the sitting parent would employ some trickery and fly off only when it has put some distance between itself and the eggs. Not the case. As its partner arrives, the incubating bird takes off vertically in an explosion of feathers and legs. That is how most nests are found, by watching for a rocket-launching curlew, as directly beneath will be the eggs. It is such a give-away that I wonder how this system evolved. If we can use it to locate a nest, then so too, presumably, can predators. The incoming bird inconspicuously sidles into place. Once settled, the pair make contact, often with a plaintive, soft, long whistle: a haunting, aching cry that drifts over the grass.

Early on in incubation curlews will fly off the nest fairly easily at any sign of danger, and both birds circle and call overhead with great urgency. If the eggs are predated at this stage, the pair may well lay again. Later on through incubation, though, when the eggs are close to hatching, they will sit tight, sometimes really tight, as described in a letter entitled 'Extraordianry Tameness of Curlew', found in the Oologists Record, June, 1937:

> 'Mr. D.H. Meares writes that on May 2nd, 1937, he took Dr. S. Sloan-Chesser to see a nest of the Curlew (*Numenius arquata*) which he had found on a Surrey common a week previously with three eggs. The bird was sitting and did not move as they approached, accompanied by two dogs. She actually allowed Dr. Sloan-Chesser to stroke her on the nest while Mr. Meares held the dogs a few yards away. She then, without a struggle, allowed him to lift her gently off the eggs in order to see how many had been laid.'

Even if this were legal, which it isn't today, it would not be easy to do this in Wales. As in Ireland, numbers of breeding curlews have fallen dramatically. *Birds in Wales*,[1] by Roger Lovegrove, published in 1994, estimated around 2,000 breeding pairs throughout the country; today it is thought there are fewer than 400 pairs, although no one knows for sure. All the main forces of agricultural intensification, increased predation and forestry have come into play, but curlews in Wales have particularly suffered from an excess of what John Muir called hooved locusts and Iolo Williams described as woolly maggots – sheep. The highly grazed uplands that millions of munching flocks produce is described by George Monbiot as a 'sheepwreck'.

The introduction of 'headage' payments, as part of the Common Agricultural Policy in the 1980s, paid farmers by the number of sheep they grazed. It led to a dramatic increase in stocking density and severe denudation of the uplands. In the 1960s there were around 5 million sheep in Wales, and curlews did well in a mixed farming environment with some, but not too much, grazing. By the mid-1990s, the number had rocketed to 12 million. Areas of varied vegetation and different types of habitat became uniform, trampled billiard tables, creating a degraded environment for both the sheep and wildlife. Cameras placed at curlew nests around Lake Vyrnwy revealed that some sheep were eating eggs and live chicks. They seem to deliberately seek them out, probably to boost their calcium levels in such a nutrient-poor landscape. Although numbers have fallen to under 10 million sheep today, the damage to ground-nesting birds has been done. Curlew, lapwing and golden plover are all in serious decline, with population crashes of over 80 per cent in twenty years. There are no more than thirty pairs of golden plovers left nesting in Wales. However, work is under way to try to bring back ground-nesting birds, and my route took me right through the heart of Welsh curlew country.

Anglesey is bathed in sunlight on the day I arrive in early May. It is well into egg-laying season. Back in 1988 the RSPB recorded up to 350 pairs on Anglesey, 'making the island a very important place for breeding Curlews'. But I know I will be lucky if I see one or two nests at most. My best chance of success is in the southeast of the island, in an area known as Malltraeth Marsh. This six square miles of wet meadows, reedbeds, pools and rough grazing is a Site of Special Scientific Interest, designated for its wet-loving plants and variety of breeding birds. Originally a large salt marsh, most of it was reclaimed for farming in the nineteenth century, when a mile-long sea wall, or cob, was built by Thomas Telford. The sea was excluded and the land was drained and tamed.

The River Cefni, one of the larger rivers in Anglesey, runs through the area and empties into the sea in a dramatic estuary, where wildlife artist Charles Tunnicliffe lived in his home, Shorelands, from 1947 until his death in 1979. His vibrant, naturalistic paintings of British wildlife, particularly birds, prompted Sir Peter Scott to say of him, 'The verdict of posterity in time to come is likely, I believe, to rate Charles Tunnicliffe the greatest wildlife artist of the twentieth century.' Tunnicliffe illustrated Henry Williamson's *Tarka the Otter*, and the Ladybird series for children on wildlife through the seasons, *What to see in …* It is remarkable how those images have stayed in people's minds for decades. Tunnicliffe had a picture window that looked out over the shifting light and moods of the estuary, and he captured the dynamism of the wildlife that came and went through the year. His depictions of the skies and water, the skeins of geese, flocks of ducks, groups of ringed plovers are not static but caught in the act of living and moving, and the viewer is taken right there, as though within touching distance. *Curlews Alighting* shows birds landing in a field with the estuary in the background. They float balletically to the ground on stiffened wings, and you can almost feel the wind ruffling your hair whilst watching them.

Today, wildlife illustrator Philip Snow lives just in front of Tunnicliffe's house and invites me for an evening meal on my first day in Wales. He tells me the story of 'Bumpy', the curlew that arrives each winter and stays on a patch of beach close by. She was given her odd name after an injury inflicted by a peregrine falcon. Three times it swooped down and struck the base of her neck, as she stood at the water's edge. But Bumpy stood her ground and refused to fly. Each time the peregrine dived she crouched low, but didn't flee. Eventually the perplexed, and no doubt frustrated, peregrine gave up. The result of those dramatic blows is a prominent lump.

The River Cefni once meandered freely through the Malltraeth Marsh, flooding the land with the tides and after heavy rain, but now it is constrained in a straitjacket, canalised by Victorian engineers. I walk along one of the banks with Dave Rees, then Senior Conservation Officer for the RSPB, listening to the chorus of singing sedge warblers, reed buntings and whitethroats. I am struck by the plethora of straight lines all around us – fences, ditches, the course of the river, stone walls and footpaths. The impression of the Malltraeth Marsh is one of organisation of the landscape by equations; it looks like a sheet of graph paper. Control was not only in historic boundaries; the RSPB reserve carefully manages water levels and the height of the vegetation, and rows of electric fences are being erected to keep out predators.

The precise RSPB management has worked, though; bitterns have returned to the reedbeds and lapwings to the fields, and it is a joy to see so many lapwings flapping and whistling against the blue sky. They swoop around a pool, excitable as ever, with their glossy dark green plumage glinting in the sunlight. A large patch of reedbed quivers with the fluty trills of reed warblers and the surprisingly loud song-burst of Cetti's warblers. A marsh harrier glides across the horizon. There is a lot of life on display in the Marsh. It doesn't feel natural, though; this is not a landscape at ease with itself. It is made, not evolved, and is more like the Fens or the Somerset Levels than a natural waterscape. The lapwings fly over fields because the formulas have been worked out correctly, not because the land has been fashioned by time into the right mixture of niches. But in such a human-modified landscape, it simply isn't possible to leave nature to it and expect a variety of life to thrive. Too much drainage, too many predators, not enough of whatever it is that wild, unmanaged roughness provides, makes life too hard for many creatures.

The curlews have stayed away. Something is not right for them, but it is difficult to know what that is. The only breeding pair we saw was calling over a patch of rough field which was just outside the boundary fence of the reserve. In what seemed like an act of avian defiance, they bubble and swoop over private farmland, putting their precious eggs just out of reach of management.

Trying to find the nest through binoculars from the roadside proves impossible. We can pinpoint the most likely spot, but the nest itself remains elusive and there is no public access through the field. The circle of eggs is well away from prying eyes. I wonder if this is what the sixth-century abbot, St Beuno, had in mind when he blessed the curlew that rescued his prayer book from the sea and said its nest must always remain hidden (recounted in Chapter 4). It is a curious story, this Christian tale of the saint and the curlew; some say it is not Celtic at all, but was written much later, perhaps in the nineteenth century, an example of myths and legends growing and accreting ideas as time goes by. Others, though, say it is an original Celtic tale, passed on through the generations. Whatever the truth, I have often wondered why the author specifically picked a curlew to be the hero that protected holy wisdom when there are so many birds to choose from. Perhaps the writer used St Beuno to bring curlews in from the spiritual cold. Celtic Christianity drew heavily on nature for imagery and inspiration, as all of life was seen as a reflection of God. By giving a curlew the role of a guardian of truths, it challenged the commonly held perception that they were birds to be feared.

The Welsh dread of curlew once ran deep. Just like in Ireland, ancient Welsh folklore associated these birds with storms at sea and oncoming rain. The Welsh tales, however, turn up the intensity, and curlews become harbingers of death, particularly if heard at night. It is an unfortunate association, perhaps formed because of their unnerving alarm calls. Nesting curlews, when disturbed by a predator such as a fox or badger, will fill the air with urgent and insistent wailing and barking. In Arfon, curlews have the old Welsh name Cwn Ebrill, 'April dogs', or the barking birds. They swoop and cry in great anxiety, trying to drive the intruder away. The sound is distressing enough heard during daylight hours, but if heard when the light is fading, the gentle daytime eater of worms takes on an entirely different character.

Could this be the origin of the terrible tale of the Welsh hounds of hell, Cwn Annwn? These mythical black dogs chase the souls of the dead across the sky, yelping as they pursue terrified spirits. John Masefield, in *The Hounds of Hell*, imagined the fear induced by hearing them as evening fell:

> And presently no man would go
> Without doors after dark,
> Lest hell's black hunting horn should blow,
> And hell's black bloodhounds mark.

Human attitudes to nature, though, are rarely simple. Throughout time we have used the creative, emotional repository of thought that is folklore and myth to explore our nuanced approach to the natural world. Curlews become Jekyll and Hyde creatures that inhabit both the bright, sunlit landscape of the day and the other-worldly realm of night. They combine joy and despair, as in the traditional Welsh ballad 'The Curlew':

> Your call is heard at high noon-day
> A wistful flute across the mere,
> As herdsman's whistle far away.
> Your call is heard at midnight clear
> then hear we, as you swell your keen,
> Barking afar, your hounds unseen.

Few birds call at night, so those that do act as a focal point for our deep fear of vulnerability in darkness. Our human senses, so attuned to light, can barely access nightscapes. The night-time barking calls of curlews translate into the hounds of hell. Composer Peter Cowdrey has made a study of curlew calls, and when slowed down by a quarter, the whaupping, yelping of the curlew is pretty much identical to the sound of a large, barking dog.

Their long whistles also become something just as fear-inducing. Again, slowed down, they are uncannily like the howl of a wolf – a chilling, haunting sound over a darkening moor. Sounds that may be joyful and bright in sunlight can quickly turn sinister. Robert Burns wrote, 'I never heard the solitary whistle of curlew on a summer noon without feeling an elevation of soul, like the enthusiasm of devotion or poetry.'[2] At night, however, the same sound was believed to issue from the dreaded Seven

Whistlers. In both Welsh and English mythology, these birds of doom fly across the night sky, and to hear them is to be warned of death. At the turn of the twentieth century, Alice Gillington wrote the menacing *Seven Whistlers of Cornwall*:

> Whistling strangely, whistling sadly, whistling
>   sweet and clear,
> The Seven Whistlers have passed thy house,
>   Pentruan of Porthmeor;
> It was not in the morning, nor the noonday's
>   golden grace,
> It was in the dead waste midnight, when the tide
>   yelped loud in the Race;
> The tide swings round in the Race, and they're
>   plaining whisht and low,
> And they come from the gray sea-marshes, where
>   the gray sea-lavenders grow;
> And the cotton grass sways to and fro;
> And the gore-spent sundews thrive
> With oozy hands alive.
> Canst hear the curlews' whistle through thy
>   dreamings dark and drear,
> How they're crying, crying, crying, Pentruan of
>   Porthmeor?[3]

The Celtic story of St Beuno and the curlew, then, takes a night-crying demon or a hound of hell and transforms it into a creature that is keeping watch over our spiritual poetry. A bird of death comes to the aid of a preacher of life. This enchanting tale asks us to be thankful to curlews, not to fear them. In return for its holy act, St Beuno decreed that a curlew's nest must always be difficult to find, thus protecting them into the future.

St Beuno joins another early saint, St Cuthbert, as one of the first-recorded conservationists. Cuthbert lived on the other side of the UK, about as far from west Wales as it is possible to go, on the Farne Islands. Cuthbert is famed for protecting eider ducks from hunters. Reginald, a twelfth-century monk who recorded events at that time, noted that eiders felt so safe on the Farnes, they allowed themselves to be stroked and often nested by the altar and under the bed or even in between the blankets in the monk's cell. Only a saint would tolerate such things, he proclaimed.

The spirit of St Beuno is tangible around the sunlit hills of Pistyll on the Llyn Peninsula, in west Wales. This was Beuno's home patch. His main church is in Clynnog Fawr, an imposing, somewhat cold building that dominates the small village. But there is a far more charming chapel associated with Beuno, just nine miles further south down the coast. Tim Higgins, a friend and former canon at Bristol Cathedral, takes me along a small, unmade track nestled alongside crags lined with gorse bushes, singing with stonechat and whitethroat. The sun shines, and ahead the ocean sparkles blue and silver. Below us, situated comfortably in the hillside and next to a stream, is St Beuno's retreat. This is said to be where the venerable preacher came to pray in solitude and to refresh his spirit. The sea view would soothe any weary soul, and the surrounding landscape of field, brook and glade creates a palpable sense of peace. Here, birds of both the sea and the countryside sing together to a musical score of wind and distant waves. It is a perfect setting in which to find the goodness in life. I listen to the mewing call of choughs and a piercing cry of a curlew whilst standing by the church, completely in awe of the beauty of this special place.

Today, St Beuno's tiny church is a popular destination for pilgrims seeking a fusion of nature and spirit. The building itself is unassuming. You enter, head bowed, through a low, narrow door. The floor is strewn with aromatic and healing herbs collected from nearby fields, which give off a rich aroma. Inside, the font is carved with Celtic knots. Yew branches adorn the windows and door. Mosses and grasses are placed around the edges of the pews. On the windowsills are lovely arrangements of wild-flowers, surrounded by small stones piled together like miniature dolmens. Standing in the cool darkness as the sun streams in through the windows, the tale of St Beuno and the curlew makes much more sense. This Christian church reaches out a firm hand of friendship to its pagan past. Nature is welcome here as part of faith, not simply as a backdrop.

That evening, as though to complete a mystical west Wales experience, I give a talk in a reconstructed Neolithic roundhouse, a wattle-and-daub theatre-in-the-round. In the centre of this extraordinary conical building is an open fire, the smoke rising up and out into the night sky through a hole in the thatched roof. Evenings of storytelling and music happen frequently here at Felin Uchaf, and the low lighting and circular shape emphasise the dancing and crackling of the flames. The centre of the room becomes a vibrant, energised space of drama, an effect it would be impossible to capture on film.

Dafydd Davies-Hughes is a compelling teller of tales. He begins by giving some facts about the building and what to expect through the evening, and then, without noticing the transition, you are drawn through a veil. You are now no longer part of an audience receiving information, but at the centre of the ancient tradition of campfire sagas, living the danger, the excitement, the tragedy and the joy of vivid characters conjured purely out of words. Stories by fire-light trigger deep resonances that refer to something long ago and unknowable, yet still powerful. Dafydd leaves you entranced by his skill. He's a hard act to follow.

My PowerPoint presentation seems more than a little incongruous. A rapidly assembled projector and a screen look ugly and awkward in a Neolithic roundhouse and I wish I had Dafydd's skill. In the discussion afterwards, we talk all things curlew and how important they had once been to the life of the locals. Curlews were once so common that at least thirty different areas had a local name for them. *Gylfinir*, meaning long bill, is mostly used in the north of Wales; *chwibanogl* is a whistle and is used in Ceredigion; and *chwibanwr* means whistler, their name in Pembrokeshire and Carmarthenshire. In Radnorshire, curlews were known as the Llanbister cuckoo as they were the most commonly heard harbingers of spring rather than the cuckoo itself. Someone mentions a nearby rise called Clip Y Gylfinir, 'the hill of the long-billed bird', or 'curlews' rise.' Curlews

returning to breed in the spring were often seen sailing over
the top before landing in the fields. As in Ireland, people
hadn't noticed when they had quietly slipped away from
the spring and summer life of the area. There is genuine
sadness and surprise. Once again, it seems that because
curlews are still seen in good numbers along the coast in
the winter months, the impression is one of abundance.
When the reality of the situation dawns, it comes as a shock.

We leave the roundhouse in the dark. The narrow footpath to the car park is lit by a thousand shining stars. It is
cold and clear and the heavens seem infinite. To add poignancy to what had already been a magical evening, a sharp
new moon hangs above the thatched roof. A talk on the
new moon bird is illuminated by a new moon – it is a
moving sight. 'May your journey pass without a twist or a
knot,' are Dafydd's parting words.

The spiritual side of west Wales is strong. It is a land
proud of its ancient culture. Flags sporting red dragons flutter from many garden flagpoles and Welsh is spoken widely,
and often as the first language, reminding the numerous
English residents that they are visitors in a land that is
anchored somewhere very different. Otherworldly tales of
wonder are celebrated as part of Welsh identity and
proudly passed down the generations. There is none of the
shame associated with history, as in Ireland with its very
different colonial experience. But what west Wales seems
to share with the island across the sea is a cultural under-
current of melancholy. 'Being Irish, he had a profound
sense of tragedy which sustained him through temporary
periods of joy,' is a saying often (and probably wrongly),

attributed to W.B. Yeats. You could argue that it is a Welsh trait, too.

The sound of the Welsh harp and the sight of drifting mist through valleys go some way to represent the sense of deep yearning that is laced throughout Welsh culture. It is summed up in the word *hiraeth*. There is no direct English equivalent, but something like pining, homesickness, yearning and unrequited love are close. *Hiraeth* has been interpreted in many ways and is often described as a longing for a past that can never be recovered. And to add a very Welsh twist, perhaps it never really existed at all. It can be for a person, a place, or an experience of home. It is a word for many complex emotions – the upwelling of feelings when discovering old love letters, or a desire to return to somewhere that can never be found. For Val Bethell, who made a short film about *hiraeth*, it is 'the link with the long-forgotten past, the language of the soul, the call from the inner self. Half-forgotten – fraction remembered. It speaks from the rocks, from the earth, from the trees and in the waves. It's always there.'

Other cultures capture the same experience in equally beautiful words. In Japan the nearest is *kyoushuu*. A Japanese friend described it as 'not at all sugary, but for me, anything that you leave behind in the country of your origin. It includes happiness you experience in the past, as well as what you miss deep inside. It is much more than homesickness.' *Sehnsucht* is a similarly powerful word in German. For C.S. Lewis it is a longing for a far-off country, but not a physical place on a map, it is intangible, always elusive. In *The Weight of Glory*, Lewis describes *Sehnsucht* as '… the scent of a flower we have not found, the echo of a tune we have not heard, news from a country we have never yet visited'. *Saudade* in Portuguese also expresses the inexpressible sense of yearning, of what was, but can never be again. It finds its expression in the traditional Portuguese song, the fado. In Polish the word is *tesknota*. In *Lost in Translation*, Eva Hoffman writes, 'I sometimes hear the peasants coming back from the fields and meadows, singing fierce, pure, modal songs that sound like no other music I've heard – and then I am filled by *tesknota*, though I don't know what for.' For African slaves, the Blues might have emerged from the same kind of emotion.

This universal feeling of yearning, or *hiraeth*, has been part of the character of Welsh culture for many generations, as in this poem from the ancient set of anonymous verse known as Hen Benillion:

> Gold will end, silver will end,
> Velvet and silk will end
> And all rich clothes will decay
> But *hiraeth* will never perish.

And somehow the call of the curlew is the sound of all of this richness – the sound of *hiraeth*. In a BBC Radio 4 programme called *From Mumbai to Machynlleth*, broadcast in January 2016, the bubbling calls of curlews were laced throughout as the documentary explored the relationship between Urdu traditional love poetry, Ghazal, and Welsh verse. There is a striking similarity between the two cultures, as both have their linguistic roots in Sanskrit and both use words and song to express a deep sense of longing for someone or something that is out of reach. 'It is easier to stop a river flowing to the sea than to quell the yearning for one deeply loved.' Cue the cry of the curlew.

Welsh poet R.S. Thomas was a master at capturing *hiraeth*, albeit in bitter phrases as well as sweet. Thomas, like W.B. Yeats, looked back to an idealised past rooted in the natural world, to 'a simple peasant culture where identity … was unproblematic, growing from a rich imaginative heritage, rooted in a particular place.' In *Welsh Landscape*, Thomas wrote, 'There is no present in Wales, and no future, there is only the past.' And when writing about the lost traditions of hafod, a seasonal migration of hill farmers to high pastures in the summer, and of Calan Mai, celebrations on the first day of May, he dreams,

When I am there, I hear the curlew mourning the people who have passed away, and I dream of the days that were, the days of Calan Mai and the hafoty; days when the Welsh went to the high pastures to live for a season at least, 'At the bright hem of God/In the heather, in the heather'.

The call of the curlew, piping, bubbling, crying in the wind, is quintessentially the sound of this deeply experienced sense of *hiraeth*. It is no coincidence, then, that one of the last breeding strongholds for curlew in Wales is in a 25 square-mile area of moorland and hills in north Wales called Mynydd Hiraethog, 'the hills of great longing'.

This mixture of moorland, farmland, rugged hills, lakes and conifer plantations lies to the east of the Snowdonia National Park. A section of it forms the control site for another of the RSPB's Trial Management Projects. It also hosts perhaps seventy pairs of curlews. On a windy day, Dave Rees and I visit an upland section that is known to have around five breeding pairs. Walking across the moor, the air seems especially fresh and the views are breathtaking. The landscape shows only four colours – the green and brown of the vegetation and the blue and white of sky and water – but every variation and hue appears and disappears as the clouds race above. Wales stretches away peacefully in all directions. We could be the only people in the country that day. The Hills of Longing are well named, though the longing they evoke on a sunny day is sweet, not sad.

It is always a privilege to go birding with people who are good at it, they have a range of senses that most of us lack.

A whirr of a wing, a flash of a shadow, a slight, barely audible tweet, is enough for an identification. And that famous 'jizz' of a bird, the overall manner and posture that is unique to each species, is enough to elicit an identification from what seems to be a mere pinpoint in the distance. We see (apparently) stonechat, skylark, meadow pipit as well as at least two curlew (which I do see). It is an enriching experience, and it never ceases to amaze me how much I don't notice, before it is pointed out to me.

What you can't fail to see throughout much of upland Wales, though, are wind farms. Personally, I find comfort in the sight of large, whirring turbines. Climate change is a reality and doing nothing to reduce our greenhouse gas emissions cannot be an option. But the power of wind doesn't come for free. Obviously, wind farms need to be built where it is windy, which is usually on the tops of hills. And they are sited on marginal ground, exactly where many ground-nesting birds breed. Setting aside all the controversy around the aesthetics of wind turbines and their effect on the wildness of wild places, putting large structures on breeding grounds comes with its own set of issues. Erecting and maintaining them creates disturbances, but there is another more worrying effect. Research carried out in 2009[4] showed that curlews and other ground-nesting birds actively avoid nesting near wind farms, leaving a margin of up to 800 metres. The study showed a reduction in the density of nests in this zone of up to 40 per cent for the curlew, golden plover, snipe and meadow pipit. Set this against the increase in the number of wind farms in recent decades throughout upland Britain, and it is obvious that curlews are now facing new pressures. A Welsh National Assembly Renewable Energy research paper published in 2013[5] shows that between 2004 and 2011 the amount of energy produced with renewables in Wales doubled from around one to two gigawatt hours, and two-thirds of that comes from onshore wind farms.

This is an increasing challenge, as our demand for non-fossil fuel energy will inevitably, and quite rightly, rise. Many of the most suitable sites for wind farms are on the very places favoured by birds like curlew: high, isolated moorland. The tension between wildlife conservation and climate-change mitigation is set to increase in the following decades. These competing green agendas show how complex it is for us to live sustainably and to also accommodate a vibrant community of wildlife. Sometimes we will be forced to choose between the conservation of wildlife and the production of low carbon energy, and I suspect our demand for energy will win.

As the afternoon sun begins to slip away, Dave and I rest on the shores of a reservoir, Llyn Aled Isaf. There is not a soul around. We have seen a few curlews flying and calling during the day, a sign they are still here, but in worryingly low numbers. But they haven't gone, and that has to be a positive sign; something to work with. Lying in the heather and enjoying the last traces of warmth, suddenly, from the opposite bank we hear the unmistakable guttural cries of curlews. The call is specific to mating, and described by *The Birds of the Western Palearctic* as 'a soft but widely audible "gri-gri-gri".' It is almost a growl or moan. Through binoculars we can see a mounted pair on a small shingle beach.

Each copulation lasts a few minutes. The female tilts forwards and loosens her wings as the male calls behind her and flaps his wings before mounting and touching her neck with his bill. After they mate they separate but stay together, eventually flying away, hopefully to nest. Desmond Nethersole-Thompson records that after mating the male often dances around the scrape he has prepared for the eggs. It is a happy, memorable moment. Curlews are here in the Hills of Longing, and they mean business. And then, to add to an already thrilling experience, a male hen harrier glides across the reservoir and over the horizon, its white feathers stark against the darkening sky. This is wild Wales at its very best.

The sunlit evening is replaced by a wet, cold dawn. The polar explorer Sir Ranulph Fiennes once quipped that, 'There is no such thing as bad weather, only inappropriate clothing'. True. Rachel Taylor, a Senior Research Ecologist for the British Trust for Ornithology, takes pity on me as I shiver in her car and lends me her spare Buffalo shirt, designed to be worn in the Antarctic. Then we step out into biting wind on the Migneint moor, which lies to the south of Mynydd Hiraethog. There are around thirty pairs of curlews here. The clouds spit rain and it is unforgiving today on the high moor. The warm heather of Hiraethog seems a world away. Immediately, three pairs of curlews bubble over the fields on either side of the small road. They are in full mating display, soaring and gliding on outstretched wings, their rising calls carrying far on the wind. Perhaps it is the weather, but there is a scratchy urgency to their calls today. These birds are not only communicating with each other, though, they are also transmitting data through a small box attached to their backs. Tucked into hedges all around the area are base stations – tall, pole-like structures with cylindrical tops, about the size of an egg box. Some of the curlews have small GPS/VHF loggers glued to their feathers, and every fifteen minutes, if they are within a couple of hundred metres of a base station, the loggers record the time of day and the birds' location. For the first time, Rachel and her partner Steve Dodd from the RSPB are finding out how curlews use the landscape during the breeding season. Tracking migratory birds in the winter has been happening for a while, but the exploration of how the birds work their breeding grounds is new, and what Rachel and Steve are in the process of discovering is both fascinating and challenging.

Although they have only managed to put trackers on four birds so far, an indication of the scale of a curlew's mental map is beginning to emerge. Far from staying local to their nest, non-incubating birds slip away in the evening, just after dark, and fly to roosting sites for the night, returning to the nest just before dawn. The distance is highly variable; some go just a short way away, but one bird went 3 kilometres to the shores of a small lake. The birds are therefore separating at night and utilising far more of the landscape than the immediate nesting territory. No one knows why they do this. Nor do we understand why the birds choose to feed in specific places during the day. One bird flew a staggering 21 kilometres away to a favoured feeding spot. Rachel and Steve's work is highlighting how curlews select some areas far more than others and are prepared to commute long distances. Is this because there are now fewer good places to feed close to their nests? Perhaps less dominant birds are forced to travel as nearby high-quality areas are taken by dominant birds? Who knows, but in all instances they seem to like feeding in areas that have been kept short-cropped by light grazing from sheep and cattle and that are, of course, rich in invertebrates.

As all the birds tagged happened to be males, it is not known, yet, if females behave in the same way, or if the pattern of landscape use changes as the breeding season progresses. But at least some results are coming in, showing us that curlews are complex birds with complex needs. They range over landscapes, but not in a haphazard way, they target specific locations and we need to understand why. We may protect a nesting area, but if the roosting and feeding sites are not taken into account, the birds may fail to breed. Does this go some way to explaining why curlews are now absent from areas that, to us, look suitable for nesting? A wind turbine, a drainage ditch, an increase in stocking density or a new patch of forest on these roosting and feeding sites may well be enough to stop them succeeding. This was new information in 2016, and yet again I was astonished at how little we know about birds that were once so common. I also wonder if their night-time sojourns to remote parts helped form the many myths about flying demons. Curlews soaring over the moors at night, perhaps calling plaintively in the wind, could be rich source material for fireside tales. Both science and folklore try to make sense of a perplexing world. These two strands of thought don't seem such uncomfortable bedfellows in this country that values different ways of comprehending.

Rachel sets up two telescopes and we watch the displaying birds for some time. Their calls are the sounds of sprawling wet moors. Their long bills are wide open as they fly. Until the late nineteenth century, though, to hear a curlew call required a trip to these high moors or bogs, as they were virtually absent from lowland and southern areas. Then something happened from the late 1800s onwards, and the moorland whistle was increasingly heard as a lowland flute. Curlews expanded their range, moving down from the hills and into the fields, a pattern echoed across the rest of the UK, too. Perhaps an increase in fire-arms and game-keeping and the maintenance of heather moorland for shooting during the Victorian era helped boost numbers and the excess birds spilled over to the lowlands, finding suitable nesting sites in rough fields. This is one theory, but no one knows for sure.

By the 1920s, curlews had arrived in the southern county of Glamorgan, and by the Second World War 'Curlews were breeding right across the county from the Rhymney Valley to the Gower.' They now sang over slag tips and on the hills above the mining villages, maybe inspiring new thoughts and ideas in those who stopped to listen. And I wonder whether the presence of those calls, heard now in the places where poets dwelt, laid the foundations for some of the most beautiful imagery from the two great Swansea poets, Dylan Thomas and Vernon Watkins.

These two close friends could not have been more different in character. Dylan Thomas was an irascible creator who played with language, invented it, tore it up and discarded convention. He was wild and unrestrained. Vernon Watkins was a quiet, reserved man of routine. His day job was a bank clerk, but his evenings were full of perfectly crafted words. Dylan Thomas described him as 'the most profound and greatly accomplished Welshman writing poems in English'. Creativity can emerge from storehouses both chaotic and calm; these poets invented imagery that moves the soul, and both found inspiration in the cry of the curlew.

For Thomas, in 'The White Giant's Thigh', the bubbling call of the curlew reminded him of the music of tumbling streams and made through 'throats where many rivers meet.' The sound expresses the pain and longing of women wanting to have a child:

> And alone in the night's eternal, curving act
> They yearn with tongues of curlews for the
>   unconceived.

But the curlew is also a raucous member of life's rich menagerie, which wails, crows and screeches its presence to the world in wonderful tumult. In 'Prelude', Thomas builds a Noah's ark of poet-creatures, a celebration of life on Earth. He surveys the variety of life from the woodland to the sea. He wonders at a 'ruffled ring dove' hooting in the darkening sky, and on the beach, where fishermen are 'crow black', the 'shells/that speak seven seas' lie on the sand as high-flying geese sail overhead. And then Thomas takes us

> Down to the curlew herd
> Ho, hullaballoing clan
> Agape, with woe
> In your beaks, on the gabbing capes!

On the other hand, Vernon Watkins used the sound and image of the curlew to give vent to his emotions when Thomas died. Despite Thomas being, at times, an appalling friend to Watkins (even though he was best man, he didn't turn up to his wedding), he provided vicarious energy and daring to Watkins' life of quiet certitude. 'The Curlew' expresses the state of deep grief as he remembers his many walks with Thomas along a beach on the Gower:

> Sweet-throated cry, by one no longer heard
> Who, more than many, loved the wandering
>   bird
> The same on rocks and over sea I hear
> Return now with his unreturning year.

In an earlier version, the lines were even more poignant:

> Alone I hear it now, Alone I hear,
> A curlew call the unreturning year.

Some years later, Watkins wrote 'The Snow Curlew'. As the world lies hushed in snow he hears the spring call as heralding the end of the desolation of winter. He can now come to terms with grief:

> Silence. Then a curlew flutes with its cry,
> The low distance, that throbbing spring call,
> Swifter than thought. It is goodbye
> To all things not beginning, and I must try,
> Making the driftwood catch,
> To coax, where the cry fades, fires which cannot
>   fall.

The spread of curlews throughout Wales in the twentieth century played its part in inspiring the poetic voice. It wove its magic through their being, drawing out phrases of depth and beauty. To lose such a bird is to lose far more than just a species, it is to let slip away that which is irreplaceable, the source of deep creativity. Wales and the call of the curlew are strongly bound together.

Chapter 8

SOUTHERN ENGLAND CURLEWS

Our relationship with curlews changes as we head further east across the country. Even today a different culture is tangible between the Celtic West and Anglo-Saxon England, but far less so than in days gone by. The borderland I visit on the Curlew Walk is the Shropshire Hills, an Area of Outstanding Natural Beauty. It is a surprising and delightful mixture of rugged hills, pretty villages, heather moor and farmland, and was the home of author and poet Mary Webb. In her 1917 novel *Gone to Earth*, set in this area, she describes a young vixen called Foxy:

Between the larch boles and under the thickets of honeysuckle and blackberry came a tawny silent form, wearing with the calm dignity of woodland creatures a beauty of eye and limb, a brilliance of tint, that few women could have worn without self-consciousness. Clear-eyed, lithe, it stood for a moment in the full sunlight – a year-old fox, round-headed and velvet-footed. Then it slid into the shadows.

Gone to Earth is a moving story of the life of a beautiful young girl, Hazel Woodus, who lived with her father in a poor cottage on the side of one of the hills. Hazel was a wild child and 'had so deep a kinship with the trees, so intuitive a sympathy with leaf and flower, that it seemed as if the blood in her veins was not slow-moving human blood, but volatile sap'.

Hazel had a loving relationship with Foxy, a cub she rescued and kept as a pet after its mother was torn apart by hunting dogs. But when the young vixen ate one of her father's chickens, he threatened to drown it. In her broad accent, Hazel gently reproaches the fox, but then she ponders its true nature:

'You was made bad,' she said sadly but sympathetically. 'Leastways. You wasn't made like watch-dogs and house-cats and cows. You was made a fox, and you be a fox, and it's queer-like to me, Foxy, as folk canna see that. They expect you to be what you wanna made to be. You'm made to be a fox; and when you'm busy being a fox they say you are a sinner!'

Animal sinners are termed vermin, and vermin must be ruthlessly eradicated. In the tragic end to the story Hazel dies trying to save Foxy from a pack of hounds (and save herself from one of the hunters), by jumping with Foxy off a cliff into a quarry. There are, of course, parallels inferred between a young woman being pursued by men and the lot of a fox being chased by dogs, but it works also at the level of an anti-hunt novel. In a review of *Gone to Earth* in the *New Statesman* in 2000, Rowan Pelling wrote:

> Hazel is the first martyr of the animal rights movement, sacrificing her life so that her pet Foxy shall not be 'cut in two and flung (a living creature, fine of nerve) to the pack and torn to fragments'. Every hunt sab should have a copy.

Hunting with dogs has now been banned, but exactly 100 years after the book was published, fate and fortune has placed foxes under renewed pressure in this out-of-the-way beauty spot on the England–Wales border. Today, rather than being the quarry of virile hunters with hounds, they find themselves in the crosshairs of the guns of fox controllers working for conservation.

The Shropshire Hills are curlew country. Their remote, rough-hewn terrain has offered perfect nesting areas from time immemorial. In *The Fauna of Shropshire*, written in 1899, H.E. Forrest states that the curlew 'is numerous on our Shropshire moorlands and breeds regularly.' Ancient and craggy, the hills rise above a sea of bright green fields and are sudden and unexpected mini mountains in the middle of tame countryside. They carry an air of greatness, of peaks much grander than their mere 500 or so metres. It is as if they have been cast adrift from some vast mountain range somewhere far away and have come to rest in the midst of humanity. These are old hills with jagged, weatherworn outlines. Mary Webb set her stories around the Stiperstones Ridge in the south of the area, which is now a National Nature Reserve. The top of the ridge is defined by tors of 510-million-year-old quarzite, a hard, crystalline rock sharpened through the action of ice and frost. In 1839 geologist Richard Murchison described them as, 'broken and serrated edges … they stand out on the crest of the ridge at short intervals, like rugged cyclopean ruins.'[1]

Where there are mountains there is poetry. Capturing their drama, in 1860 Walter White saw 'the bare spines of some fossil monster, huger than imagination ever dreamt of.'[2] And Magdalene Weale, who travelled through the area on horseback in 1935, describes 'that gaunt range … virile and hard with the hardness of immense age, and crowned with its strange outcrop of black quarzite like so many ruined fortresses.'[3] As Weale cantered over the hills she revelled in their wildness, 'with the wind whistling in one's ears and the curlews flying overhead.'

Curlews are woven into this evocative landscape. Their calls capture the spirit of the place like no other bird. This hidden, distinct world of crag and damp valley was once full of bubbling curlews in the spring, as evocatively described in H.W. Timperley's *Shropshire Hills*, written in 1947:

Let a cloud drift across the sun on a spring day, darkening the green of the damp bottoms and the brown of the hillsides where the new bracken has not yet begun to cover up the old, the air feeling chilly as the sunlight is quenched, and if it happens when curlew are up and calling, the dimming of the sun will completely restore the valley to the birds. They will fly like shadows along the green or the brown, or cast their strange silhouettes against the cloud; but they will lose something of tangibility as birds but as the voices of birds they will be clear and close; they will be the voices of the past, filling the valley with notes and cadences learnt in prehistoric solitudes, voices which sound unearthly to us because we have no remembrance of those times, though perhaps the faintest wraith of inherited recollection, ten thousand times removed from clearness, drifts across our minds when we hear the curlew's call. With the curlew there are snipe and pipits in this valley, both birds of rushy or upland places, but if they live in the valley they do not possess it like the curlew.[4]

The valley to which Timperley refers is between the Stiperstones and another ridge to the east, the Long Mynd. Further on are the Clee Hills. To the west sits Corndon Hill and Stapeley Common. Waves of high ground dipping into lowland farmland roll across southern Shropshire. They are 'curlew places', where the last populations of the birds hang on. Today, following the general dispersal of curlews into lowland areas throughout the UK at the turn of the twentieth century, curlews have changed their habits and rarely now nest on the high ridges amongst the heather. Instead, they have moved to the lower slopes and into the flat, damp fields, siting their nests amongst the hooves of cattle and sheep.

My visit to the Shropshire Hills is a detour south off the main route, but I had planned to coincide with a weekend of curlew-centred activities run by the Stiperstones and Corndon Hill Country Landscape Partnership Scheme (thankfully, LPS for short). As my walk takes me into these environs of quaint villages nestled into the hillsides, I feel as though I have gone through the back of the wardrobe and into another world. Here, it seems, is a Narnia for curlews. A meadow festival is under way, complete with little girls in floral dresses carrying bundles of hay, with wildflowers woven into their hair. For the energetic, there is a bale-lobbing competition and a how-to-scythe-hay-by-hand demonstration, swiftly followed by a scything team competition. There are guided flower and bug walks, and demonstrations on how to build a hayrick. Some stalls sell home made food and drink, and another has information leaflets and posters explaining how curlews need these meadows for their nests. Herb-rich hay fields, cut late in the year, are a curlew's best friend. The curlew is hailed as the celebrity bird of Shropshire, a local wonder of nature that must be protected for the future.

Aside from the meadow activities, in Hyssington village hall, artist Bill Sample is holding a 'make-a-curlew-lantern-out-of-wire-coathangers-drinking-straws-and-tissue-paper' workshop. The room is full of mainly women and children assembling white, curlew shapes. There is a noisy, fun atmosphere. The ghostly creations hang around on pieces of string attached to bamboo poles. They swing gently and are strangely animated. These lanterns will have a practical use later in the year, when they will be used to guide an evening procession to see an outside curlew installation, also designed by Bill. He is in the process of fashioning seven luminous, fibreglass curlews, which are to be placed in the middle of a small lake on a local farm, giving the impression of a flock of glowing birds flying over still water. I don't ask Bill if he has chosen seven curlews deliberately to refer to the seven Shropshire Whistlers. Maybe it is by accident that he is creating ancient myth in modern materials.

But this isn't all. In nearby Priest Weston village hall, choirmaster Mary Keith is holding a curlew-themed singing workshop. All the songs are about curlews and much of the music mimics curlew calls. Writer and fellow curlew enthusiast, Karen Lloyd, had previously held a workshop to write the words for curlew songs, which allowed the locals to express their feelings for the birds in lyrics. These songs will be sung as the curlew lantern procession makes its pilgrimage to the glow-in-the-dark sculpture later in the year. I feel I have left Planet Earth and entered Planet Curlew, a magical curlew world, folded away in a crease in the space-time continuum. It is extraordinary and wonderful. In the afternoon I am interviewed for a local radio station about the walk so far, and in the evening I give a talk in Snailbeach village hall, to a room full of people who love their local birds and are determined to bring them back.

This outpouring of love for curlews is not so surprising, considering that their decline in this area has taken place quite recently, and memories are still strong. The effects of agricultural changes in the second half of the twentieth century were felt here, of course, but the terrain and isolation meant progress reached it later than further east and south. Up until 1990 the *BTO Breeding Bird Atlas* recorded a good population of curlews throughout the county of Shropshire – around 700 pairs. But the inevitable transformation of the land meant that by 2010 no more than 140 pairs remained – a catastrophic decline of 80 per cent. Even the remote curlew stronghold of Mary Webb's Stiperstones region saw a 30 per cent decline in numbers in eleven years, with just forty nests dotted through the fields. By any measure, this region that has always been regarded as a curlew hotspot is in real trouble.

The reasons for their falling numbers are the same as elsewhere. A varied, nuanced landscape has been replaced with uniformity, little variation in sward height and no mosaic of wet and dry. The timings of agricultural activities have also been disastrous. Early in the spring, when birds are establishing their nests and beginning to lay their eggs, fields are flattened by heavy rollers and harrowed by chains to improve them for pasture and planting. Then, grass is cut for silage from late April onwards, when the eggs and young are still vulnerable. Even if they survive the machines, predation by foxes, badgers, crows, gulls, stoats, weasels and ravens can take a heavy toll. The tide has turned against the curlews in Shropshire and their days seem numbered. The local communities, though, come from gritty, ancestral stock rooted in the land. In his novel, *St Mawr*, D.H. Lawrence wrote of the people of the Stiperstones area, 'It was one of those places where the spirit of aboriginal England still lingers, the old savage England, whose last blood lingers still in a few Englishmen, Welshmen and Cornishmen.' Perhaps this is too romantic a description to apply to the team and helpers of the Stiperstones and Corndon Hill Country LPS, but it is not far off.

Despite its unmemorable mouthful of a name, the LPS does impressive work. Funded mainly by the Heritage Lottery Fund, with others contributing, its membership is made up of local organisations, community groups and professional bodies from both England and Wales, and they undertake projects on a variety of different areas, from archaeology to restoring meadows. The LPS asked local people what specific wildlife project they would like them to undertake, and the overwhelming response (97 per cent of respondents) was that they wanted to help curlews. Curlew Country, as the project is called, was established in 2015 and is focused solely on working with locals to discover why the much-loved Shropshire birds are in decline and what can be done to help their recovery.

Curlew Country initially concerned itself with giving farmers advice about managing their land better for curlews. Although farmers appreciate the birds and like having them around, they were suspicious of yet more conservationists telling them what to do. They were also doubtful that any amount of monitoring or changing the routine of cutting fields would help unless predator numbers were reduced. Amanda Perkins, the Project Officer, had her work cut out to get them on board. Scarcely had the project started than it already seemed bogged down in negativity, with conservationists viewed as farming unfriendly and unsympathetic to the problems of producing food – of not living in the real world. After listening to their feedback, the project was redesigned. The key to success lay in stressing the effectiveness of local, independent action, concentrated solely on curlews, and not run by established, mainstream organisations. By working with farmers right from the beginning, the majority of farms that hosted curlews eventually agreed to help. In this part of the world, the farming community wants to save the curlews no less than anyone else. With permission granted to go on to farmland, the project began. Working farm by farm, field by field, it was possible to protect most from machinery; but keeping them safe from predators proved far more challenging. No one knew for sure which predators were doing the most damage, as observing the act is nigh on impossible. The nests are well hidden amongst grass that gets longer through the season, and most predators strike at night.

Simple detective work can give some clues, but this isn't by any means an exact science. If the nest is suddenly emptied overnight, the finger of suspicion points at foxes. They tend to sneak in, scare away the sitting bird, and carefully take the eggs to eat them away from the nest, or perhaps bury them for later. Foxes are clean and tidy thieves, leaving the area with barely any disturbance. The eggs simply disappear. Badgers, on the other hand, are blunderbusses. They also mainly predate at night, but they are much messier eaters. They trample the ground, crunch up the eggs *in situ* and leave broken fragments scattered around. The surrounding vegetation is often flattened and their trail is obvious. Crows and ravens eat curlew eggs in the daytime. Ravens, being large, can carry the eggs away, but more often than not curlew eggs are too big for a crow's bill. They have a go at eating them at the nest site by making a characteristic hole in the shell with their beaks and then draining the contents by lifting the egg and letting the insides pour into their gullets. The fragments are mostly left around the nest.

At the beginning of the project, Curlew Country employed a professional ornithologist, Tony Cross, to monitor twelve of the forty known nests. A 24-hour camera, triggered by movement, was placed next to each nest. He also put a temperature logger (a thermochron) inside the nests, which recorded the time of day the nest went cold; another clue to help with the identification of the predator. Farmers agreed to leave the areas of fields that had curlew nests and didn't cut that section of grass until later in the year. Tony also radio-tagged any surviving chicks. The results of the first year of observation were shocking. Out of the twelve nests, nine failed before hatching. Six were predated by mammals (one fox and one badger were filmed in the act; the other four nests were almost certainly taken by a fox, but this was not caught on camera), and one nest was deserted for unknown reasons. One nest was destroyed by an avian predator, possibly a crow, and another by an unknown cause.

The remaining three nests did go on to produce a total of nine chicks. Seven chicks were eaten by day four, another lasted ten days, and the last chick made it to twenty-eight days before it too was predated. Twelve nests, not one surviving chick. None of the community wildlife groups throughout the wider area saw any chicks or reported adults behaving as though they had young. The awful conclusion from 2015 was that no chicks at all were produced in the Stiperstones and Corndon Hill area. It was a dispiriting result, to say the least.

Earlier in 2016, the year of my visit, the project had employed a field assistant, David Tompkins, to help Tony. Now, twenty-one nests had cameras installed next to them and again thermochrons were placed inside the nests, and the chicks radio-tagged. Once more, the results were profoundly shocking. Seventeen nests failed at the egg stage. One nest was abandoned for reasons unknown. Two badgers and three foxes were caught on camera in the act of predation, a further two nests were most likely attacked by a badger, and a further five probably by a fox. One nest was trampled by a sheep and a further three nests were lost to unknown predators. In light of the seriousness of the situation, a decision was taken to protect the last few nests with electric fences to stop foxes and badgers getting too close. Seven chicks were successfully hatched, but once outside the protection of the fence (curlew chicks are mobile almost immediately), they too were lost, one to farm machinery, the rest to predators. Once again, out of twenty-one nests, not one chick survived to fledging. In two years, out of a total of thirty-two nests, not a single chick was successfully raised to help replace the ageing population.

Being long-lived birds, curlews can cope with high levels of nest failure and don't need to produce many chicks to keep numbers stable. Each pair needs to raise only one chick every two years to keep a level population, but even that is not happening in Shropshire. In 2017 Curlew Country stepped up their action. The first thing they did was employ a fox controller to keep numbers down during the breeding season. It was not a decision that was taken lightly, but there seemed to be no alternative, as the study showed that foxes were the main problem. The second step was to try out a technique called 'headstarting'. Done strictly under licence, ten eggs were removed from nests in the wild and incubated artificially, protecting them from predation. They were returned to the nests just before hatching. Five chicks fledged from these eggs. Another three chicks fledged from wild nests. For the first time in years, the interventions deployed by Curlew Country meant a new generation of curlews flew away from their fields.

Headstarting is a desperate measure, but these are desperate times. It can only ever be short term and is illegal without a licence from Natural England. If it works, though, it can quickly boost the population, which buys more time to work with landowners to restore suitable habitat. The Shropshire Hills will never return to the time of Hazel and Foxy, when Mary Webb walked its rocky paths and curlews were abundant. But the fields could be made more wildlife-friendly, and the birds helped to return in sufficient numbers so that they can protect themselves from predators, and make intervention unnecessary. In the meantime, Curlew Country is doing whatever it can to stave off local extinction.

In *The Singular Stiperstones*, a beautiful book of the history and natural history of the area, published in 2014, Tom Wall ponders the changes to the land that inspired Mary Webb to write her novels and poetry:

> The topography remains the same of course, but the loss of the detail, the grain of the countryside, the richness of its wildlife, has been dramatic. In terms of agricultural livelihoods there have been considerable improvements – production has greatly increased and subsidies have underwritten profitability – but in terms

of habitats and wildlife, texture and colour, the
enriching fabric of the countryside has been torn away.

Also writing of Mary Webb's Shropshire, Paul Evans, nature
writer and broadcaster, observes that 'so much of the
ecological weave of the countryside has unravelled that the
once commonplace is now extraordinary.' The widespread
curlew has become a bird teetering on the edge of survival.
From what I have seen on my walk, and from numerous
environmental sources, this change in the abundance of
curlews is not an anomaly. The Curlew Country report
from 2015 states:

> These declines are not restricted to the LPS, with
> comparable declines seen in Shropshire as a whole and
> other parts of the UK. In Shropshire, comparison of
> the Breeding Bird Atlas maps, published in 1992, with
> comparable maps from the 2007–12 Atlas survey,
> shows that Curlew now has a much more restricted
> range. Local surveys suggest that the Curlew
> population has fallen by 85% in only nine years in the
> 50 survey plots monitored by the BTO Breeding Bird
> Survey in Shropshire.

The Stiperstones LPS project, Curlew Country, does seem
to be a well-studied representation of what is going on in
much of lowland, farmed Britain. The results match what
has been recorded in many other places, namely that birds
are arriving to breed but their eggs and chicks face an overwhelming onslaught: the might of modern farming

methods, dramatic changes to the landscape, any number of foxes, badgers and crows in the area, all of these bear down on them at the most vulnerable time in their lives. How we decide to respond to this crisis goes right to the heart of conservation. Protecting the curlew is the art of balancing the needs of a bird that requires large complex landscapes against the requirement to feed and house a large population in a small country. It's a fiendishly difficult problem to solve, and whether to tackle it a local level, or through national initiatives, is a key question. The Curlew Country project is small and therefore fast-acting. It is local conservation involving local people aimed at local birds. It knows the ground, knows the people and is not constrained by having to keep a diverse membership happy, as is the case for many large NGOs. But it lacks the pulling power and confidence of the larger organisations when it comes to applying for grants and funding. On a human level, it relies solely on the passion and persistence of a small team. While that energy is there it can achieve many things. If, for whatever reason, it fades, there is no large organisation to fall back on for support and the project could collapse. Small and local or large and national, both have their advantages and disadvantages, and the solution probably lies in a combination of the two approaches. But there is no doubting that the curlews of Shropshire are benefiting from the minimalist Curlew Country. And being able to act fast might be the key to conservation in the future, as the pace of change in the countryside increases.

On the weekend of my visit, we are offered Sunday lunch at Hollies Farm, under the Stiperstones Ridge. The

Pinches have farmed beef cattle and sheep there for four generations. Kila Pinches provides a delicious spread as the family, including grandfather, father and daughter, gather around the table – three farmers whose combined working lives have spanned immense changes. This is a kind, generous family who care about the landscape and their animals, but without sentimentality. Mrs Pinches (grandmother) tells me that she loves the sound of curlews and wanted the bungalow they had built on the farm for their retirement to be called 'Curlew Fields', because 'this was their home – they were here before us.' I then ask the same question of all three farmers: if you were offered the equivalent money to scale down your livestock interests and farm to produce wildlife instead of food, would you be interested? Both grandfather and father say they certainly would; it is the way of life and working on the land that matters, and the product is less important. On the other hand, the daughter, Rhian, a talented young farmer in her twenties, shakes her head. She would prefer to leave farming and do something else, because tending wildlife is not what she has been trained to do. Her interest is in maximising output and running the farm as efficiently as possible to supply demanding and volatile supermarket customers, where the price on the shelf dictates everything and competition is fierce. As food today costs less than at any time in the last sixty years, and the drive is towards ever more, ever cheaper products, Rhian has to be a business woman as well as a farmer, and she sees herself as a manager of land for livestock, not a wildlife ranger. She also says that although she knows and likes curlews, an interest nurtured by her parents who are interested in wildlife, she would be surprised if her young farming friends knew about them, or had even heard of them. I ask if they are taught about wildlife in agricultural college, but she confirms that they aren't. It is an enlightening conversation over Sunday lunch and it sharply illustrates the changes in attitudes to farming and to the land that have taken place since the Second World War.

Afterwards, a group of us walk the nearby hills. En route, I stop at a viewing point to look out from the Stiperstones Ridge to the flat landscape below, chequered with the squares of bright green fields. This is the factory floor that supplies food to the growing population of Britain, and increasingly further afield. Exports of meat, dairy and cereals to Europe and Asia grow year on year, provided by business-savvy farmers like Rhian. How non-productive wildlife fits into this industrial landscape is far from certain, and I wonder if we have the will to find a way to make sure it does.

In his book *Meadowland*, John Lewis-Stempel, who farms in Herefordshire on the Welsh/English border, frets about curlews returning each year to his fields, '… as though it is their migratory wingbeats that turn the Earth, and should they fail to appear we will have entered some ecological end time.' I fret about curlews, too, not because their disappearance is a sign of an environmental apocalypse, but because it will be immensely sad that we cannot find it in our hearts to make room for the wild. If the Eurasian Curlew disappears it will be yet another of this Earth's wonderful species that slips into oblivion for no other reason than it cannot pay its way in the global economy, and is therefore considered dispensable.

The dispersal of curlews from the uplands to the lowlands in the early part of the twentieth century saw them fly to landscapes on the cusp of change. The *Birds of England*, published in 2005, outlines their expansion. They were present in the Somerset Levels by 1900, Sussex by 1912, Wiltshire by 1916, Oxfordshire by 1925, Nottinghamshire and Berkshire by 1944, Buckinghamshire by 1946, the Brecks in Suffolk by 1948 and in Norfolk by 1949. Although never as numerous as birds on the northern moors, good populations sang their way through the spring and summer, weaving their way into the lives of the people of the south. For a while they could adapt and thrive. Their rise and fall in one small corner of Warwickshire is documented in Brian O'Shea's delightful *The Call of the Country*, published in 2005. It is a record of his birdwatching experiences in the twentieth century. The back cover states:

This is the story of the rural environment as seen through the eyes of a lifelong birdwatcher. It is a nostalgic return to the old haunts remembered from early post-war days; a journey of discovery to find how the countryside and its birds have changed.

O'Shea first became aware of three pairs of breeding curlews in hay meadows around the hamlet of Maxstoke in the late 1950s. This 'peaceful haven lying in a fertile vale of mowing grass and pasture' lies between Birmingham

and Nuneaton, just north of the M6. He recalls his aston-
ishment at seeing one for the first time:

> The bird looked simply too large for such compact,
> restrictive, well ordered, agricultural land. A bird like
> this was surely made for the freedom and wildness of
> the moors and seemed out of place here … The
> incongruity of this agrarian setting had the effect of
> making the birds seem even more appealing than they
> would have been in traditional habitat.

O'Shea returned to Maxstoke in the 1980s, and curlews
were still there. Twenty years later, in 2003, he was
surprised and delighted to hear one bird calling in a distant
field, 'its bubbling notes "trembling" the air with the clarity
of crystal'. But now he worried about how the land was
changing. Back in the 1950s, he noted how quickly he got
wet feet as he walked the fields. By 2003, however, he went
for miles in dry trainers. Drainage channels had sucked
away the moisture to make better grazing for sheep and
cows, and a flat, uniform field was the result. 'The ensuing
poorer habitat will make eggs and young easier to find by
ravens, foxes and other predators,' he wrote. A large brown
bird is much more conspicuous in flat, bright green fields,
especially in shorter grass. In the riot of colour and form
that is a hay meadow, full of grasses, flowers, dips and
ridges, it can blend much more easily into the background.
His concern was well founded. A recent request for curlew
sightings from Warwickshire bird clubs revealed no new
records. It seems they have now gone.

It is a common story, and today there are fewer than 300 pairs of curlews left in the southern part of England, with virtually none in the southeast. The birds exist in remnant pockets of a few tens of pairs in Gloucestershire on the Severn and Avon flood meadows, the Somerset Levels (West Sedgemoor RSPB reserve), the heaths and mires of the New Forest, the Upper Thames in Oxfordshire, Breckland, and a handful of birds on Salisbury Plain and Dartmoor. It is a paltry number, but something to work with nonetheless.

Just before setting out on the Curlew Walk, I went to see some southern birds in curlew-friendly hay fields along the floodplain of the River Avon in Gloucestershire. I had been contacted by Phil Sheldrake (then RSPB Conservation Officer for Gloucestershire and Wiltshire) and Mike Smart (a Gloucestershire birdwatcher) who invited me to see the work they were doing monitoring the birds that still came back, and even managed to raise a few chicks.

In early April 2016 we stood under the raised section of the M5 motorway, near Gloucester (a thunderous, disconcerting experience) and looked out across the large expanse of Upham Meadow, an SSSI (Site of Special Scientific Interest). Half a kilometre away, the gently flowing Avon formed the far boundary. Pensive and melancholic willows dangled their branches into the water, and the masts of moored dinghies swayed slowly from side to side. The elegant, pointed church spire in Bredon village was outlined against Bredon Hill, which marks the start of the Cotswold hills. It is a landmark made famous by A.E. Houseman's poem of the same name:

In summertime on Bredon
The bells they sound so clear;
Round both the shires they ring them
In steeples far and near,
A happy noise to hear.

Happier than the roar of the motorway, that's for sure, but it is in this noisy place that the curlews still hang on. Upham Meadow is a surprising sight. Most English farmland is framed by hedges into small packages, and it is not until you reach the vast tracts of East Anglia that open, expansive agricultural fields become common. But here the seasonal flooding of the river has made the ground too wet for intensification and this large, flower-rich grassland is a welcome and spacious sight to behold in the West of England. Not only is the grass alive with insects, it is cut late by a consortium of farmers who manage it traditionally. Upham is a Lammas meadow, so-called because it is cut around Lammas Day, an Anglo-Saxon festival where bread is brought into a church to mark the beginning of harvesting the grain, usually on 1 August. Lots of insects, late cutting of hay and restricted access for people – what more could a curlew want?

Standing tall and proud, looking as though it owned the place, was WBY (White, Blue Yellow, named after the colour combination of rings on its legs). WBY is a female and has returned to Upham for the past three years (possibly for longer), and to the same places on the Severn estuary in the winter months for six years. Not only is this female faithful to Upham, she nests in the same spot in the meadow, almost by the same patch of dandelions. Behind, another, unringed, pair were chasing each other in characteristic pre-mating behaviour. Each bird took turns to lower their heads and charge, running past and around their mate, making a touching and amusing display. Yet another pair bubbled and glided through the air. The sun shone and a gentle breeze scurried through the trees as returning curlews danced through their spring rituals.

Mike is coordinating a small band of volunteers who are monitoring the birds throughout the Severn and Avon meadows, and Phil is collating the results. He is also monitoring the few pairs settled on Salisbury Plain. There are around 40 pairs dotted along the Severn and Avon vales and they are doing better than many other southern locations, with at least six pairs managing to produce young. Personal contact with farmers to negotiate late cutting in the intensive fields, as well as the age-old agricultural routine in Lammas Meadows, is making life easier for West Country curlews. This is one of southern England's prime curlew sites, right beneath the M5.

There are pockets of breeding curlews dotted around the southern part of England, and most have small numbers of local volunteers monitoring them. With little involvement from major conservation organisations (apart from the RSPB involvement in the Upper Thames and Somerset Levels), the dedicated curlew field workers are isolated. Immediately after the walk, Phil, Mike and I met again and began to make plans for a southern England Workshop, the Call of the Curlew, where all the disparate southern groups could come together to share information and ideas. The UK has a legal obligation to protect the range of curlews, not just the populations in the north, and so more must be done to help bolster the southern birds before these last few hubs dwindle to nothing. The good news is that half the battle has already been won, as curlews are greatly loved in the south. Despite being relative newcomers, we have reached out to them and taken them to our hearts.

In some places though we will need to love them very much to bring them back. On Dartmoor, just four pairs return each year and only one pair usually attempts to breed. They hardly ever succeed. Predation and disturbance by dogs and walkers frustrate their efforts, and the Dartmoor curlews have only managed to fledge three chicks in twelve years.

My visit to the Shropshire Curlew Country project comes to an end, and it is time to head north and east. Amanda Perkins says goodbye to me in a car park by the Stiperstones National Nature Reserve. 'You look like someone who just wants to go home,' she says, and gives me a hug. Every journey has its downtime, and this is it for me. In a couple of hours I could be back home in Bristol, but there is another three-week trek ahead before I can entertain any thoughts of going home. The situation for southern curlews is not good, handfuls of birds hang on, scattered through dangerous fields. But they are still here, and there are good people working hard to save them, and that gives me heart to carry on.

The next part of the Curlew Walk will take me to the Staffordshire Moorlands, the place where I was brought up, and then beyond into the Peak District. This is the start of upland England with its crags, heather moors and mountains. It is very different in character to the south, and part of this higher ground is quintessential grouse-shooting country. I know I will find far more curlews further north, but I will also come face to face with some of nature conservation's most bitter conflicts.

Chapter 9

CURLEW MOORS

There is the comfort of a cream tea about English country lanes. As I walk from Shrewsbury to Stoke-on-Trent, the May sunshine is filtered through fresh leaves that cast a soft mantle over the land. The rugged tracks of Ireland and Wales seem a world away, as do the mini mountains of Planet Curlew on the Welsh/English border. Heading further into England, I am aware of another transition, of leaving behind not only different landscapes but also the remnants of a different state of mind. Traces of the ancient Christian synergy with nature can still be found out west, living on through old stories, folklore and the ancient symbols carved into rock, but it was eradicated more thoroughly further east.

Early Christian missionaries to the British Isles converted the pagans to worship one God, but instead of presenting them with complex theological arguments they communicated with these earthy, practical people through a shared experience of nature. The natural world was a language everyone understood, albeit with a different take. For the pagans the Earth was redolent with meaning and nature was to be feared as much as revered. The gods could wreak havoc as well as bless humanity at will, and had to be praised and soothed. People dwelled in the midst of spirits whose minds were capricious. The Christians introduced just one God and one creator who was entirely good, and the natural world was seen as a great book that told of his greatness. The merging of these two mindsets produced an early Christianity that was visceral and rooted in the very stuff of the Earth, as the story of St Beuno and many other tales show. To begin with, therefore, Christians were outdoor people. As Mary Low writes in *Celtic Christianity and Nature*:

> Long ago, before there were churches, it was normal
> for people to practise their religion out of doors. In the
> Hebrew Bible, Abraham meets his God under an oak
> tree and Deborah prophesied under a palm. In the
> New Testament, Jesus prays in the temple at
> Jerusalem, but also in the hills of Galilee. Nature was
> an acceptable place of worship, as it still is in many
> parts of the world … These are the old wild
> sanctuaries, the first places of worship.

As a consequence, the first Christian churches were bright places, mirroring the landscapes surrounding them. The walls were covered with paintings telling of biblical tales

and often featuring trees, birds and natural features familiar to the congregation. Martin Poulsom, a friend, theolo-
gian and Catholic priest, wonders about the effect of
pre-Reformation churches on the spiritual imaginations of
the faithful. Going into one of these brightly painted sacred
spaces, he reckons, 'might have felt like they were stepping
into a building and out into a vast landscape of biblical
imagery, the wide cosmos, and the world as it was meant
to be'. But over the following centuries huge forces came
into play that eroded these connections. The Christian-
Pagan fusion, characterised by the cross and the circle,
increasingly gave way to straight lines and rigidity, as a
centralised, hierarchical Church became established. The
battle for the heart of Christian practice raged through the
centuries, producing significant turning points for the natural world.

Over time, money and power corroded the message of
Christian holiness and simplicity, but the suppression of
this opulence by the reformist monk Martin Luther in the
sixteenth century, in favour of a back-to-basics, uniform
religion, had consequences other than just dismantling a
wealthy hierarchy. Nick Mayhew-Smith, an author who
has written extensively about spirituality in the landscape,
believes the Reformation played a part in the removal of
nature from worship. The reformers wanted no distractions
from the pure word of God, and the vibrant paintings in
churches were whitewashed not just from the buildings
but also from the minds of people:

Rather than stopping the march towards human power structures in favour of something more sympathetic to nature, it simply shifted focus to the individual's relationship with God, which in many ways widened the gulf between the spiritual and the physical worlds. No sacramentality, no need for priests, no need for the transformation of material objects (bread, wine, baptismal water) into anything special, just a person and a Bible.

Many leading reformers deemed colourful paintings a temptation to wrong-thinking, and God was rendered sepia and only accessed through words. This in turn must have helped to separate faith from nature in the worshipper's heart and mind. Add to this the great intellectual revolution of the Renaissance, when science was divorced from the sacred, and the death knell for a spirit-filled natural world tolled through Christendom. The Celtic-Christian approach to religion clung on in the far west, but for the most part it was suppressed and St Beuno and his curlew faded from view.

This shedding of a Christian practice imbued with nature took many hundreds of years, but eventually the natural world was excluded from liturgy and daily worship. The church swept wildness out of its buildings and back into its place, which was decidedly not at the altar. The joys, fears, challenges and dangers of a wild world were kept outside of the four-square walls in favour of a system that required order and predictability. As Mary Low describes:

Church buildings, temples, mosques and synagogues all
represent a retreat from this raw encounter with
nature. In many parts of the world it is simply assumed
that proper worship needs a roof over its head.
Outdoor spirituality is seen as a fringe activity or
private affair, and on Sundays throughout the year
Christians turn their backs on nature to worship its
creator in a house of their own making.

The only nature commonly seen in churches now is in the
potent symbolism of water for baptism, images in stained-
glass windows, flower arrangements, seasonal holly and
Christmas trees, or the produce that represents harvest
festival. On the whole, Christian nature has been tamed
and confined. God has become an indoor spirit.

Indeed, Christian theology looked with increasing suspicion on the natural world, concerned about a return to a
more pagan mindset. Non-human life was seen as integral
to the fall of Man, nature was unbridled, lustful and
immodest in every way. The Book of Genesis tells us that
a snake deceived Eve by offering her the forbidden fruit
from the tree of life. Wilfully tempting, she fell for its wiles,
and in so doing condemned all of humanity to lives of toil
and hardship. 'By the sweat of your brow you will eat your
food until you return to the ground, since from it you were
taken; for dust you are and to dust you will return.'

Far from being bright and spiritual guides to our inner
lives, a view held by the early Church, the non-human
world was now deemed incapable of reaching heaven. To
truly be created in the image of God, said theologians,

animals need both rationality and intellect, two qualities present only in human beings. Creaturely life was downgraded from co-creators on a spiritual Earth to irrational creatures in a fallen one. This shift in vision was a wretched analysis and has ever since dominated the fate of nature in the mainly Christian west. The ruthless way in which some Christian people treat the world around them follows from that re-visioning of non-human life from spirit-filled to soulless.

These themes I explore with Martin Poulsom, my Catholic priest friend, who accompanies me for two days on this Midlands stretch of my walk. His offer of company is well timed. I am tired and in need of encouragement for the long, curlew-free walk to the Staffordshire moors. I also feel the need to let off some theological steam about the loss of nature from religious doctrine. Back in 2005 I gave a talk in Clifton Cathedral, in Bristol, urging the Catholic Church to rediscover its original connection to nature. After all, some of the most precious habitats on Earth are held in its hands. The whole of the Amazon basin and the Philippines, large parts of the Congo and sub-Saharan Africa are in areas where Catholicism is the dominant form of organised religion and still has political and social influence, yet enormous environmental destruction takes place. In recent years, all of the world's major religions have paid more attention to climate change, particularly because it adversely affects poorer nations, but the protection of species is low down on their agendas, if it is present at all. Martin is a kind, non-judgemental listener and he lends a sympathetic ear, though he can offer no solutions.

Some poets have looked enviously upon non-human creatures, and the freedoms that they enjoy as a result of their downgraded status. Being devoid of an eternal soul means life can be unfettered and unbound by the moral choices that dominate human existence. Creaturely life is not torn between the temptations of bodily desires and the rigours of holy living, nor is it tormented by visions of heaven and hell. R.S. Thomas considered this ignorant bliss in his poem 'The Minister'. Looking at a cow, he wryly observed that:

> No one ever teased her with pictures of
> Flyless meadows,
> Where the grass is eternally green
> No matter how often the tongue bruises it,
> Or the dung soils it.[1]

And in 'Tales from the Twilight', W.B. Yeats playfully describes the Christian natural world as 'Nations of gay creatures, having no soul, nothing in their bodies but a mouthful of sweet air.'

Martin and I sit in the sun, drinking tea by a canal a few miles outside Market Drayton, and we watch children feeding noisy ducks. Gulping sweet air and squabbling over bread, much to the amusement of onlookers, doesn't seem such a bad existence, and I feel heaven will be the poorer if it does not welcome such bright and beautiful beings.

The next stage on my walk is an emotional stopover in Stockton Brook, a village in the Staffordshire Moorlands where my family lived for forty-five years. Instead of going home I stay for two nights with our next-door neighbours, Maggie and Mark. Just a few months earlier, we sold the family house after the death of my parents, and another family lives there now. It is strange to stand in the garden and look over a high hedge to the trees my father had planted and to the greenhouse I helped him dismantle and clean out one summer. There are people talking and noises of activity coming from the garden, but they are not voices I recognise. The same birdsong fills the air, though, and I am sure my dad's spirit drifts among the flowers that he so loved. It hits me hard that I can no longer talk to him sitting on his bench by his pond, or watch my mother pick soft fruit from the vegetable patch by the bottom hedge. It was my father who often took me to the Peak District, just a few miles up the road, and showed me the fossils in the limestone walls and the remains of old mineshafts. We stood on bridges and marvelled at the dry river beds in summer, when just a few months earlier there had been rushing water. We took identification books and tried to remember the names of common wildflowers, but neither of us was much good at it. We walked quietly around the Arbor Low Stone Circle, trying to imagine who raised these slabs and why. I saw how sad he was at the pulling up of the railway to form the Tissington Trail (he was a great steam train enthusiast), but he always laughed at the 'Winking Man', a natural stone feature on The Roaches. The rock formation looks like a man's face, and as you drive past he seems to wink at you. One day we broke open a piece of limestone and revealed a perfectly preserved shellfish. I must have been about twelve years old. The feelings of awe and wonder were so powerful. I knew we were the only people ever to see this creature and I had so many questions. How come a shellfish was now in a landlocked valley? What else lived alongside it? How old was it? What colour was it when it was alive? That moment set me on a path to study geology at university, and my curiosity about the Earth and its life came directly from those shared times. All these thoughts and more came back as I look at what was once our house. Maggie and Mark are sensitive souls and understand how emotional it is to be so near and yet so far from home. They make sitting next door a warm and fun-filled time.

I reach the Staffordshire Moors in the Peak District a couple of days later and a cross curlew is transforming the blustery air into full-throated anger. I must have been near a nest or chicks. Its harsh, anxious, klacking call is a full-on curlew bombardment, described by poet Clyde Holmes in 'Curlew's Nest':

> Incensed wing flames.
> An aerial attack
> sputtering his aggression
> in machine-gun rhythms.

The male (I assume by the length of the bill) swoops first one way then another in a desperate attempt to drive me away. I search briefly to try to see what he is protecting. Through binoculars I look for the periscope neck of a sitting bird, scanning and alert. Or perhaps glimpse some tiny curlew fluffballs, with their impossibly large feet and

bright black eyes. But the incessant screeching of the curlew is too distracting. The experience of being attacked by a curlew is something I share with poet Jonathan Humble in his charming poem, 'Incoming'. Jonathan was so astonished at the ferocity of a curlew he fell off his bike:

I am not your enemy dear messenger,
but still your intent feels murderous …
I cannot help but admire your bravery and the
    skill
with which you missed my skull by inches. How
    are you
to know, my crescent beaked Nemesis, that I am,
in fact, a fully paid up member of the RSPB and
    have
no designs on the eggs you've hidden …

I leave, and my curlew assailant retreats. It is silent once more. The intensity of the male's reaction shows how high the stakes are – it's all or nothing for their nest. If it is predated they most likely won't lay again, unless the eggs are lost very early. So much time and effort goes into getting this far, so much pair bonding, energy for egg production, defence of territory. Through curlew eyes there are dangers everywhere, from snakes to foxes to birds of prey. Add to those problems the modern ones of domestic dogs, cows, sheep, horses, hill walkers, joggers and mountain bikes, and there is no room for complacency and little time to rest.

Walking The Roaches is to feel the sky vast above your head and little shelter from the wind. But the starkness of the moors is electrified by the call of a curlew. 'A moor without a curlew is like a night without a moon, and he who has not eyes for the one and an ear for the other is a mere body without a soul,' wrote naturalist George Bolam in 1912. Whether it's the bubbling song, the soul-searching *curlee*, or the harsh alarm calls, all of a curlew's repertoire is part of the magic of the moorland. I don't particularly remember hearing them when I came here as a child, but I think they must have entered my subconscious, weaving themselves into my psyche.

The Roaches is an escarpment of rock and heather, the closest patch of moorland to Stoke-on-Trent. It sits at 500 metres above sea level, between Leek and Buxton, an area known as the South West Peak, part of the Peak District National Park. And it happens to be one of the places on Earth I love the most. Although only a few square miles across, it is surprisingly wild and dramatic. The area was supposedly named by French prisoners from the Napoleonic Wars who called it *Les Roches*, The Rocks, because of the slabs of dark millstone grit that jut out of the heather like blunt teeth. The coarse sand that makes up the gritstone was carried by rivers into a vast delta where layer upon layer built up, the bedding planes crisscrossing as the rivers altered course. These laminated, shifting sands are now visible in the outcrops that stick out of the moor. Rounded by aeons of weathering and erosion, the crags provide sloping ledges for nesting peregrines, and testing routes for rock climbers. They say that scaling them is like climbing an elephant's bum, all rounded wrinkles and gritty friction. The dark towers of rock look like they've had a hard life and seem to stare resentfully out towards the genteel and far more frequently visited White Peak to the east, where green rolling hills and creamy limestone walls create a Postman Pat-like landscape that many find more appealing.

But this brooding dark moor is curlew country, and it is here that they nest amongst the wet rushes and cattle-grazed fields. A jolly band of Staffordshire Wildlife Trust volunteers accompanies me over The Roaches and we pass two of my favourite landmarks. On top of the ridge is the supposedly bottomless Doxey Pool, said to be home to a mermaid with the unalluring name of Jenny Greenteeth. Ms Greenteeth is supposedly the manifestation of a woman who drowned in the pool one foggy day, and who now takes her revenge by enticing unwary walkers to their deaths. And below us, hidden from view, is the mysterious Lud's Church, one of the most evocative and atmospheric natural features in Britain. Rarely visited, it remains a treasure to be stumbled across (and hopefully not into) by hikers wandering from the track. Formed by a landslip, the narrow chasm is 100 metres long and 15 metres tall. It is said to have been a hideout for Robin Hood and the site of the Green Chapel in the medieval poem *Sir Gawain and the Green Knight*. What is certain is that in the fifteenth century the Lollards, the heretical followers of John Wycliffe, met here to hold their services, hence the reference to a church. But it is also thought to be a site of worship with more sinister connotations. Water constantly trickles down the walls. The interior air, even on the warmest of days, is dank and cold. Not much light reaches the nave of this natural sanctuary, and the weak shafts that do penetrate the ferns seem too afraid to reveal the crevasses. Legend has it that this is the place where the Devil chooses to say Matins.

Full of tales and mystery, The Roaches mark the start of vast tracts of upland that define much of northern Britain. Rolling hills, moors and mountains over 800 metres make up 40 per cent of Britain's topography, and most of this high ground is in the north. These are varied landscapes, some dry and heathery, others wet and bog-like. Upland farms and areas of rough grassland are part of the mosaic. Heather moorland like The Roaches makes up a quarter of the upland areas, and indeed 75 per cent of all heather moorland in the world is in Britain. While these high areas may seem wild, and in our imaginations we may like to think of them as wildernesses, the truth is that they are all worked and managed to some degree. Traditionally, farming was the mainstay, with livestock periodically moved up and down the hills with the seasons. More recently, hill farming has decreased, and forestry, wind farms and the leisure industry have become ways of making a living. Grouse shooting developed over the nineteenth century, and although it has declined, shooting estates still make up 12 per cent of heather moorland. The vast majority of breeding curlews in Britain nest in this complex landscape; in fact, one-quarter of the world's population of *Numenius arquata* breeds in these uplands. How we decide to develop Britain's mountains and moors in the future is vital to the survival of curlews, and many other ground-nesting birds, too.

The changes wrought over the centuries in The Roaches, small and compact as the area is, also apply to the story of the larger tracts of heather moorland further north. It is a tale of isolation, farming, shooting, abandonment and then a re-imagining and reclamation. It can pretty much be told through the history of one unusual building – Don Whillans' Hut.

An overhang of rock in the middle of the escarpment shelters an eerie, mock Gothic house. It protrudes directly from the rock face, which forms its back wall. Were it larger it would no doubt have been used in horror films, where hapless young women find themselves marooned for a night in a thunderstorm, but it is actually a rather small two-storey building designed to look grand. Made out of the same gritstone it is built into, the roof is turreted and the windows arched. The rocks and trees shield it from sunlight and the walls are green with moss. Don Whillans' Hut, or Rockhall Cottage as it used to be called when I was familiar with it, is dark, damp and hugely atmospheric. It is as much a part of The Roaches for me as the heather and

the crags, and it commands a breathtaking view over the valley to the west.

It was built in the nineteenth century on the site of a cave formed from fallen blocks. In the eighteenth century this dark and cold cavern housed the 'old crone' Bess and her beautiful daughter. They sheltered ne'er-do-wells and law-breakers and surrounded themselves with intrigue. One legend says Bess's daughter could be heard singing haunting ballads amongst the rocks at night in a language that wasn't English. Add to this atmospheric scene numerous appearances of the anguished ghost of a local murderer called John Naden, who was hanged for cutting the throat of his lover's husband, and this place takes on a mysterious and dangerous aspect. With just a scattering of farms, few tracks and no transport, The Roaches of old was wild, a perfect place for eccentrics and outcasts who couldn't, or wouldn't, live in society. I am sure many British moors have housed such characters, real or imagined. Daniel Gumb was a cave dweller on Bodmin Moor in Cornwall about the same time, for example. As a repository for our fears and dark imaginings, moors are hard to beat.

At the beginning of the nineteenth century The Roaches was absorbed into the Swythamley Estate, owned by the wealthy Brocklehurst family. They developed it for shooting red grouse, following the pattern of so many moors at this time. Shooting grouse for sport was increasingly popular through the nineteenth century as an emerging wealthy elite developed an enthusiasm for pastimes in the romantic uplands. They travelled there on the railways built on the back of the Industrial Revolution, and shot birds with the new, mass-produced, breech-loading guns, which were quick to load and fire. The grouse moors became the equivalent of today's expensive golf courses – exclusive places to do business and make influential friends, even to arrange marriages. As Lady Aberdeen put it in her *Memories of a Scottish Grannie*:

> An informal and pleasant mode of intercourse sprang up which ... had important results to the country, for when politicians of different parties were fellow guests under the same roof for a week, differences were apt to be smoothed over and compromises effected.

The Roaches were part of this very British trend. Locals were kept away and poachers dealt with severely. Access to shooting estates for ordinary folk became increasingly difficult, as the UK census of 1871 records as many as 17,000 gamekeepers across the country. In 1862 Rockhall Cottage was built specifically to house gamekeepers, and it was located on the site of Bess's old cave dwelling. It had no facilities and was little more than a shell, but it certainly looked the part, a cross between a small castle and a folly. One of the keepers who lived in Rockhall Cottage apparently brought up twelve children there.

The moor gradually changed character as the Brocklehursts put in roads and bridges, and cut footpaths through the estate. The management of the land for grouse became increasingly intense, as shooting proved to be a good way to gain revenue. Drainage channels were dug to dry out the ground to encourage heather growth, and the heather itself was managed by a cyclic pattern of burning and by sheep grazing. The resulting mosaic of fresh new growth provided food for grouse, and the older, denser patches were ideal for nesting. The gamekeepers also controlled predators, shooting foxes, stoats, weasels, pine martens, polecats, crows, jays, ravens and rooks. Birds of prey such as red kites, buzzards, peregrines, hen harriers and some owls were also eradicated. Anything that compromised the production of grouse chicks was removed, classed under the catch-all derogatory term: vermin.

Not only did the grouse benefit from this intense management of heather, tooth, beak and claw, but meadow pipits, curlews, golden plover, black grouse and lapwings also thrived. The springtime air was filled with the call of waders. *The Birds of Staffordshire*, by T. Smith, records that the gamekeepers liked curlews and encouraged them, using their loud protestations at intruders near their nests to alert them to foxes or poachers. It also states that curlews were 'numerous' on the moors. In fact, they were still so common on The Roaches in the first half of the twentieth century that a curlew was chosen as the symbol on the crest of the Staffordshire Moorlands District Council. This heraldic shield shows one rising out of the heather, and the motif is stamped on the sides of household rubbish bins throughout the moorlands region. Not many people nowadays realise their bins are decorated with a curlew; most of the people I ask think it is a phoenix rising out of flames.

The burgeoning of curlew numbers on the moorland in the nineteenth and early twentieth centuries led to them spreading down the hillsides and colonising the rush-filled fields of the farms on the lower slopes, a pattern seen throughout the UK. This was the curlew's heyday, the time when they bred over most of the country, their numbers swollen by successful breeding on upland areas. As predator control was also common in the lowlands, not just on pheasant-shooting estates but on farms more generally, the scene was set for curlews to become farmland birds. They had made the transition from spirits of the wilderness to birds of the fields, entering our lives and more fully engaging with us in everyday places.

The two World Wars, however, changed everything – for people and the landscape. Many keepers went off to fight, and the social and political upheavals shifted society away from the old order. By the end of the Second World War, activities like grouse shooting faded in many areas, as it did on The Roaches, and many estates resumed grazing as the main source of income. Another pastime of the wealthy also declined. Like many wealthy landowners of the time, the Brocklehursts had built up an exotic menagerie that was housed on the moor near their shooting lodge. After the main animal lover of the family, Courtney Brocklehurst, was killed in action, the animals were simply released into the 'wild'. Most died very quickly (emus, Asian antelopes, peacocks), but the Bennett's wallabies and a single yak roamed the moor for a while, regularly surprising walkers and car drivers. The yak apparently lived until the 1950s, but the wallabies survived longer and often appeared in the local paper. At their peak there were about fifty of them, but cold winters and poor food saw them gradually dwindle to the odd one or two. A local farmer, Frank Belfield, wrote on a Peak District website, 'In 1963, which was an exceptionally cold winter, with daytime temperatures below freezing for a number of weeks, I fed hay to the wallabies along with my sheep. However, at the end of the cold spell, one night the foul weather returned with a vengeance and the next morning I found 13 dead wallabies behind the north wall bordering Rockhall wood'. Occasional sightings still come in, but the last confirmed one was from a photograph taken in 2009.

The last of the Brocklehurst family died in 1974, and Swythamley Estate was broken up and sold. A large part of The Roaches was bought by sheep farmers in Macclesfield, who crowded it with animals and restricted access to the public. Despite no drainage, electricity or running water, Rockhall Cottage was bought by an unconventional couple who wanted to get away from it all, namely 'Lord Dougie, King of the Roaches' and his wife Annie. An eccentric to cap all eccentrics, Lord Dougie wore an eyepatch and prowled around the boulders and trees, having altercations with the climbers and snarling at walkers. I often walked here as a child with my dad and we loved seeing him, and he was totally harmless. The poor man was driven mad by thoughtless climbers, and nosy people who would hang around trying to get a look at him and his garden. To be fair, it was quite a sight. Painted on the side of a huge boulder in the middle of his garden was a none-too-subtle warning, 'Keep Out Or I'll Shoot You!' Over the gate was a hangman's noose. Next to a wall was a grave with the name of his wife (despite the fact that she was still alive) carved into the headstone. Set against the backdrop of an eerie house, there's little wonder he attracted so much attention.

Lord Dougie kept the magic of his little patch of moorland going, but the rest was under serious threat. Fuelled by farming subsidies, sheep took over. The Peak District saw a five-fold increase in sheep numbers over the twentieth century, most markedly in the last half.[2] They did untold damage. Overgrazing destroyed the heather and their many hooves trampled the nests of waders. Further drainage was put in place to make the land better for livestock, increasing the damage to the soils. Many areas not grazed were turned over to Sitka spruce plantations, which sheltered foxes and crows. The face of The Roaches became battered and scarred. With no predator control, no management of heather, and widespread wildlife-unfriendly farming and forestry, curlew numbers plummeted. For the last quarter of the twentieth century the number of breeding curlews on the Staffordshire Moorlands fell by more than 60 per cent, and there are now not many more than a hundred pairs in total for the whole area, around 230 square miles. Stemming this decline seems a Herculean task.

In 1980 the Peak District National Park bought a large part of the land, and sheep numbers were reduced. Access was reopened and walkers encouraged back into the area. In 1990 Rockhall Cottage was deemed unfit for human habitation, and Dougie and Annie were moved to a warm, sanitary flat with all the mod cons. Their dilapidated castle was restored and upgraded by the British Mountaineering

Council, and turned into comfortable accommodation with heating, water, hot showers and a well-equipped kitchen. It was renamed Don Whillans' Hut after the famous climber, who established some iconic routes amongst the crags. This development symbolised a revival of outdoor sports seen across Britain. The Roaches is now incredibly popular, not just with rock climbers and hill walkers but also with mountain bikers, birdwatchers, photographers, horseriders, dog walkers and picnickers. It is estimated that 100,000 visitors each year come to The Roaches, making erosion of footpaths and disturbance to nesting birds an increasing problem. As car parking has become more difficult, restrictions have been put in place along the narrow roads below the escarpment and a shuttle bus operates at weekends. The Roaches has been 'discovered' and The Ramblers has placed it in 'the top 50 walking routes for Britain's finest views'.

It is not only people that are returning. Since 2008 a pair of peregrines has nested once more on the crags, the first pair for a hundred years after the sustained persecution by gamekeepers and farmers. The Staffordshire Wildlife Trust set up 'Peregrine Watch' to show the birds to the public through a telescope in a car park, but it also helps keep an eye on them. Anti-raptor activists and the illegal falconry trade are a constant threat, and in 2015 four chicks disappeared from their nest just two weeks before fledging. With the increase in visitor numbers through the area, disturbance is a major worry, but it is heartening to see that walkers and climbers are generally cooperative in keeping away from the breeding ledge each year. Merlins are also seen in the area during the breeding season, although no nest has been recorded. Buzzards are once again a common sight, and red kites can also be seen flying over the moor.

In 2011 the Staffordshire Wildlife Trust took over the management of The Roaches and began a programme of restoration. Drains have been unblocked and wet areas restored to try to persuade redshank and snipe to return. Footpaths have been upgraded. The Sitka plantations are being felled and the rushy pastures, with cooperation from the farmers, are being managed to encourage curlews back to the fields. The aim is to join up the fragmented landscape of this small patch of moor to create a coherent fabric. Slowly but surely, The Roaches are being managed back into a more bio-diverse landscape, but always with the restrictions imposed by the sheer number of visitors.

Whether the few remaining pairs of curlews (there are only around six pairs left in the immediate Roaches area) can increase is anyone's guess; there may well be just too many pressures. Dean Powell is a blogger who writes about Staffordshire Moorlands' wildlife. Just a couple of days before I reach The Roaches myself, he writes the following post on his site, Nature's Parliament:

What would the Staffordshire Moorlands be like without Curlew, the largest wader species in the western Palearctic. For me, Wolf Edge, Knotbury, Three Shire Head, Gibb Tor, The Roaches, Morridge, Ipstones Edge and the fields around Cheadle and Denstone would be empty of song and voice, of poetry and musical beauty, empty of a wonderful feathered friend.

No doubt I would weep and there would be pain, loss and grief. Perhaps I would sit, watch, wait and listen to the ghosts of this species in vast moorland spaces, with only memories of what was once a thriving bird in this part of the world, only memories of what used to be.

The stories of Bess's Cave, Rockhall Cottage and Don Whillans' Hut are the stories of The Roaches, and they resonate across moorland Britain. Once remote and isolated, this landscape has undergone numerous transitions, and curlews have found themselves both the beneficiaries and the victims of our upland endeavours. What the future holds for these birds is not at all certain. Brexit, social and political trends and climate change will all play major roles as the twenty-first century unfolds. The world for curlews looks very uncertain indeed.

It is time to make my way to the White Peak, a few miles to the east. As I say my farewells to my fellow walkers, and to what will always to me be Rockhall Cottage, I give thanks for Lord Dougie and the wallabies, and to my dad for bringing me here all those years ago when it still felt wild. That time has gone and the eccentricity and unpredictability of The Roaches have been replaced with something far more controlled. But the magic of the moorlands is still there in moments of solitude. At dawn or late in the evening, I am sure that Bess, the tortured ghost of the hanged murderer, and the long-dead gamekeepers reclaim their time and space:

Like the white waves that lap at lonely beaches
Like the windsong where there is no ear to hear,
I know they call in vain to us –
The old forgotten things of man.

Chapter 10

CURLEWS AND CONTROVERSY

Like *hiraeth*, *cynefin* is another rich, Welsh word with no direct English translation. It captures our relationship with homeland, the place of birth and upbringing. It is where one's soul is no longer restless but knows and understands the physical land; where there is an ease of mind and spirit. As with any good relationship, it is two-way. The trees, rocks, birds, even the grass, seem glad to see you return home. 'The whole wilderness seems to be alive and familiar, full of humanity. The very stones seem talkative, sympathetic, brotherly,'[1] wrote John Muir when returning to his beloved Sierra Nevada in California, after a period in the city; he may well have been defining *cynefin*. The Welsh language is rooted in the landscape and has developed a lexicon that is finely attuned to our emotional connection to the Earth.

It is *cynefin* that I feel as I leave The Roaches and walk towards the White Peak on a beautiful day in May. I know this high road well; it runs straight across moorland and rough farmland, between what used to be the isolated Mermaid Inn and the Domesday village of Warslow. It is an old trackway that has always felt remote; far wetter and more windswept than the valleys below, and is often shrouded in cloud. Sturdy millstone grit walls hold back the heather and rushes, preventing them spilling out onto the tarmac. Even on a bright day the moor wears a sombre face, but it has an ancient heart that has beaten strong and steady for millennia. While the surrounding lowlands were completely transformed by the Industrial Revolution, this landscape has retained a feeling of wildness. Pot banks, coal mines, silk mills and ironworks became the centres of life in the Midlands' towns, but the moor was far less easy to tame.

The road has given access to this high land for generations. From medieval times it was a route for packhorses taking travellers across the moorland pass, some in search of wealth from the seams of lead and copper in the limestone valleys to the east. In the eighteenth century, hill farmers used it to take milk, butter and meat to markets in Leek, or to be loaded onto trains and sped to London. By 1900 one-fifth of London's milk was being supplied by north Staffordshire and Derbyshire. It is easy to imagine those men and women of the moor, carts laden, facing the wind, which always seems to blow strong and cold no matter what the time of year. The old farmsteads of the area have names that fit this sturdy landscape: Lumbs Farm, Cave Farm, Hob Hay Farm, Hillside Farm.

A hundred and fifty years ago, a new cohort appeared in this out-of-the-way part of the north Midlands. Attracted by sport and status, upper-class men brought their guns, and local lads made money out of beating the heather to flush birds towards the line of fire. Grouse shooters had arrived to make the most of the many red grouse produced by specially trained gamekeepers. The moor became a playground for the rich and powerful. But by the 1940s, the seismic shake-up of the world order saw old and young, rich and poor joined together for a common cause: to fight fascism. Now American accents joined the local, flat-vowelled dialects, as US troops moved in to practise shelling and mortar fire to support the allies. The intense activity scared away the birds and trampled nests, helping to bring to an end the predominance of grouse shooting. Today, there are still guns on the Warslow Moors, but of a different type and with a different aim; the Territorial Army practises covert manoeuvres here. A local keeper tells me that at night, as he waits to shoot foxes, he can track the troops with his infrared spotter as they crawl through the heather, their camouflaged faces and clothing glowing brightly.

As with The Roaches, the history of the land defines its character. And somewhere out there, either side of the old road, new curlew families are, hopefully, emerging, adding their stories to the saga of this moor. Around twelve pairs of curlews nest here. A local ranger tells me that they are still on their eggs, which are tantalisingly close to hatching. This is one of the most exciting times to watch them.

After a month of quiet incubation, there is a sense of agitation and energy in the air. The sitting adult, which can either be the male or the female, seems unable to relax or get comfortable. It is restless and frequently shifts position. Every now and then it stands up to delicately move the eggs with its long bill and feet, nudging them gently to turn them around. Sometimes it just watches them before settling down again, wriggling gingerly to cover the eggs as well as it can. After twenty-eight to thirty days, hatching begins, and it can take many hours. The wader expert Desmond Nethersole-Thompson recorded a chick taking seventy-seven hours to wriggle free, and ornithologist Tony Cross told me that a chick in one of the nests he was watching took four days to extricate itself from the egg. It looks exhausting.

All the while the activity around the nest increases. The two adults communicate far more frequently, bubbling and curlee-ing loudly, but also with low whistles or three-note piping. At other times they sing softly to each other, a curlew duet, but then, astonishingly, they can break out into a surprisingly full-on crescendo of trilling before they swap incubation duties. The sitting bird throws back its head and opens its bill wide, its whole body quivering with the effort of forcing so much sound out through its throat and into the air. After all the furtiveness of the weeks of incubation, this noise is surprising. Surely a fox can hear it, too?

As hatching progresses, vocalisations take on a greater range. The incubating bird starts to whistle quietly, its throat extending and contracting. It also emits a range of low growls, piping, clucks and hoots, or it uses its bill to clack and snap. These calls are directed at the unhatched chicks, and the tiny chicks reply with audible peeps. They are conversing with their parents, learning their calls. On the day they break out they will immediately make miniature, two-note, high-pitched, truncated curlees, thin and reedy but definite precursors to the full-throated notes of the curlew.

The guard bird is some metres away. It yaps and whaups at any sign of danger and its partner responds by sinking low, stretching its head and neck out flat on the ground. Or it may sit bolt upright, peering around. Every sinew is tense and the feathers on its head erect. Eventually, it relaxes, and cooing softly it turns to snuggle its long bill deep into the feathers on its back. Even in this position it still calls, whistling into the warmth of its own down, staying in touch with the eggs. The curlews' world is changing. As each chick emerges it peeps and the adult replies, often tucking its head beneath its belly and touching the chick gently with the tip of its bill. There is now an almost

constant curlew conversation, and over the following few hours the chicks will peer out for the first time from under the wings to take in their new world.

Right from the start they feed themselves, eating insects around the nest with their small, shiny black beaks, which won't grow into the long, new-moon shape for a year. Curlew chicks have wanderlust in their blood, and within a day or two they are off. Tiny bodies, little more than fluff with feet, are all too easily damaged. Huge agricultural machines, hooves of cattle and sheep, running dogs, carnivores catching food for their own young – all of these pose a threat. They need to keep alive for five weeks before they will be big enough to fly, and from then on, their survival rate is good. But for now, in the tender weeks after hatching, they need vigilant parents, lots of insect food and peace.

This drama is just beginning on Warslow Moor as I pass by. A group of lapwings, pumped up with angst and anger, chase off a sparrowhawk. Their weird whining screams and their dizzying flight are disorientating, and the sparrowhawk gives up. It is a demonstration of how important numbers are in tackling predators. Mobbing a bird of prey is effective, but a few birds are simply not intimidating enough and are easily ignored. At least one lapwing family survives. I watch an adult lead its chicks away from the road, strutting proudly over patches of bare ground and around bits of old farm machinery. Its upright stance and long crest blowing in the wind give the impression of a highly strung nursemaid. Both curlews and lapwings are breeding more successfully on heather moors compared to other areas, benefiting from the management.

All around this part of the South West Peak District telltale patches of burnt heather show where the grouse moors, belonging to Lord Derby, are still active. Historically this was rich shooting country. In 1935 a record 2,724 red grouse were shot here.[2] After the Second World War, however, the Peak District lost over a third of its heather cover, as land was reclaimed for forestry and sheep grazing, but some grouse shooting still hangs on. In a layby I stop to talk to a gamekeeper. He is somewhat taciturn and wary of questions, but he believes, along with other keepers I have talked with, that the general increase in raptors (birds of prey) such as buzzards, sparrowhawks, red kites and peregrines over the last few decades is taking its toll on grouse numbers. Not only are they depleting grouse chicks, he complains, they are devastating the other ground-nesting birds alongside them. He would dearly like to control raptors, and the evidence indicates that some gamekeepers do so, despite the birds' blanket protection.

The control of birds of prey by gamekeepers, on both the uplands and lowlands, has a long and bloody history. The red kite, once one of the most common raptors throughout Britain, was extinct in England and Scotland by 1879. By the end of the nineteenth century, another species – once so numerous it was named after its habit of taking domestic chickens, the hen harrier, had gone from mainland Britain. Only about forty pairs were left in the more remote parts of Scotland. Persecution confined buzzards to the far southwest and northwest of England. A combination of farmers, shepherds and gamekeepers, all targeting meat-eating birds, meant similar devastating scenarios for goshawk, Montagu's harrier, white-tailed eagle, marsh harrier, golden eagle, peregrine falcon, spar-rowhawk, osprey, kestrel and merlin. Anything with a sharp beak and talons was considered a threat to grouse productivity, classed as 'vermin' and treated as such. Persecution, combined with widespread landscape and environmental changes in the twentieth century, meant birds of prey became extremely rare.

The legacy of those intense years of predator control is still present on some shooting estates, where vestiges of a mindset that wants to eradicate any threat to grouse still holds sway. Raptors were included on the list of Schedule 1 species and given the highest protection under the Wildlife and Countryside Act 1981. It is illegal to disturb

or kill any bird of prey, but the law, it seems, is frequently broken and persecution continues on some grouse moors of northern England and Scotland.

Despite the great reduction in heather moorland across the UK over the last sixty years, grouse shooting is still popular. In England and Scotland there are in the region of 250 shooting estates and between 12 August and 10 December each year they host 40,000 shooters. Producing grouse, however, is an unpredictable business. Whether a grouse moor can actually hold a shoot depends on keepers producing a surplus of red grouse above a baseline, which each grouse moor sets for itself. As a rough guide, that is about twenty pairs per hundred acres. Red grouse are wild birds that are native to Britain and confined to heather moorland. Their numbers can be boosted by providing ideal breeding conditions: good food, good habitat, and keeping predators, diseases and parasites to a minimum. If everything works well, and the weather is good during the crucial breeding season, many birds will survive, providing the shootable surplus. But that isn't always the case. Cold wet springs, or years with high infestations of ticks and gut parasites, can kill young chicks, meaning too few adult grouse for shooting in the autumn/winter.

The moors are therefore managed to maximise chick production, which includes heavily suppressing things that

eat them. Many predators are legally controlled, making the killing of foxes, crows, mink, stoats and weasels the bread and butter of a keeper's job. Killing birds of prey, however, is now illegal and comes with a heavy fine or even imprisonment; but that hasn't stopped some (not all) shooting estates breaking the law. In 2015 the RSPB revealed that out of the 176 convictions for raptor persecution since 1990, 68 per cent were gamekeepers, although it doesn't specify if they were from the uplands or lowlands. But in the last couple of years it seems to have been more difficult to catch criminals. In 2016 there were 81 incidents of persecution of birds of prey, but no convictions. In 2017, despite video footage of a gamekeeper shooting a hen harrier on its nest, the evidence was deemed inadmissible and the case dropped. Criminal acts still take place, but it appears to be fiendishly difficult to convict the perpetrators.

Birds of prey are killed throughout the year, not just on moors in the breeding season, for many are also targeted on their wintering grounds. In 2015 the RSPB confirmed sixty-four cases of shooting and trapping. There were also thirty-two confirmed incidents of poisoning, including fifteen buzzards, four red kites and three peregrine falcons. In 2017 the Scottish government increased its pressure on the grouse industry after one-third (forty-one out of 131) of tagged golden eagle chicks went missing between 2004 and 2016 over or near grouse moors in eastern Scotland.[3] The Scottish Environment Minister, Roseanna Cunningham, wrote:

The continued killing of protected species of birds of prey damages the reputation of law-abiding gamekeepers, landowners and indeed the country as a whole. Those that carry out these crimes do so in defiance of the will of Parliament, the people and their own peers. That must end … By looking at ways of strengthening the legal protection for birds of prey we are sending out a strong message that Scotland's wildlife is for everyone to enjoy – not for criminals to destroy for their own ends.[4]

All raptors are at risk, but it is the hen harrier that wears the dubious crown of Britain's most persecuted bird of prey.

Just a few miles from Warslow Moor, a hen harrier's nest was destroyed in 2011. The eggs were smashed and the feathers of a female were found nearby. The male disappeared, too. It is impossible to prove this was malicious. It could have been the work of a fox or dog, but as the number of hen harriers remain stubbornly low across England, it is hard to believe crime isn't a major factor in some of these incidents. In 2015 five male hen harriers simply vanished, causing their partner birds to abandon their nests. This is covert persecution. The bodies are rarely found and evidence is nigh on impossible to gather.

The reason hen harriers are particularly targeted is because they nest on the ground, often in heather, next to grouse, and their presence shifts the dynamic of the moor. Hen harriers are large birds of prey, and, when hunting, their silhouette gliding over the hills causes grouse families to scatter. Young chicks often lose contact with their parents, and if the weather is cold and wet, many die from exposure. The grouse chicks are also a favoured food for hen harrier chicks. During the breeding season parent harriers can take a grouse chick every three hours to feed their own young, which means as many as 270 chicks in a few weeks just to supply one hen harrier nest.[5] That sounds high, but it can be dealt with. Hen harriers can be distracted from taking game-bird chicks by what is called 'diversionary feeding', where keepers put out dead rats and chicken chicks near the harrier nest as an alternative food supply. This has been shown to work very well and reduces the take of grouse chicks by nearly 90 per cent. If hen harriers stayed at one pair on a moor, all this would not be a problem, but they don't.

The lack of ground predators, along with plentiful food and good heather condition, benefits harriers as well as

grouse, and harriers breed very well on grouse moors: too well for the grouse-moor owners. Unusually for raptors, they like to nest in loose colonies. One pair of harriers will attract others, and numbers quickly build up. A study on Langholm Moor in southern Scotland showed that hen harriers increased from two pairs in 1997 to twenty pairs in 2002. That is too many pairs for a keeper to manage by diversionary feeding, and the harriers ate over a third of the grouse chicks, preventing a shootable surplus. As shooting parties can pay up to £30,000 for a weekend, grouse have to be made available, and therefore the pressure to eradicate the enemies of red grouse is great.

The startling fact is that in England in 2016 only four pairs of hen harriers bred successfully, despite there being enough habitat for over 230 pairs.[6] In 2013 no hen harriers bred successfully at all. In Scotland the number of breeding pairs fell from 505 to 460 between 2010 and 2016. Despite high-profile campaigns, protection schemes, satellite tagging and monitoring, harriers continue to 'disappear', mainly over shooting estates in northern England and Scotland. It is, though, worth noting that they continue to decline over Wales and the island of Ireland too, where there is very little grouse shooting. Large-scale losses of breeding habitat due to forestry and intensification of farming are also factors that have to be considered.

In 2016 a Hen Harrier Action Plan was launched by the Department for Environment, Food and Rural Affairs (DEFRA), which brought together 'organisations that are best placed to help drive actions forward for the hen harrier on the ground and who are committed to doing so'.[7] The members of the group were the RSPB, Game and Wildlife Conservation Trust, the Moorland Association, the National Gamekeepers' Organisation, the National Parks and Natural England. One solution on the table was 'Brood Management'. This has proved to be highly controversial. It involves an estate allowing a small number of hen harriers to nest and rear young, but it allows moorland owners to stop the build-up of colonies. The suggestion is that the nests of hen harriers be kept at one pair per ten kilometres. If another pair nests within that distance, the moor owner can request that the second pair is removed to an aviary and then released in suitable habitat in the same region. This approach was not accepted by the RSPB, who want persecution to stop altogether before any intervention at their nests is considered. The negotiations reached a stalemate as hen harriers continued to be targeted by several estates, and the RSPB withdrew from the process.

The result of this very human conflict is that some grouse moor managers make sure no harriers nest on the moors at all, rather than risk a build-up of numbers, which they then can't control. The result is high levels of persecution. Some of the blame for this appalling situation must lie with those who pay high sums to shoot red grouse. Grouse moors are a service industry; if their clients demanded a criminal-free moor with a wide range of wildlife thriving on it, that would happen. If they continue to demand very high numbers of grouse, and turn a blind eye to raptor persecution, criminal acts will continue. But I know of no pressure being put on the shooting fraternity themselves to shift their expectations.

Despite two hen harriers being found shot in 2017, there are some signs of hope. In the same year, ten young fledged from three nests in Northumberland. At least seven nesting attempts were known, but they failed due to natural causes. It is a pathetically small number, but at least it is something. This, along with the continued increase in the numbers of other raptors in the UK, is, hopefully, a sign that things are beginning to change.

As in so many wildlife conflicts, while the arguments rage, the losers are the wild creatures, in this case hen harriers. And caught in the middle of this particular struggle between grouse moor management and raptor survival are the other ground-nesting birds: curlews, lapwings, meadow pipits, ring ouzel, skylarks and golden plovers.

To experience an all-out breeding wader extravaganza, a grouse moor is a good place to go. Curlews are twice as likely to be found on a grouse moor than outside of one, and their success at raising chicks there is over three times greater.[8] This is heartening when so much is against them in other areas. I saw this concentration of curlews for myself before I set off on the Walk. It was the result of a blog I wrote on curlews for Mark Avery, a high-profile conservationist, wildlife campaigner, hen harrier champion and former Director of Conservation at the RSPB. Off the back of that article a grouse moor owner invited me to his shooting estate in Wensleydale, next to the magnificent, medieval Bolton Castle. It was with some trepidation that I set off to meet Tom Orde-Powlett (who is introduced in Chapter 2), the latest in line to take over the running of Bolton Castle, which has been in his family for 600 years.

I felt nervous driving to Leyburn that February afternoon. I knew I was out of my comfort zone. I know nothing about shooting and don't know anyone who shoots, nor do I have any experience of the wealth and the culture that usually go along with it.

The castle is both impressive and intimidating. A combination of age and history stirs the emotions, especially as Mary Queen of Scots was imprisoned here. Most of the building has fallen into disrepair and the jagged stonework and tumbledown walls seem to be straight out of the romantic paintings of Jacob van Ruisdael. The turrets rang with the harsh calls of jackdaws. We met in Tom's office at the top of a spiral staircase in one of the intact wings. It felt cold, as only a stone building can, but Tom was warm, welcoming and polite and immediately provided tea and sandwiches. 'How are we going to get on, Tom?' I asked. 'I'm left-wing, vegetarian with vegan tendencies and have never even held a gun, let alone shot anything. I'm not sure we have much in common.' He smiled: 'We will get on just fine,' he replied. And we did.

On that first visit in February we watched a hundred or so curlews flying into their evening roost in wet fields below the castle (described in Chapter 2). My second visit, in early April, was just a couple of weeks before setting out for Ireland. As evening fell I gave a public talk out in the middle of the moor. About fifty locals, farmers, landowners and keepers gathered on a chilly hillside to hear about the walk, and to have a barbecue. The bubbling of displaying curlews provided an evocative backdrop, and £1,000 was raised for the British Trust for Ornithology Curlew Appeal. By nightfall it was very cold and an awesome panoply of stars shone overhead. As the last of the 4x4s disappeared down the moorland track, I took a sleeping bag and spent the night in a stone hut that stood proud on the hill crest. The silence was profound, broken only by the occasional cry of a bird. At 6am I went outside as an ashen sky bled through the darkness. The air was sharp and the ground glistened with frost. The outline of the moor was just gaining definition but already the sound was magnificent. 'The whole world was this symphony, and there was not enough of her to listen,' wrote novelist Carson McCullers, describing listening to an orchestra, but it could equally apply to the music of nature, to the feelings of immensity that come from the power and purity of birdsong in that hour around dawn.

Never before had I heard so many curlews bubbling and calling their name, flying high in the washed-out sky on

stiffened wings. They were dotted everywhere – a curlew panorama. In between, lapwings whined like space invaders, visitors from another planet. Below me a small tarn glinted like a bead of mercury, and from its shoreline rose a flock of black-headed gulls, their harsh calls trailing away as they streamed over a hillside and out of sight. And, barely audible, the liquid, plaintive whistles of golden plovers floated across the heather, perhaps the loneliest sound in Britain. Added to this mixture was the cackle of red grouse. It is clear that this grouse moor in April is far from a monoculture of game birds. Much of Bolton Castle moorland is designated as SSSIs (Sites of Special Scientific Interest) for the variety of wildlife they support, and they are considered by Natural England to be in favourable condition.

This variety and number of ground-nesting birds is possible only because of management. A lot of time and money goes into nurturing this landscape. Left alone, there would be more trees, more predators and less heather. Much of this open, minimalist palette of soft yellows, purples and browns would eventually be closed in by woodland. It isn't 'natural', and only hard work and money keep it this way. It relies on the profits from around thirty shooting days in the four months of the grouse season, subsidies to which all upland landowners are entitled and payments for environmental services, so-called HLS (Higher Level Stewardship) payments. This is a cultural landscape, shaped by history, economics and sport. But little, if any, of our crowded island can be described as wild in the true sense of the word. Everywhere is tinkered with,

altered and tweaked, to fit our requirements, from gardens
and golf courses to nature reserves and National Parks, and
of course, farmland. They are all managed; the differences
are a matter of scale and intensity. Here in the uplands it is
easy to confuse dramatic and remote landscapes with
untouched wildernesses, but they are not necessarily the
same thing. Grazing by sheep, cattle and deer, deforesta-
tion, mining and the extinctions of species have all changed
the land through time. Our needs have dictated everything,
and over the centuries we have decided what we want
from a piece of land – be that food, housing, industry,
parks, leisure or nature. The choice has always been, and
still is, ours, and the decisions made usually depend on
public opinion and money.

It wasn't long before I saw one of the two full-time
gamekeepers on his morning rounds to check traps for
stoats, weasels and crows. There is no need to do much fox
control here; they are rare, taken out by neighbouring
farms and estates before they reach the grouse moors of
Bolton Castle. This happens on nature reserves, too, but
usually, the control of foxes and crows is done quietly away
from public view. The RSPB, however, publishes its data
online. Figures for 2015/2016 show that 368 foxes were
killed on twenty-eight reserves and 487 crows on eleven
reserves. Other wildlife culled for conservation include
red, fallow, roe, muntjac and sika deer, the eggs of gulls,
feral Canada, greylag and barnacle geese, mink, rats, mice,
goats, grey squirrels and rabbits. If rarer, more specialist,
species are to survive, lethal control is often necessary, but
always alongside habitat management.[9] The RSPB figures

are there for all to see, but figures are nigh on impossible to get from other wildlife charities, which are worried about losing members if predator control is done in their name. It is usually contracted out and removed from immediate association. This is, understandably, a difficult problem for conservation organisations to reconcile; their raison d'être is to protect and nurture wild creatures and landscapes, yet to do so they have to engage in unpalatable control. The bloodied and ruthless side of conservation is too often hushed up, but an understanding and open acknowledgement of what is done, and why, is sorely needed.

Tom arrived with tea and energy bars, and as the sun rose we sat against the wall of the hut and viewed the brightening moor. What would he do, I wondered, if a hen harrier arrived to nest here? 'I'd be delighted,' he said. 'They are magnificent birds. But coping with more than one pair might be a problem and threaten the moor's viability.' He would, though, be more than happy to help relocate extra eggs safely – the brood management tech- nique, or brood 'meddling' as it is called by those who oppose the idea. The peace of that beautiful April morning suddenly had an edge. It is always a difficult and uncom- fortable discussion to have with people on either side of the debate.

I had never expected to find myself face to face with this controversy; curlews are as conflict-free as you can get. They stay out of our way and are increasingly rare, so much so that many people nowadays are barely aware of them. Although once on the quarry list, they are no longer shot for sport or for food, nor are they agricultural pests. They are not valuable for their feathers and they don't carry diseases that affect humans or our livestock. For the whole of my 500-mile walk I never met anyone who wanted to kill curlews. Yet they are embroiled in this bitter conflict. The uncomfortable fact remains that I saw more curlews on grouse moors than anywhere else in the country. They are, by default, in the middle of this conservation battleground. What happens to grouse moors affects curlews, too. The fate of an enigmatic spirit of the wild is bound to the aggressive world of sport and politics. It is not a good place to be; the demands for reform, or even a ban, on grouse moors are growing.

The criticisms of grouse moor management are not confined to the persecution of hen harriers. Some believe that the rotational burning of heather pollutes water courses and causes increased flooding in the lowlands. Burning is also thought to release carbon dioxide, which exacerbates climate change. The number of predators that are routinely controlled, such as foxes, stoats and weasels, is considered too high. So, too, the control of mammals such as hares and deer that carry ticks that can kill ground-nesting birds. Arguments rage over all these issues, with no clear-cut answers to any of them, as surprisingly little data exists. As yet it is not possible to make definitive, science-based statements about the environmental effects of managing a grouse moor, but there are of course different sides of the arguments to consider with an open mind.

In terms of carbon dioxide emissions, the cycle of burning can be seen over a long timescale. If burning is done badly – that is, widespread, uncontrolled and allowed to go down the soil – it is certainly damaging and may well contribute to pollution and flooding. On the other hand, if it is done according to recommendations – that is, over a small area and only to burn off the heather canopy, so-called 'cool burning', it is less so. There are, of course, immediate effects as the plants burn, but only perhaps 10 per cent of a moor is burned annually, with the remaining 90 per cent left to regrow on a ten- to fifteen-year cycle. So, seen over the long term, a healthy moor with vigorous new growth is a constant carbon dioxide sink. Other wild-life habitats are also managed in what may seem to be destructive ways, but are in fact beneficial. Hedgerows are cut back, woodland is coppiced and wetlands cleared of encroaching scrub, for example.[10]

The control of predators like foxes and crows is not confined to grouse moors and is also carried out on nature reserves too, but to a lesser extent, and the number of generalist predators like foxes and crows remains high across the country. The culling of mountain hares, which can carry the ticks that infect ground-nesting birds, is undoubtedly upsetting. Hares do very well on grouse moors, along with rabbits and waders, because of the depression in predator numbers. While hare numbers are naturally kept low by fox predation, they increase rapidly when that threat is removed, and controlling them is part of the management strategy when tick infestation rises. However, mounds of dead mountain hares in the back of trucks and piles of animal carcassess on so-called 'stink pits' used to attract predators, is a potent symbol of the intense nature of grouse moor management and very hard for those not involved in the industry to accept.

It is also difficult to accept the many dead rabbits scattered over the roads where there are active grouse moors. Rabbits thrive without predators, and many of them are killed by traffic, especially the kits. In other situations, the carcasses would be welcome food for meso-predators like foxes, but in grouse moor areas they lie on the verges, untouched.

There is, of course, another side to the same coin. Red grouse that are shot in the winter months are eaten, either by the shooters themselves or by selling them to game dealers and restaurants. It is therefore possible to see grouse moors as a form of farming, specialising in producing a high-end product. Other forms of food production found in the lowlands are arguably far worse environmentally and ethically. The ground is regularly ploughed and drained and in many cases the use of chemicals for fertiliser and pesticides is very high. Millions of animals are slaughtered each year to meet an ever-growing demand for meat. Around 950 million birds, 2.6 million cows and 10 million pigs are killed in the UK annually for human consumption. The milk and meat industries in particular are highly damaging to the environment in their production of greenhouse gases, use of water and destruction of habitat. Intensive agriculture produces 10 per cent of Europe's carbon emissions and is responsible for a decline of over 50 per cent of farmland birds since the 1970s., not just curlews but also yellowhammer, skylark, grey partridge, turtle dove and starling to name a few. The ever-increasing demand for large quantities of cheap food is environmentally devastating. The terms 'green concrete' and 'green deserts' are often apt for vast swathes of monocultures. When grouse moors are viewed as farms, it can be argued they are less environmentally damaging than the way we produce most of our food.

However, it is undeniable that many people find shooting birds for sporting entertainment distasteful. Increasingly, there is a feeling that killing for fun has no place in modern Britain. However, purely on ethical grounds, if the bird is eaten it is hard to argue that shooting grouse is worse than electrocuting chickens. Viewing it in terms of animal welfare, the life of a red grouse is better than that of a chicken. The birds are wild and living in a good habitat right up to the minute they die, which is more desirable than the short life cycle (usually only five weeks) imposed on broilers, those imprisoned bags of chemicals and hormones that fill our supermarket shelves. It is undeniably true, though, that grouse will only ever provide seasonal food for the well-off, like truffles, wild-caught salmon or hand-picked scallops.

The primary issue that sets grouse moor management apart from other forms of land use is the illegal killing of birds of prey. Until that is dealt with, public and political demands to tighten regulations, or even to shut down grouse moors, will increase. It is difficult to see how birds like curlews will not decline even more rapidly if grouse moors are closed quickly and with no exit plan, especially as the lowlands are increasingly hostile to ground-nesting birds.

All in all, grouse moors are one piece in a mosaic of managed areas in Britain. There are costs, and there are benefits. The future lies in getting the balance right. For the sake of hen harriers, waders like curlew, lapwing and golden plover and for the future of heather moorland itself, it would be a great pity if all attempts to find a solution fail. Fresh winds need to blow through the debate; it feels tired, and the opposing arguments are entrenched. More money for new initiatives has to be provided, and a reconciliation service established to bring together different interests with a renewed sense of purpose. In addition, the grouse shooters themselves must be brought to the negotiating table, as their influence is vital. There is too much at stake for this to fail, but finding a solution is made all the harder by the increasingly toxic stance taken by factions on both sides.

Roughly 12 per cent of the UK's uplands are managed as grouse moors. What this land will look like if grouse shooting is banned will vary from place to place, and will be dependent on the money available for management after the revenue from shooting is withdrawn. Most likely, landowners will turn to sheep grazing or forestry for income. Other areas may be abandoned and allowed to evolve into woodland, so-called rewilding. No doubt there will be areas that will be protected as heather moorland and managed for moorland wildlife. The Warslow Estate in north Staffordshire, which I visited on my walk, is now a mixture of farmland and nature reserve. This once-grand grouse moor once belonged to a wealthy Victorian shooting family, the Harpur Crewes, who lived at Calke Abbey, near Derby. At its height, 1,365 brace of red grouse was shot here in 1935, but, like The Roaches, the estate was split up and sold after the Second World War. Today it is owned by the Peak District National Park Authority, who employ Tim Robinson as a Conservation Predator Control Contractor. Tim does what he describes as 'wildlife keepering', which is less intense than what is done on grouse moors. It is aimed at maximising the greatest range of wildlife, rather than focusing on the production of grouse. He and his assistant keepers reduce the number of crows, foxes, stoats and weasels around known wader hotspots over the winter and early spring months, so that, come the breeding season, there are fewer predators around. In the summer, when breeding is over, they concentrate on habitat management by blocking up old drains to re-wet the peat, remove encroaching shrubs, monitor the amount of grazing by sheep and cut back dense rushes. Predator control is still part of the mix, but there is less of it.

Tim and his team cover an area similar in size to Bolton Castle Estate, about ten square miles. Although he doesn't officially monitor the curlews, Tim estimates that about twenty pairs breed on the moor and surrounding fields, although he doesn't know how many manage to fledge chicks. The change to a mixture of farmland, forestry and nature reserve could, if still keepered to some extent, support some curlews. By way of contrast, Bolton Castle grouse moor, a highly managed, thriving shooting estate, has between 100 and 150 pairs of curlews.

Curlews and grouse moors are an uncomfortable mix for many conservationists. A nationally declining wader, for which we have international responsibility, is being supported by an industry that struggles to find acceptance in the conservation world. In some ways, the fate of hen harriers and the fate of curlews are interlinked, and both are dependent on the resolution of an increasingly volatile, bitter dispute.

As the dark, millstone grit, heather moorland transitions to the White Peak, the grouse moors are left behind. The drystone walls change from grey to creamy white. Winding roads thread through the limestone hills and valleys. The fields are now bright green and the deep valleys wear a rich cloak of broadleaved woodland. The White Peak is a miniature Dordogne. I walk with Tim Robinson to Bakewell, discussing predator control and his feelings on grouse moor management and the raptor conflict. He has never been a grouse moor keeper, but he enjoyed beating for grouse shoots when he was younger. He acknowledges the pressure that grouse moor keepers are under to maximise the number of red grouse and agrees that the Victorian mindset of vermin eradication is still present in some areas. He has also been on the receiving end of abuse by animal-rights activists who waited for him to check a fox trap early one morning. Two men shouted in his face, pushed him around and took photographs of his car.

I wonder how Tim, a sensitive man who clearly loves the natural world, deals with a job that for six months of the year involves culling wild creatures. 'You've always got to be sure why you are doing it and what you are trying to achieve. I do it to help waders, they're in serious trouble. If I didn't believe it made a difference then I wouldn't do it.

I respect and admire foxes and crows for their intelligence and how they adapt to different situations, but it's a matter of balance.' Tim is delightful company, the mortal enemy of foxes and crows by day, a ballad singer in a choir by night.

One thing is clear to me from my visits to grouse moors, both extant and re-imagined: very little about conservation is easy. There is a general perception that protecting wildlife is soft and nurturing, but the reality on the ground is often raw and bloody. Some animals may have to die so that others can live, and those decisions are fraught with conflicting views. Conservation frequently requires highly political decision-making, where heightened feelings can spill over into aggression and entrenched positions. Its place in the complex mix of cultural and social activities is always subject to debate, and as society evolves, species will be kept or lost depending on our societal choices. During the walk I saw for myself the conflicts around turf-cutting, commercial forestry, silage production, grouse shooting, livestock farming, wind turbines, dog walking and even jogging. All of these can directly impinge on a curlew's wild world. Curlew conservation therefore focuses on the discrepancy between what we want and what birds like curlews need, which is to be left alone over large, varied landscapes. That is a big ask in today's world. In my more pessimistic days on the walk, I wondered if keeping curlews in our countryside simply demands too much of us, and what we are observing is an inevitable trailing off to extinction. Thankfully, those days were less common than the more optimistic ones, which were certainly underpinned by my many wonderful encounters with the bird. Until the last curlew sings, there is still hope and the story is far from over.

My moor visits are not quite done. Next, I visit the Eastern Moors, just to the west of Sheffield. Once a grouse moor, then owned by the water board, then intensively farmed, it is now managed by a partnership between the National Trust and the RSPB. Ten square kilometres of it is one of the six RSPB Trial Management Projects, the paired sites (with active and control areas) dotted around the north of the UK, working out what is best for upland curlews. This is an active area where foxes and crows are controlled and a range of habitat changes is being carried out. There are twelve pairs of curlews nesting here. I chat with the site manager, Danny Udall, and we discuss the idea of widespread curlew farming as a last-ditch attempt to save them. It seems a desperate measure. Danny has seen an increase in buzzards in the area over recent years, but he thinks curlews still manage to chase them away fairly successfully. One of the biggest problems in this particular spot is the sheer number of people.

This patch of the Dark Peak, the name given to the mill-stone grit moorland from here northwards, receives ten million visitors a year. It is the first area of 'wilderness' that is easily accessed from Sheffield, Derby, Manchester, Leeds, Chesterfield and Huddersfield. Walking across it on a wet, dreary day, it seems such an over-used moor, much like The Roaches but on a bigger scale. It is expected to be some-thing for everyone: a wildlife sanctuary, a leisure facility, a climbers' paradise, a wilderness experience, an archaeological site, a bridleway, a dog-walking area and a sanctuary for ground-nesting birds – hardly one inch of it is left untrodden. It is a piece of the wild that has been packaged up and presented to the public as a one-size-fits-all piece of moorland for any activity. The Eastern Moor's website features a large picture of a curlew on the front page and boasts:

> … breathtaking scenery and an abundance of wildlife, the Eastern Moors has something for everyone! The site offers open access with a network of bridleways and footpaths and internationally renowned climbing edges.

As an amenity close to cities it works well and is much loved. Even on a wet day there are lots of people setting off on walks or exercising their dogs. As the rain comes down more heavily, we walk away from the car park and into the heart of the moor, and here there are fewer people. Shrouded in mist, a herd of red deer graze at a distance from the tracks, hiding themselves behind a bluff. I try to ignore the signs and information boards and imagine I am watching these deer in a wild setting, but it is far from wild. Just beyond the curtain of mist, only a few miles away, are the densely populated conurbations and industry of northern England. If these large, impressive mammals can find a home here, can moorland birds? Ring ouzels are being helped to share their space with rock climbers, but it remains to be seen if curlews can increase and thrive in this multi-use site. The aim of the RSPB is to increase the number of pairs of curlews in both the active and trial areas by ten pairs. At the moment there are twenty-seven pairs in total, but I wonder how even that modest increase can be achieved. On the way back, an adult curlew flies over our heads, calling in alarm. Maybe it has a nest nearby. A family and their labrador walk across the heather while the bird circles anxiously. There are few places that have the same cheek-by-jowl nature of wildlife, wilderness and people as here on the Eastern Moors. The team working on the Trial Management Project are kind and helpful and I wish them every success in a very challenging environment.

My last two nights in the Peak District are spent with Tim Birkhead, a professor of zoology at the University of Sheffield and an acclaimed writer on natural history. He and his wife Miriam kindly offered to put me up and give me some space for downtime. On a sunny morning, Tim and I walk the hills on the fringes of the Eastern Moors near the Redmires Reservoirs, three man-made lakes providing water to Sheffield. This is also an active grouse moor. A ring ouzel flits amongst the crags while curlews fly up from the heather, trilling brightly. We watch a keeper checking traps in a valley below the track. Signs on stiles and gates ask people to stay on paths and to keep dogs on leads to protect the nesting birds, and on the whole this seems to be obeyed. Tim comments that people walking in this area would be surprised to hear curlews were in such trouble, as they seem to be doing fine.

My visits to the moors of Staffordshire, Derbyshire and North and South Yorkshire are intellectually and emotionally challenging, so it is good to have some time to talk things over with Tim and absorb some wisdom – and to touch base with the dreaming spires of academia. I ask if I can wash some clothes. 'Sure,' he says. 'I think it goes in there,' pointing to the dishwasher. I am grateful to be in such kind company and to soak up some much-needed peace in a calm house full of knowledge. Over breakfast I happen to mention how much I like bullfinches, such handsome birds. 'Did you know the males have tiny testes, and very simple sperm? Compared to a reed bunting, which has enormous testes for its size and very long and complicated sperm?' I didn't, but only Tim would think that this was a perfectly normal conversation over coffee and toast.

I return to the Eastern Moors later in the summer to look for curlew chicks with naturalist Kim Leyland, employed on the RSPB Curlew Project. The day is so misty it is impossible to see even a few metres ahead. For most of the time we wander a small patch of what is called Big Moor, which is well away from the main tourist areas and where Kim had seen chicks just days before. Trying to spot tiny camouflaged birds in long grass in the fog, whilst constantly being bitten by midges, is a little trying. Crows in the trees caw and flap as they scan the ground. In Irish mythology the crow is associated with Morrigan, a warrior goddess and a bringer of death. Harsh on crows, perhaps, but from the perspective of curlews, not too far from the truth. The crows readily take curlew eggs and chicks, and if they work as a team, which they seem to do, the parents find it hard to fend them all off.

As two adult curlews become increasingly distressed by our presence, we retreat to the car and watch them from behind a drystone wall by a busy road, but the curlew family remain frustratingly hidden. Eventually, right at the end of the day, a wary adult curlew appears out of the long grass and walks into a section of shorter grass with the air of being on duty. As the traffic zooms past behind us, tiny yellow and grey chicks emerge. They are as bright as buttons, confident and cute. Unaware of the big world outside of their heathery nursery, the two fluffballs of hope for the future pick their way over the vegetation with their enormous and rather comical feet. The adult wanders behind, and like any parent of toddlers, seems afraid to take its eyes off them, even for a second. Standing tall on a rock near a twisted hawthorn, about 50 metres away, the other parent keeps watch. Occasionally they call to each other. It is a wonderful scene and we watch until the family potter back into the undergrowth and out of sight. The Eastern Moors, with all their complexity, are still producing the curlew goods, and it is truly a delight to behold.

After my stay in Sheffield I am rested and ready for the last section of my walk, to head for the agricultural lands of the east and then on towards the sea. But first, one last detour. I am invited to supper with someone who had phoned me a few days before. 'Come to Belper station, I'll meet you. I want to give you some chocolate and say thank you for helping curlews. We'll give you a roast dinner.' I have no idea who this man is; all he told me was his name, but it is too good an offer to refuse.

Chapter 11

SEEING THE
LAST CURLEW

'I try to find a piece of magic in nature every day – a bee in
a foxglove, the sunrise, rain on leaves, a line of ants, perhaps
a curlew calling (nods at me), that'll do me, it's all I need
to keep me going.' This is Ashley – tall, rangey, with a
strong Derbyshire accent. He has a crew cut and a handsome face that is lined with experience. I can't tell his age;
maybe he's in his fifties. His job is as a heating engineer – a
troubleshooter for central heating and air-conditioning
units all over the Midlands – but in his heart he is a wildlife
campaigner and a naturalist. Ashley straddles contrasting
worlds, where boilers and computers sit cheek by jowl
with birds and wildflowers. It is a bitter-sweet life because
he doesn't like his job, 'but it gets me out all round central
England, and means I can keep an eye on things.' Perhaps
he needs the tension between the part of his life that pays
the bills and his inner burning passion for the natural

world, providing him with the impetus to get him out of bed every day before dawn and walk the local hills, watching and recording the natural world shift and change by the hour.

I'd received a phone call from Ashley a few days earlier as I walked along a road in the Peak District, asking me if I'd like to join him, his partner, Anita, and her grandchildren for their weekly family dinner. 'I'd also like to give you some chocolate, because I think what you're doing is amazing.' I have no idea how he found out about me, and he couldn't remember. Certainly not through the internet as he doesn't have a computer at home and has never sent a text in his life. His Mark 1 mobile is only ever used to receive and make calls. 'It must have been through Anita – she does all that kind of thing.' It would be true to say I wasn't sure about accepting his kind offer, nothing to do with the prospect of dinner, but I felt I had a lot of catching up to do with my notes. I'd booked a bed and breakfast, the first one in weeks, and I was looking forward to quiet anonymity after so much walking, talking, visiting, listening and remembering. But Ashley sounded genuine, and I was here to meet as many curlew people as possible, so I agreed to meet him at the station near his house.

I arrive in Belper at 4 o'clock in the afternoon and no one appears who could possibly be Ashley. It is pouring with rain, and I have to take shelter in a doorway at the back of Poundland, near a car park. If asked at this moment, I'd be disingenuous if I said I wasn't feeling grumpy. The rain bounces off the pavement, sending people dashing for their cars. The sky is dark and thundery and the air feels close. A young man carrying a toddler races in beside me, both soaked to the skin. 'Bloody hell duck, where'd this come from!' I nod in sympathy, open a bottle of shaken-up fizzy water and accidently spray us all over again.

Ashley speeds into the car park in a white, work-worn van. For some reason, the binoculars sitting on the passenger seat, surrounded by oily papers and grubby equipment, cheer me up as we hurry home. In their unpretentious, welcoming cottage in the country his delightful family are going through homework and chatting quietly. The smell of roast dinner adds to the homeliness and Anita is delightfully welcoming. Jack, aged eight, lists his favourite animals as dogs, megalodons, blue whales and cats. Granny, aged ninety-one and originally from western Germany, speaks the language of the northern lowlands – Plattdeutsch. Eventually, she remembers the local name for curlews as 'Wasser-tuten', literally, water toots. When she was a child they were common birds, flying around them as they cut peat for fuel. Wasser-tuten, birds that toot as they stalk the sodden ground. It is a good image. Rain still falls outside the cottage. Perhaps some Derbyshire Wasser-tuten are somewhere nearby, their feathers beaded in raindrops. I'd like to think so. Granny tells me she recently returned to the area where she was born, but the peat and the tooting birds have gone.

On the walls of the sitting room are two striking paintings. One faces the windows and is large, serene and light-filled. The other, on the opposite wall, is smaller and dark, facing away from the light. The larger painting features two diminutive gulls standing at the edge of the ocean, gentle waves lapping around their legs. A vastness of quiet water extends to the horizon and beyond. Wispy white clouds, tinged with pink, break up a translucent, porcelain blue sky. A strong patch of yellow at the top of the canvas indicates the sun, but it is only a suggestion; the fireball is out of the frame. Even so, its light seems to permeate the entire painting.

The whole image exudes peace and I yearn to step inside and sit on the sand, to soak up its warmth and tranquillity. I can't imagine anyone not wanting to be on that beach. It presents a place that is at once changing but permanent. 'I bought that to remember my mum and dad,' says Ashley, noticing that I keep looking at it. 'You can't tell if the tide is coming in or going out or if the sun is rising or setting.' As someone who has recently lost both parents, I know exactly why he finds it comforting and I find myself lingering over the details whenever I can.

On the opposite wall, in shadow, the darker painting is of a lapwing, a single bird that takes up the whole frame. It is an unusual composition; they are usually shown flying in flocks or in a 'deceit' of lapwings gathered in a field; 'deceit' is their collective noun. Noisy and frantic, they cry 'peewit', which is also a name for them, as they try to deceive a predator into thinking their nest is elsewhere. It's the reason why Chaucer thought lapwings to be 'ful of trecherie'.

In Ashley's painting, this striking black and white bird with its distinctive crest is stepping out of blackness and into weak light, walking over the dark soil straight towards the viewer. The metallic green of its wing feathers flashes like armour, its beady eyes look determined. This is a lapwing that challenges the observer, daring you to blink. Walking off the earth and straight into your life, it demands that you reassess your opinion of peewits as dizzy and alarmist. This is a lapwing on a mission to re-frame the deluded and educate the ignorant. I am impressed. 'They're my favourite bird,' says Ashley. 'I know curlews are yours, but I watched twenty peewits making such a noise flying and swooping over a meadow, must have been a fox set them off. I'd happily swap with a blind person for a day so they could see that. The local butcher painted it for me.'

Before we eat I go with Ashley up onto the hill behind his house, striding quickly through the old woodland that grips the steep slope. His long legs absorb the incline with little bother. My aching muscles and short legs try their best to keep up. He points out a hill in the far distance. 'There's still curlews nesting up there, in the rougher bits, called Alport Heights. I'll take you later.' I'm hoping he means by car. 'There used to be loads of curlews through-out this valley but most have gone – just a few hang on. Saw two pairs last week up there. None around here, though; they went years ago from this bit. You'll see why in a minute.' At the top of the path the land flattens into fields and we stand by a fence and look out over a large, freshly planted area of crops. 'There were three lapwing nests in there a couple of weeks ago,' he says. 'I marked them all out with sticks and told the farmer where they were so he could go round them when he was rolling. I left some beer on his doorstep. The next day the whole lot was flattened. Happens all the time. All you can do is keep going.' I can hear the despair in his voice and understand the lines on his face a little better. The neat rows of whatever crop it is that is so important that not one inch of soil can be left for the birds, looks unnatural. Nothing in nature appears in such straight lines. Curlews couldn't live here. There is no long grass to hide their nests and there's too much disturbance. Their clutch would also have been flattened by the roller. A couple of men walk past with their dogs; maybe they are part of the problem as well. Dogs look like foxes and foxes will set a curlew off a nest in no time, allowing crows to get in and take the eggs. Curlews would have given up long before the lapwings, they are much more nervous and flighty.

I wonder where the poor peewits have gone. Did they dive-bomb the machine as it went closer to their eggs? Maybe they ganged together, trying to distract it, practising their 'deceit'. If it was still early in the season, did they go somewhere else to try again? Or had they given up this

year and decamped to wherever lapwing failures go? Another year older, another year with no chicks, another year closer to deserting this place for good. The lapwings are following the same trajectory as curlews, inching closer to local extinction in many areas of farmland. By the time I return from my reverie Ashley is disappearing down the path, striding determinedly towards home.

The evening meal is delicious and the company a joy. As we drive to my bed and breakfast after dinner we pass a little owl perched discreetly on a lamppost. We are climbing up to the highest point between Derbyshire and London, Alport Heights, which Ashley had pointed out earlier. The fields are rougher up here, less intense and more untidy. Suddenly, a curlew flies over the road and Ashley slams on the breaks. I can't believe one has made a last-minute appearance. We watch it sail majestically into the distance – long, downward-curving bill and small head attached to a hunched back, the rest of its body boat-like and streamlined. It is silent, and it looks calm and in control. Maybe its mate is waiting for a change-over at their nest. 'Fabulous birds. I know why you love them.' And even though the curlew disappears into a distant field, we stay parked in the middle of the road, staring at the horizon, hoping to see it again, or at least to hear it call out over the gathering dusk. It doesn't oblige, but at least it is still here in this highly managed landscape. It must have found a little bit of peace, maybe a patch of fallow field which is too difficult to tame. 'It breaks my heart what we're doing to this planet,' says Ashley. 'We need to be more gentle with the land. It can't all be about us. Icecaps

melting, forests chopped down, these birds disappearing.
We aren't the only ones who live on this Earth.'

The car park for Alport Heights suffers from littering,
but provides a great view over the counties of central
England. To the north and west lie Yorkshire, Staffordshire
and Shropshire. To the south and east are Warwickshire,
Leicestershire and the West Midlands. Tomorrow I am
heading east into Nottinghamshire and through to
Lincolnshire. The rain has stopped and this land of ancient
oaks and mugs of tea is bathed in evening loveliness. But
through curlew eyes it is a very different vista. The southern half of England is not a welcoming land for a singer of
wild songs. Curlews are increasingly rare below a line from
The Wash to Shrewsbury, slipping away from the lowlands.
This is hard-working land where the job of producing food
outweighs all else, and curlews, lapwings and many other
creatures that share the soil fall by the wayside, unable to
add to the bottom line of a financial spreadsheet. I feel a
knot of tension as I wonder what lies ahead for them, and
I have a strong feeling I've seen my last curlew for this trip.

At the door of the bed and breakfast, Ashley, true to his
word, gives me a bar of posh dark chocolate. 'Just two
squares with a mug of coffee in the morning – any more's
too rich.' Ashley, and many like him I met along the way,
constantly try to make the world better. They haven't given
up, even though the odds are stacking ever higher against
them. Nothing is over until it's over, and as long as curlews
fly over the road and lapwings keep trying to nest in fields
these local heroes will keep on doing what they see to be
right. To me, they are like stars that shine more brightly as

the sky gets ever darker. But it's worth remembering that many stars together produce enough light to see by, lighting the way for the rest of us. I put the chocolate into my bag and give him a hug. Within seconds he's gone, speeding down the drive back to his cosy cottage. At dawn he'll be striding the hill again and by mid-morning he'll be fixing his first boiler.

I lie in bed in the forced prettiness of my room in the bed and breakfast, thankful for people like Ashley and his family. Conservation is widely regarded as the preserve of the monied middle class. Membership of conservation organisations is biased towards the white and affluent sectors of society. Yet time and again it is people like Ashley who are typical of the doers, the ones who get up-close and personal with the organic matter of the planet. They are the people digging, planting, mending and fixing. One minute they are up a tree hammering in an owl box, the next they are looking for otter poo along a river bank. You may well find them staking out lapwing nests in a farmer's field. Ashley doesn't have the luxury of time, or the headspace, for too much existential angst about the woes of the planet; there is work to be done to help wildlife, so it's best to get on with it. As I wrestle with a frilly pillowcase that is infuriatingly tickly, I give thanks for the no-frills Ashleys of this world and their dogged determination to keep going. They inspire hope. I go to sleep, knowing I'll wake up tomorrow with a renewed sense of purpose for the last few days in eastern England.

Except for a few populations on some of the lowland heaths, curlews didn't breed in the eastern counties before the mid-1940s. They were brief visitors, spirits from the higher moors that touched these flat lands with their songs for only a few decades, then left again, driven out by environmental changes. The early nineteenth-century Northamptonshire peasant poet, John Clare, doesn't mention them. They would surely have featured in his real-world, emotional poetry if they had been a part of his life. Over the years, most of the heaths were ploughed for farmland, but one anomalous colony of around thirty pairs does hang on in Breckland on the Norfolk–Suffolk border. Little is known about them, but they are still there, nesting on an island of remnant heathland in a sea of intensively managed farmland and forestry. Unfortunately, they are way to the south of my route, which ends on the Lincolnshire coast.

The borderland between Derbyshire and Nottinghamshire is undulating and pastoral. There are lapwings in the fields and all kinds of songbirds in the bushes and woodlands. The verges are bright with wildflowers, 'little poems of wildness', as John Muir would have put it. The sun has also returned and I have excellent company in the form of an ex-Dominican friar, writer, journalist, broadcaster, environmentalist, gay-rights activist and Catholic commentator, Mark Dowd. A fan of the Eurovision Song Contest, Mark had made 'a tidy sum' on betting on the winner in 2016, and generously offered to keep me company for one day's walking, to pay for the evening meal and even for a bed and breakfast.

For fourteen hot, tiring miles, Uncle Sparkle (as he is known by his family) keeps me entertained by singing former Eurovision Song Contest winners in their original languages, and in between he muses on how I might measure the success of the walk. Our utilitarian society demands facts and figures. If, after five years, there is no proof that there has been any increase in curlews on the ground, has the whole 500 miles been a failure in terms of curlew recovery? Are graphs and pie charts the only way to demonstrate success? Or, maybe, he suggests, it is better to see the whole enterprise as an act of faith that doesn't need short-term, tangible outcomes. Rather, it belongs to the unknowable, instinct-driven realm of acts of hope; a 'lead kindly light' type of walk, as he puts it, quoting John Henry Newman. I agree with him. It has to be in the category of a journey into the unknown, with the hope that a better world for curlews, and for wildlife in general, might, in some mysterious way, be a future outcome.

Sometimes, vulnerability to the elements, and to the whims and vagaries of human nature, can produce wonderful and unpredictable things: not necessarily now, or even soon, but sometime. I carry in my wallet a copy of one of my favourite poems-come-prayers, 'A Step Along the Way'. It was written by Bishop Ken Untener as a reflection on the martyrdom of Bishop Oscar Romero, who was murdered in 1980 for upholding the rights of the poor in El Salvador. The central section is a call to work for a better world with a light heart, not one that is weighed down by the enormity of the problems we face:

This is what we are about.

We plant the seeds that one day will grow.

We water seeds already planted, knowing that
    they hold future promise.

We lay foundations that will need further
    development.

We provide yeast that produces far beyond our
    capabilities.

We cannot do everything, and there is a sense of
    liberation in realising that.

This enables us to do something, and to do it very
    well.

It may be incomplete, but it is a beginning, a step
    along the way …

We may never see the end results, but that is the
    difference

Between the master builder and the worker.

It is very difficult to know what exactly it is that leads to
lasting change, whether action is triggered by a single spark,
or by a concatenation of events. There is no formula that
anyone has been able to write down. The Save the Whale
movement was ignited by two things. The first was the
public being made aware that whales 'sing'. Their haunting
calls were recorded underwater and broadcast around the
world, forming a connection between ourselves and these
giant mammals. The second was the sight of a small, flimsy
boat, *Rainbow Warrior*, putting itself between a whale and
a huge Japanese whaling ship with harpoons at the ready.
It was a David and Goliath image based on hope against all

the odds. Eric Hoffer was an American sociologist who studied the causes of revolutions through history, and tried to decipher what it was that inspired people to change the world. In his book *The True Believer: Thoughts on the Nature of Mass Movements*, he concludes:

> Those who would transform a nation or the world cannot do so by breeding and captaining discontent or by demonstrating the reasonableness and desirability of the intended changes or by coercing people into a new way of life. They must know how to kindle and fan an extravagant hope.

Emily Dickinson famously created a fragile and particularly beautiful image of hope in her poem, '"Hope" is a Thing with Feathers':

> 'Hope' is a thing with feathers
> that perches in the soul,
> And sings the tune without the words,
> and never stops at all.

Although Einstein suggested that not everything we measure is useful, and not everything that is useful can be measured, pie charts and graphs do have their place in persuading people with purses to open them. There is increasing empirical evidence that being surrounded by a thriving natural world that is full of diverse form, colour and sound is beneficial to our health and wellbeing. In 2007 Dr William Bird wrote a report for the RSPB: Investigating the

Links Between the Natural Environment, Biodiversity and
Mental Health.[1] The opening paragraphs are stark:

> It is a paradox that as a society we find it unacceptable
> to take wild animals to be kept in captivity, yet older
> people in residential care homes can stay indoors for
> years with no access to the stimulation of the outside
> world. We spend millions to create ideal conditions for
> our garden plants, balancing the right soil with the
> correct amount of shade and the right moisture, yet we
> allow our children to grow up in a hostile urban
> wilderness with concrete walkways, heavy traffic and
> no contact with nature.
>
> Humans are a species with as much need for the
> natural environment as any other … By disconnecting
> from our natural environment, we have become
> strangers to the natural world: our own world. This has
> challenged our sense of identity and in some more
> subtle ways has had a significant effect on our mental
> health.

The report highlights all of the positive benefits that nature
brings to those recovering from illness or operations, in
alleviating loneliness, building communities, encouraging
development in children, and lessening aggression.
Birdsong, it appears, is crucial. Not only does Nature's
visual stimulation act as a balm, but sound is just as important to our psyche. Listening to the phrases and melodies
of wild creatures calms our nerves and soothes our minds.
Birdsong triggers the release of endorphins, inducing

tranquillity through an ancient, inner language that we instinctively understand.

The voices of birds are formed in a structure called the syrinx, which sits just above the lungs, at the point where the trachea (windpipe) branches into the two lungs. The syrinx is a double-barrelled structure, two pipes working in harmony, giving the range and variation of notes that some birds use to produce their complex songs. A musician friend, Peter Cowdrey, described to me how curlews produce the bubbling, trilling call. 'It's a bit like having two trumpets in their throats, able to slide over scales and tones, but they work as a pair to produce harmonic richness.' The double nature of the syrinx allows the curlew to orchestrate both the major and minor keys, a thrilling weaving of sounds that can evoke both joy and sorrow, and play on our emotions, producing what poet W.S. Graham called the curlew's 'loveweep'.[2]

Much has been written about why we find the sound of birdsong so powerful. In 'Investigation of Musicality in Birdsong',[3] the authors suggest it works in the same way as music, 'a combination of rhythms and pitches – and the transitions between acoustic states – affecting emotions through creating expectations, anticipations, tension, tension release, or surprise.' The pauses between phrases are just as poignant, 'building up an arc of suspense, confirming or violating the expectations of the listener, forming phrases containing a typical beginning, middle, or end.' The Japanese have a word for the meaningful gaps between objects or sounds – 'Ma'. It is the nothingness, the empty space that gives definition to the positive and concrete. In other words, Ma is the recognition that the story is in the gaps as much as in the words. This is how we speak and sing, how we tell stories, full of phrases interspersed with meaningful silences. We understand this form of language, we share it with birds. And it has been used to great effect in the arts.

Watery landscapes transmit haunting bird calls. They float over the surface of the water, rolling away into the distance. A curlew calling over wetlands is one of the most evocative sounds on Earth. Benjamin Britten used it to create an opera of great power, *Curlew River*. It was first performed in 1964 in the Church of St Andrew in Orford, Suffolk. Set in the water-filled landscapes of East Anglia, *Curlew River* is a re-telling of an ancient Japanese tale, *Sumidagawa*, translated as Sumida River, a real river that flows through Tokyo. It is traditionally performed as a Noh play, a form of classical Japanese theatre using masks, ritual and music. The story is tragic; a distraught woman sets out to find her lost son, aged 12. Eventually she reaches the banks of the Sumida and a ferryman tells her about a memorial service, held the previous year, at a burial mound on the opposite bank. It was for a child who had died of exhaustion after being captured and abandoned by a slave trader. It becomes clear that the child was the woman's son. She sinks into despair and is given a gong to beat an invocation to the boy's spirit, which rises out of the mound. As the mother desperately tries to hold on to the ghost, he retreats back into the tomb, leaving her alone, weeping on the banks of the river. The end of the Noh performance is darkness and silence.

This story moved Britten, who refashioned it for a Western audience, whilst still retaining its original profundity. To Westerners, Noh theatre may seem rigid and static, but the emphasis is on the contemplation of the philosophy, rather than the story of the drama. The ritualised actions unclutter the mind, allowing the audience to ponder the great mysteries unfolding before them. Britten transformed Noh into something his British audience could relate to. The Sumida River became Curlew River, based on a fictional 'wide and reedy Fenland river'. Japanese travellers were replaced by monks and pilgrims, who chant and pray as they walk the river bank, setting a liturgical tone. The abbot becomes the narrator.

Sumidagawa, a Buddhist Noh drama, was transformed into a Christian morality play. Buddhist philosophy was mainly replaced with Christian ideas. The original ending, for example, highlights the evanescence of life, one of the basic tenets of Buddhist thinking. All of existence is impermanent and fleeting, and, therefore, the ghost of the boy returns to his grave. Britten Christianised this final scene, and instead of transience he portrayed hope. Instead of a tomb being the boy's final resting place, his soul is carried to heaven, signified by the grieving mother watching soaring curlews over the river. As if to say goodbye, his spirit circles silently over her head, accompanied by the birds, before departing.

Interestingly, curlews were not initially part of the story. The original working titles were *Across the River*, or *Over the River*. But as Britten's ideas developed the curlew emerged as the most fitting bird to symbolise the emotions he wanted to convey. Britten wrote to the librettist for *Curlew River*, William Plomer, 'Oddly enough, as the work progressed, the Curlew grew in significance.' Perhaps Britten was aware of the myths and folktales that surrounded them, their associations with death, water, storms and departed souls. Or maybe he was simply moved by the sound of the cry of a curlew over wetlands, a spiritual sound floating over the water and through the mist: 'Where in the plash of streams a lone curlew cries,' said poet John Coulter.[4] Whatever the reason, curlews were woven into the fabric of the text and the music, and the title was settled just a few months before the first performance.

In both the Japanese and Britten's versions, the mother of the dead boy asks the ferryman what the birds are that are flying over the river, and in both versions the ferryman replies that they are gulls. In *Curlew River*, though, the mother then says:

> Gulls you may call them
> Here by the Curlew River
> Call them I beg of you
> Curlews of the Fenland.

The curlew motif became essential to the character of the whole opera. Britten even invented a new musical annotation, the 'curlew pause', which he used on the score. Its shape is the profile of a flying curlew, a classic M outline, and is placed over a note or rest to denote that at this point the singer or instrumentalist must wait until the others have caught up. It is a way of allowing the music some of the freedom of expression found in Japanese music. It is a malleable pause in the drama that allows a re-gathering of the performers: a 'controlled floating', as Britten described it.

Bringing together the ancient associations of curlews with a Christian narrative, *Curlew River* is a masterpiece of emotional storytelling, showing that the new moon bird is still bound to our inner, secret lives. Our hopes and fears intertwine and harmonise, like the cry of the bird itself.

The cry of the curlew has attracted the attention of others, too, but for very different reasons, especially in the eastern counties as the birds return from their breeding grounds to spend the winter on the coast. For generations, hunters have pursued them for the pot in the late summer and early autumn, and recipes are explored in Chapter 1. By all accounts, shooting wary curlews is not easy, since they are likened only to crows for their wiliness. Getting within firing range used to be one of the great challenges of wader shooting, before they were taken off the quarry list. In an article in the journal 'Shooting UK', a hunter describes his last trip to bag curlews before it was made illegal at the end of 1981. On a late autumn evening on a windswept and freezing marsh, 'The light had all but gone, and I could hear the surf breaking above the roar of the gale ... I spotted a ragged mob of maybe a dozen curlew being whisked along by the wind about 100 yards to seaward.' By hiding in a ditch until they flew over him he managed to shoot four birds, despite their twisting and turning flight. His reward was a curlew casserole with onions, herbs and brown beer, and lunches of roast curlew sandwiches, which were welcome protein for 'a penniless PhD student'. The hunter rued the day hunting curlews was banned; 'this old fowler learned a lot about fieldcraft on the marsh from curlew. If you could outwit this wiliest of waders, the rest were pretty much plain sailing.'

Not everyone who shot curlews, though, had such a rose-tinted experience. John Fowles, literary giant and author of *The French Lieutenant's Woman*, *The Magus* and *The Collector*, also hunted in his youth. In his autobiography, *Wormholes*, he recalls becoming interested in shooting and fishing in his late teens:

> That phase ended dramatically one dusk when I was wildlfowling in the Essex marshes. I winged a curlew. It fell in the mud beside the Thames, and I ran and picked it up. Curlew scream like children when they are wounded, and in too much haste I reversed my gun in order to snap the bird's head against the stock. The curlew flapped, the gun slipped, I grabbed for it. There was a violent explosion. And I was left staring down at a hole blasted in the mud not six inches from my left foot. The next day I sold my gun. I have not intentionally killed a bird or an animal since.[5]

The desperate cry of an injured child can be added to the repertoire of curlew calls. It has to be a good sign that hunting curlews is banned or under a voluntary moratorium throughout most of Europe. Even so, the latest figures for 2014 show 7,000 curlew were shot in France, alongside up to 120,000 lapwings.

On the penultimate day of my walk, I find myself making my way through the middle of a vast field of crops. The footpath should take me to a main road. These green deserts are void of life, and not a bird sings. I notice the dry and cracked earth, hard as concrete despite the light rain. No ground-probing bird could feed in here. But the absence of life makes it a perfect place to sing out loud. The footpath is blocked at the far end and I can't find the way through. Eventually I make my way to a road off my route and have a long walk to get back on track. I spend the last few miles trudging along an A road in drizzly rain with traffic thundering just inches away from a very narrow footpath. It is miserable. I give up with 5 miles to go and stand at a bus stop. I feel cold and shivery. I buy a bag of chips to try to get some energy, but I can't eat them. Within minutes of sitting down on the bus I am asleep. I end up at the hotel where I've booked a room. It's hot and uncomfortable, but I simply don't care. It is quiet and by now I am exhausted.

It feels like the end of the 500 miles has come quickly, like suddenly hitting a wall. On the last day I meet the head of the Lincolnshire Wildlife Trust, Paul Learoyd. Paul takes me to Woodhall Spa, one of their reserves where two curlews had been heard displaying earlier in the year, and he is pretty sure they bred here the year before. The reserve is an old airfield, once home to the 617 Dambuster Squadron, but now the concrete is being reclaimed by wild flowers covered in butterflies. We walk to the spot where the curlews had been seen and a little ringed plover scuttles away, but there is no sign of curlews. It seems inconceivable they could nest successfully here. There is not enough cover and the ground seems so open and vulnerable to every predator in the area. Many are probably using the looming backdrop of a large area of forestry, Ostler's Plantation, which juts up against the northern boundary. Like so many others, it was planted in the nineteenth century on heathland that was considered waste ground. Curlews used to nest on those heaths. Maybe this pair, who keep trying to raise a family here each year, have some ancestral memory of what this concrete and tree-covered landscape used to be like. Paul considers the question of whether some of the trees should be removed. 'There is no doubt a large number of foxes and badgers live there, making it hard for the birds in the reserve. Crows nest in the trees, too. But you have to weigh it up against the community benefits these woodlands provide. They are such important places for dog walkers, cyclists and all kinds of family activities, so they have a really important job to do. Everything has to be balanced out. It can't just be about wildlife; people are part of the mix, too.'

It was a good, sound message to end the walk. We leave the reserve and head for the sea. Paul is sensitive and stands back as I walk out alone to the edge of the water and let it wash over my worn-out boots. In just a few weeks the winter birds will be back here, spending the cold, wind-blasted months getting ready for another breeding season. Some of the curlews that had failed to nest successfully inland could already be on their way back.

Six months earlier, I had stood by the sea just down the coast in Norfolk and wondered what a 500-mile walk would reveal. It was not surprising that I found a mixture of joy and sorrow, but some experiences were delightfully unexpected. Curlews apart, one obvious truth that emerged was that kindness is everywhere in Ireland and the UK. I never ceased to be touched by people's generosity and willingness to help me. It is easy to feel that the world is becoming more hostile and dangerous, but I found nothing but goodness in the everyday lives of the people I met, and most had had no connection with me before the walk. On the other hand, there is also bitterness and resentment flaring up between different conservation communities. Conservationists, farmers, landowners, developers, businesses, hunters and locals seemed locked in battles all over the country. People are generous but they are also protective of their territories, quickly establishing camps and building walls. If there is one thing I learned, it is that conflict resolution is the key to the future for wildlife throughout Britain and Ireland, and no doubt further afield, too. Nowhere is it taught to future conservationists, farmers or wildlife rangers as a matter of course, but it is needed everywhere.

So what now? Is there a next step after the 500-mile walk? It seems to me that people needed to come together to develop and to share a vision for the future of the wildlife they love. A series of conferences-come-workshops felt like a good way to bring together different factions, to begin a fresh dialogue based on shared passions. Perhaps curlews could be a bird around which many different interests could coalesce? After all, it is good to have a specific focus, rather than a general principle. Claude

Lévi-Strauss pointed out that animals can be 'good to think with'. I think curlews might fit the bill, might help us work through the whole range of problems in a safe space. It is a big dream, but within our dreams there is hope. The American poet Langston Hughes uses suitable avian terminology when stressing the importance of dreams. Hold onto them, he says, for if we let dreams fade away, life becomes 'a broken-winged bird, that cannot fly'.

As the Walk and all that it meant sank in, I realised the work had just begun. Now there are conferences to organise – meetings for the new moon bird – to try to find a way through this quagmire of emotion and conflict, and identify a clear path that could lead to a kinder world for all of wildlife. The 500-mile journey was, it seems, just the first step.[6]

Chapter 12

REFLECTIONS

There is a phrase I often heard in my childhood in Stoke-on-Trent that has stuck in my memory: 'Stop mithering an' get on w'it'; a Midlands exaltation to quit moaning and just do whatever it is that needs to be done. It is a mantra I have tried to live by in adulthood, with varying degrees of success. But as I became aware of the decline of curlews, it rang loud and clear. I had been increasingly mithering about the plight of the curlews, but I didn't know what to do about it. The only way to find out for sure was to go and walk through their land. Not just to the hotspots, but to the places where they no longer call over the hills and fields. I couldn't be sure it would help, but it felt like the right thing to do.

The 500-mile odyssey I planned took me over mountains, along rivers, into towns, across moorland and through fields. I wandered happily along car-free tracks and plodded down main roads, buffeted by the backdraught of passing lorries. I rowed across lakes to explore islands and searched for curlews on shooting estates, nature reserves and amongst the practical muck and clutter of farms. I marvelled at their abundance in some places and despaired at the silence of the landscape in others. Standing on the edge of an Irish peat bog, I heard the lonely cry of curlews in the distance, a solitary pair defending their nest when there should have been many more of their kind alongside them. But on a heather-clad hillside in Yorkshire I was transfixed by the surround sound of bubbling calls, a soul-inspiring and uplifting experience. By the end of the summer, the same moor resounded with gunfire aimed at grouse.

Along the way, I learned a lot about the rollercoaster fortunes of curlews on these small islands at the western edge of Europe; how numbers have waxed and waned depending on our activities. At times they have been accidental beneficiaries of our endeavours, but now they are unintended victims. But even though numbers have been falling for some time, it has not been until very recently that we have done anything specifically for them; we simply haven't thought of curlews in that way before, as birds in need of our help. They have always just been there in the background, flying over bog, meadow and moor, transforming birdcalls into music. They have been acknowledged and appreciated, certainly, but we have been blind to the threats that we pose to them. Now, there is a race against time. But *what* to do about it is another matter, not helped by their still being so mysterious. Even though the UK holds around a quarter of the world's population of breeding curlews, we have learned surprisingly little about them over the years. There are so many unanswered questions, and that knowledge gap seems a painful omission as they slip away.

What we are sure of is that the last 150 years have changed everything. Their traditional upland breeding areas once had enough calling curlews for them to become inextricably part of our imaginings, inspiring myth and folklore in abundance. Then, at the beginning of the twentieth century, the great curlew migration was under way. The invention of the breech-loading gun, which made shooting widely accessible, and the maintenance of heather moorland helped their numbers increase. The growing populations spread their wings and spilled downhill and into the lowlands. For the first time, they made new homes in lowland farmland, finding good nesting sites in insect-rich, damp fields and wildflower meadows. We had tempted curlews into our lives and we marvelled at the new songs that enriched our lives. Very quickly they joined the familiar coterie of loved farmland birds, to become as much a part of spring and summer as skylarks, yellowhammers and turtledoves. It was as though they had always been there, and we assumed they always would be.

The old-fashioned farming regime suited them well. The landscape was diverse, higgledy-piggledy, full of niches that served a whole array of wildlife. Many species of bird, mammal, insect and wildflower thrived. As 75 per cent of the land surface of the UK is used for either growing crops or grazing, this was valuable living space. Then, quite suddenly, we moved the goalposts. The shock of national food shortages in the Second World War increased demands on farmers. We wanted abundant, home-grown cheap food, and the only way to achieve this was to turn slow-paced, mixed farms into uniform, fast-paced killing fields. The agricultural revolution speeded up, intensified and increased production. It upped the use of chemicals to kill insects and to fertilise the soil. Hedges were removed to extend the growing areas and to allow ever-larger machines to work the land. As a means of getting more out of the same area, it's been highly successful. We have seen a four-fold increase in yield between 1945 and 2000.[1] About 55 per cent of our current food consumption is home-grown, which is the same as in the 1950s, even though the population of the UK has increased by 50 per cent. And it has been achieved without a large hike in prices. The average family in the 1950s spent a third of their income on food; today it is half that.

Nothing, however, is given for free. The cost was passed on to the land in the form of pollution of fresh waters, degradation and loss of topsoil, increased greenhouse gas emissions, flood damage and massive declines in wildlife. Human health was also affected as the incidence of asthma, certain cancers and allergies increased.

For those parts of the natural world that had come to rely on our traditional ways of producing food, the writing was on the wall. For curlews, the onslaught is constant. In early spring, large rollers flatten the ground ahead of planting, and shortly afterwards swift blades cut the pastures multiple times. Untold numbers of eggs and chicks perish. And if the machines don't get them, many fall prey to foxes, crows, ravens and badgers, the omnivorous predators that survive well in this new, disturbed landscape. Insects, a food source for the curlew chicks so crucial in the spring and summer months, have succumbed to pesticides and thinned out. Death through starvation is not unknown.

A hundred years after the new moon birds colonised our farmland, the decline was clear. Curlews are remarkably site-faithful and they continue to arrive each spring, drawn back to the same fields year on year, but they now touch down in the midst of trouble.

The intensification of farming didn't affect the uplands, but there are huge pressures here, too, and numbers are dropping. Drainage and improvement of the land for agriculture, forestry, leisure activities, increased livestock densities and predation continue to take their toll. And it is on the hills, peat bogs and heathlands, in what is commonly thought of as wild and remote land, that they are unwittingly embroiled in the most aggressive conflicts in conservation – namely turf-cutting, grouse moor management, predator control and renewable energy development. Curlews themselves excite no angst, but are

surrounded by anger and division, caught up in the cross-fire of cultural, social and economic conflicts.

Up on the moors and down in the fields we have created an incongruous situation where a bird of the wilderness, described by the author and naturalist W.H. Hudson as '… some filmy being, half spirit and half bird', now depends on us for its survival. The trouble is, we're not very dependable. We are highly political animals with differing agendas, very often separated by bitter divides.

And if all this conflict and tension isn't enough, looming on the horizon for curlews, along with everything else, is that most formless and formidable of man-made threats, the ever-growing menace of climate change. In 2016 the increase in carbon dioxide levels in the atmosphere surged to an astonishing 50 per cent higher than the average of the last ten years, and is now over 400 parts per million. The last time the Earth experienced a comparable concentration of CO_2 was three to five million years ago, when the climate was up to 3°C warmer, the polar icecaps were virtually nonexistent and sea levels were around 20 metres higher. The UK has already seen a one-degree rise in temperature over the last 100 years, and 0.5 degrees since the 1970s. This warming climate is predicted to bring wetter springs and summers, more torrential downpours, frequent floods and droughts and a shift in timing of the seasons. It's bad news for all of us, but for birds like curlews it could be devastating. Tiny chicks cannot withstand wet weather for too long before dying of hypothermia, and if there is a period of drought the ground becomes too hard for the adults to feed by probing the soil. An increase in heavy rainfall in winter also affects adults trying to tough out the coldest months of the year by the coast. There is already a measurable shift in the locus of wintering populations towards the east of Europe, perhaps because they now don't need to travel so far to find warmer winter weather.

It is, of course, of paramount importance that we continue to reduce greenhouse gas emissions if we are to contain the effects of a shifting climate in the long term. Some of the solutions on the table for reducing carbon emissions involve planting more forests to absorb carbon dioxide, and an increase in the numbers of wind and solar farms. These are often sited on damp, marginal areas to protect valuable land for crops, and they threaten to reduce further the places where curlews and other waders can nest and feed. Curlew conservation highlights how green agendas are increasingly clashing in these small crowded islands, where the landscapes of Britain and Ireland are more and more being forced to multi-task. As I walked across the British Isles, tracking the birds through their breeding season in both the lowlands and the uplands, I saw for myself the mismatch between what curlews need to thrive and how we use the land. Overlay a map of ideal curlew breeding habitat onto a map of the UK and Ireland showing present agriculture, industry and leisure, and the problems are obvious. Change that map to one of future land use, and the problems increase.

The issues that impinge upon this bird of meadow and moor are huge, no less than an ever-growing human population and the transformation of the Earth's atmosphere.

We will have to dig deep into our reserves of compassion for wild things to secure their future. And curlews can give us nothing in return but songs of the soul and a glimpse of wildness.

Some would argue that this is the way of things, that curlews were always living on borrowed time on these densely populated and busy islands. Only creatures that can fit into our agendas should keep their place – adapt or die. But then, I fear, we are heading towards what the eminent biologist Edward Wilson calls 'The Age of Loneliness', a time when only generalist scavengers will survive alongside us. The creatures of the niches, of an unpredictable, diverse and surprising world, cannot continue to exist. Faced with this miserable vision of a monochrome future, is it not better to hold on to beauty and wonder wherever we find it? At the moment curlews provide both all year round.

But how to hold on to them? I saw precious few curlews on my walk. Dispiritingly, much of the land they once occupied no longer rang with their calls. But on the upside, I met engaged, determined people doing what they can to hold on to the birds where they still survive. They mostly work alone, or in small groups, and most are financially unsupported. True passion, though, isn't driven by money (but it does help enable it). These fast-acting, pragmatic and dynamic conservationists are fired by the human engine of enthusiasm. I like to think of them as small mopeds, whizzing around the streets and dodging in and out of the traffic jams caused by the large and often lumbering trucks of government departments and some large conservation organisations. Unencumbered by having to please a large membership, or wait for the approval of a hierarchy, they can just get on with it. They are bright spots in an otherwise darkening sky, bringing hope of fair weather ahead, but they are largely isolated and unconnected. This was particularly true for Ireland and southern England. The northern moors of England and the uplands of Scotland and parts of Wales have the attention of the RSPB. Its top-down, uniform, more rigidly structured management allows the coordination of the complex and expensive five-year Trial Management Project (detailed in Chapter 3). This plan is using scientifically based management to tease out the main problems for upland curlews and find out what needs to be done to stem their decline, which is alarming even in their heartlands. Also, curlews seem to be benefiting from some of the ruthless management of grouse moors. It is in the low-lying peat bogs and marginal grasslands of Ireland and the lowland farmland of the UK where the situation is, quite simply, desperate. With this in mind, a series of Curlew Workshops, concentrating on curlew populations away from their strongholds, seemed to be a good way forward to build on the momentum of the walk, and the idea has been met with widespread support and enthusiasm.

The Irish workshop happened very quickly and took place just six months after I finished walking, at the end of 2016. It was supported by An Taisce (the National Trust for Ireland) and the Irish National Parks and Wildlife Service. It was hosted by the New Forest Estate, a golf club at Tyrrellspass, County Westmeath, situated right in the centre of Ireland. Poignantly, it is surrounded by peat bogs being cut for power generation. New Forest generously offered their venue for free, without which I doubt the meeting could have taken place. This happenstance came out of a fun night of drinking and storytelling in the house of Jean McMahon, who offered to put me up as she lived close to my route. The welcome was genuine and warm. The evening of craic with Jean's family made this one of the best nights of the trip. Her partner, Jimmy O'Sullivan, was the connection to New Forest and he offered to try to secure the free use of the venue. He was true to his word. A light of hope for curlews was born out of pure Irish generosity.

The workshop took place in the dining room of New Forest on a bright and sunny November day. The dining tables and chairs were rearranged to make a meeting room to accommodate 100 people from all kinds of backgrounds. Here, the real world of the curlew, wild, windy and rich in sound and atmosphere, was represented in a series of PowerPoint presentations showing graphs with precipitous declines. The most startling and sobering statement of the day was made by Alan Lauder, an environmental consultant: given the present population level of only 130 pairs of curlews nesting in Ireland, and the woeful number of fledglings they produce each year, they will be extinct as a breeding bird on Irish soil in around seven years, i.e., by 2023. The population graph showed a steep downward curve, plummeting to nothing in a very short time. The room was hushed, as the reality of the outside world became horribly clear.

The disquiet in the room at the end of the presentations gave way to a collective determination to turn things around. The result was the establishment of a Curlew Task Force, approved by Heather Humphreys, then the minister responsible for natural heritage, the government department with responsibility for wildlife and conservation. The Task Force's job is to drive the conservation of the last 130 pairs of curlews dotted throughout the country. It is being led by Barry O'Donoghue from the National Parks and Wildlife Service and is chaired by Alan Lauder.

Thirty people make up the Task Force, representing a wide range of interests from beef and milk producers to forestry and turf-cutters, as well as conservationists, academics and government agencies. They have no easy task. Southern Ireland is a complex place around which to manoeuvre, with powerful groups representing different interests, often at odds with conservation. Tradition and rights play a big part in how Ireland operates, and so, of course, does money. Wildlife organisations are much smaller and less mainstream than in the UK, so there is less organised pressure to help counteract the huge forces driving economic development. BirdWatch Ireland has around 14,000 members and is by far the largest (for comparison, the RSPB has over one million), and it does its best, as do An Taisce and the Irish Wildlife Trust. Even though these voices of protest punch above their weight, they are all too often drowned out by the roar of what is seen as economic progress. The Curlew Workshop therefore trod a delicate line, but it was determined to be inclusive, and to listen to all views. It offered a place at the table to anyone who could make a difference to the future of the curlew in Ireland. It was bound to be a robust meeting, and at times it certainly was, but it produced results.

An ingenious structure for what is now called the Curlew Conservation Programme was devised by the National Parks and Wildlife Service. It operates in the six main areas where curlews nest – hotspots identified in 2016 as holding sixty-eight breeding pairs, 55 per cent of the known total. Specific posts have been established, including Curlew Advisory Officers, who carry out surveys and advise on the practicalities of conservation; Nest Protection Officers, who protect the eggs and chicks during the breeding season (for example, with electric fencing, predator control and so on); Curlew Research Officers, who collect data; and, importantly and uniquely, Curlew Champions, who are the vital link between the project and the local people, a part of the conservation jigsaw that is all too often forgotten. The programme is still being developed, but having people out in the fields and in the communities with a specific remit for curlew protection has to be something to celebrate. This, combined with a new system of payments for farmers who have curlews on their land and who undertake to look after them, should bode well for the future. This initiative hasn't come a moment too soon. The results for 2017 show a further drop in curlew numbers; even in the hotspot areas just sixty pairs were found, compared to sixty-eight the year before. The report states, 'Of these sixty pairs, the breeding success of forty-four pairs was determined; with just fourteen pairs believed to have reared chicks. The total number

of juveniles recorded to have fledged was sixteen, representing a breeding productivity of 0.38 fledglings/breeding
pair, which is below the threshold required for a stable
population.' Southern Ireland has its work cut out, but the
Task Force is under way and determined to do what it can.

As I walked through the peat bogs of central Ireland, I
witnessed at first hand the devastation of the inland raised
bogs. The once vast areas of unique habitat have been fragmented and turned into farmland, or ploughed up and
burned in peat-fired power stations. It was a highly visible
cause of curlew decline. The use of the bogs is one major
concern, but industrial levels of peat extraction are being

phased out over the next decade in favour of greener fuels. Perhaps the biggest threat that curlews face in Southern Ireland is the proposed increase in forestry to offset increasing carbon emissions. Ireland is failing to meet its European obligations to reduce CO_2 by 20 per cent by 2020. Emissions from agriculture are, in fact, expected to rise by 7 per cent, and as farming contributes nearly half of Ireland's greenhouse gas emissions, the trend is decidedly going the wrong way. For example, the expected 16 per cent increase in dairy cows by 2020, with the associated demands for silage, can only result in more emissions and present more challenges for field-nesting waders like curlew. Ireland's Environmental Protection Agency report states, 'It is clear that Ireland faces significant challenges in meeting emission reduction targets for 2020 and beyond. Further policies and measures above and beyond those already in place and planned in the period to 2020 are essential in order to position Ireland on a pathway towards a low-carbon, climate-resilient and environmentally sustainable economy.'

Faced with this stark assessment, the mitigation of increasing CO_2 emissions is essential, and more forestry is seen as one way to do that. Encouraged by government subsidies, 46,000 hectares of new forest is planned by 2020, along with nearly 1,000 kilometres of forest roads. Private investment companies are taking advantage of the Government's tax-free incentives and buying up marginal grasslands and what is called High Nature Value farmland, in order to plant trees. All too often these are densely packed stands of non-native Sitka spruce. Sitka is a fast-growing conifer that already makes up more than half of all Ireland's forests. Even small-scale farmers on marginal land are being encouraged to devote their 'non-productive' land to trees. Not only can this eat directly into areas needed by wildlife like curlews, skylarks, meadow pipits, cuckoos, red grouse, hen harriers, marsh fritillary butterflies, orchids and so on, it also further fragments the landscape and provides more habitat for foxes, badgers and crows. Many species of ground-nesting birds, including curlews, won't nest in an area of up to 500 metres around woodland because of the presence of predators. The amount of suitable nesting land that is taken out of use is therefore greater than just the area of plantation.

A bewildering situation now exists in Ireland, whereby one farmer with nesting curlews on his land may receive subsidies to protect them, while their next-door neighbour could be being paid to plant forest that removes feeding and roosting areas, as well as sheltering the predators that threaten them and their young. In effect, tax payers' money is being used to plant up the last few remaining habitats needed by rare and declining birds like the curlew and the hen harrier – birds that Ireland is required by European law to protect.

It may seem like a hopeless situation, but we have to believe it isn't. Paddy Sheridan, the conservationist in County Kildare (introduced in Chapter 6), wrote to me at the end of 2017 to tell me that progress is being made with turf cutters in the area and there is a renewed spirit of cooperation to find a solution. There is still a love of curlews in Ireland, especially amongst the older generation, who can remember what a positive presence they were in their younger lives. Hope lies in that ancestral love of wildlife and, once tapped into, it may be powerful enough to turn things around. And, as an early Christmas present, in December 2017 it was announced that a number of projects in rural Ireland are to be funded under the new European Innovation Partnership. One of the projects that was successful in receiving support under this programme was for Curlew Conservation. It is a welcome boost for the Irish birds, and it is one step at a time, but each step takes us closer to saving curlews in Ireland.

Going deeper into the issues affecting curlews reveals what a complex, contradictory web of legislation we weave around ourselves and the natural world. Birds like curlews depend on this fragile tapestry, but at any moment it could unravel if the economics fail to stack up. In Ireland, it may already be too late, but at least for the time being the birds have, in just a few areas, been given a reprieve from the onslaught of economic development. They have been granted some time to build up numbers that may give them the resilience they need for future survival. But they must respond quickly and increase their numbers to a sustainable level as there is no guarantee that help will continue beyond the next few years. The measures put in place by the Task Force seem to be the only hope they have.

An injection of hope is also needed in the south of England. The Walk revealed the gaping north-south divide, where the vast majority of resources given to curlew conservation are concentrated in northern upland moors and hill farms. Therefore, the Call of the Curlew Workshop

took place in February 2017 at the headquarters of the
Wildfowl & Wetlands Trust in Slimbridge, Gloucestershire.
It was also supported by the Gloucestershire Wildlife Trust
and the RSPB. Just as the Irish workshop had shocked
people into urgent action, so too did this meeting. The area
under review encompassed everything south of an imagi-
nary line between The Wash and Shrewsbury. Before the
meeting, knowledge about southern curlews was sketchy
and incomplete. What the day revealed was that fewer
than 300 pairs still hang on, in pockets of up to forty pairs.
They are dotted through the land from Cornwall to
Shropshire and over to Breckland. Widespread and thin on
the ground, for sure, but still a definite presence. As in
Ireland, small groups or individuals were doing conservation work in their own patches, but there was little commu-
nication between them.

As the day progressed, a number of things became clear.
The first was that southern birds occupy a surprising variety of landscapes. They nest in wet flushes on the top of
Dartmoor, in hay meadows along the River Severn, and the
Upper Thames valleys; elsewhere their nests can be found
in silage fields in Shropshire, in the seasonal wet fields of
the Somerset Levels, and peatland in the New Forest and
acid grassland in Breckland. A small but increasing number,
around ten pairs, are even nesting on the dry, chalky vegetation of Salisbury Plain. The pressures facing the birds and
their habitats are very different to their northern relations,
and there is work to be done to understand their needs.

The second revelation was the breadth of the problems
they face, from intensive agricultural activities to the

extraordinarily high levels of predation. Often over 90 per cent of the nests are destroyed at the egg stage, mainly by foxes and crows. And there is an awful lot of human disturbance. The south of England is densely populated, and increasingly so. People are everywhere doing all kinds of activities, and the impact on wildlife is growing. Birdwatching and photography were cited as a major cause of disturbance on Dartmoor, while dog walking is affecting the birds in the heathland of the New Forest and the Hams around Gloucestershire. While codes of conduct can be imposed in nature reserves, curlews rarely nest in them (the RSPB reserve of West Sedgemoor, in Somerset, is one exception). Their fate therefore lies in the hands of private landowners, many of whom have no idea that the birds are there in the first place or that they are in such a perilous state. Dartmoor, for example, has only four pairs left, but only one pair regularly attempts to breed. Dartmoor has seen just three fledglings survive in twelve years. The population of curlews in the New Forest has plummeted from 120 pairs in 2007 to just forty today, with only a handful of chicks recorded. There has been a decline of over 50 per cent of pairs of curlew in the farmland of the Upper Thames valley in Oxfordshire over the same period, with fewer than forty known pairs, and little is known about how their fledglings have fared. The study described in Chapter 8, carried out in the Curlew Country of Shropshire, saw no chicks fledge from a total of forty nests in 2015 and 2016, every egg and chick was predated or fell foul to agricultural machinery.

The situation in the south of England is therefore as desperate as it is in Ireland, with the birds heading for local extinction in many places. The solution that emerged during this workshop day, however, was not a Task Force along the Irish lines, but a Forum. There was overwhelming support for a central hub, to be called the Curlew Forum, which could disseminate information and act as a link between the various southern groups. Phil Sheldrake from the RSPB, Geoff Hilton from the Wildfowl & Wetlands Trust, ornithologist Mike Smart and I now collect reports from the groups for each breeding season, gather and disseminate ideas and practical advice and organise yearly meetings for group representatives. An ambitious mission statement was agreed:

> Our goal is to work with farmers and land managers to reverse the current decline, and continue monitoring the status of breeding curlew across southern England. We will do this by sharing knowledge and experience, raising awareness, offering advice, and securing funding to implement effective conservation measures.

All of this information is available on a new website, www. curlewcall.org, which is available to everyone who wants to know more about the practicalities of curlew conservation. The interest generated has attracted others in the south who would like to take part, and who think they may have curlews nesting in their areas. The network is spreading, as are new initiatives, such as the technique known as 'headstarting', whereby eggs are taken out of the wild under licence, incubated in captivity and then either the eggs or chicks released back into the wild again.

Headstarting has now been trialled in Shropshire and is being considered by other groups such as in Dartmoor, with advice provided by WWT. The Forum is also establishing a standardised method of collecting and recording data so that the observations and numbers collected about southern curlews can be used for a national database.

The Curlew Forum can only work because of the deep-seated and profound love of wildlife that exists in British society. Britain is unique in having so many wildlife charities dedicated to everything from seaweed to red deer. Monitoring, recording and documenting the flora and fauna of the UK have been centuries-old pastimes. Gilbert White, Charles Darwin, many country vicars and Edwardian ladies, plumbers and professors have all contributed to a long and rich history of a love of nature, and have furnished us with a vast wealth of data. Britain must be the best-studied country on Earth. Everything that flutters, flies, blooms or creeps has had the undivided attention of armies of fascinated observers for generations. There are fewer field naturalists today, volunteers who can name and record their local wildlife; the skills of the naturalist are fading away, but they still exist, and birdwatchers are by far the largest group. Southern curlews are therefore fortunate to have bands of passionate birders concerned about their future. Providing a focal point for curlew groups, in the form of Curlew Forum, has so far proved very successful in bringing everyone together.

'Torrential rain, hurricane-force winds and snow are about to batter swathes of the country as Storm Georgina tears in from the Atlantic,' shouted the *Express*, the day before the third curlew workshop in Builth Wells in central Wales, on 24 January 2018. Throughout the night I lay awake listening to it rattle and pound the window of my bed and breakfast, worrying that just the main organisers might turn up. But at 7.30am, it was as though someone turned off the switch. Georgina flounced out of Wales as quickly as she hurtled in. The hills overlooking the Royal Welsh Agricultural Showground were lit by a timid sunrise, peeking out to make sure the coast was clear. As light glinted off the puddles in the car park, we all breathed a sigh of relief.

The workshop was funded by Natural Resources Wales (NRW), the RSPB, the Welsh Ornithological Society, Ecology Matters and the Game and Wildlife Conservation Trust. In total 121 people turned up, more than we had planned, and at least another forty would have liked to have come. TV presenter and naturalist, Iolo Williams, opened the meeting with a speech that marked the tone for the rest of the day: positive, forward-looking, collaborative and anchored in a love of the natural world. He described that, for him, the call of the curlew captured the spirit of the Welsh hills. As a young boy, he remembered walking with his grandfather, or *taid* in Welsh, in the Berwyn mountains, absorbing his gentle wisdom as curlews flew overhead. It reminded me of John Muir's stories of his early years in Scotland. He too learned about wildlife from his grandfather, finding joy in the everyday creatures of local places. Discovering a nest of mice in a haystack took the three-year-old John to the edge of ecstasy, and I imagine Iolo was the same. Then, said Iolo, he became 'a bag of hormones, more interested in girls and beer than nature,' and moved to London. But even in the middle of cars and concrete, remembering the call of the curlew anchored his soul in the valleys and hills many miles to the west.

Iolo's messages could not have been more apt. He touched on the Welsh love of the bird that signifies *hiraeth*, a deep yearning and longing for the Welsh homeland. He appealed to memory and culture by reminding people that there are at least thirty different local names for curlews, many relating to the bill and the beautiful calls. And, importantly, he asked everyone to approach the solutions to their peril with open hearts and minds. There is no time for assumed boundaries, he warned, the birds will disappear from the Welsh landscape if we don't honestly and openly consider all options on how to help them. It was music to my ears as I looked around the room at the RSPB sitting next to the Countryside Alliance sitting next to farmers sitting next to local government sitting next to the Gamekeepers Association, and of course, many enthusiastic birdwatchers.

Iolo's inspiring start to the day was underlined by a morning of presentations on the status and fortunes of curlews around Wales, including a sobering assessment of the Welsh population by Patrick Lindley, Senior Ornithologist for NRW. There are, he said, perhaps fewer than 400 breeding pairs left. There was a shocked silence in the room as the figure most often quoted is around 1,000. There is no doubt that much needs to be done, and done quickly.

The fact-finding talks were rounded off by Steve Redpath, Professor of Conservation at the University of Aberdeen. Free of PowerPoint and graphs, he simply stood in front of the audience and stressed the importance of working together from the start: 'It isn't going to be easy getting curlews back, but without building strong collaborations, exposing ourselves to different views, debating and listening, getting political and public support for some difficult choices and funding collaborative science to our advantage, I would argue it will be nigh on impossible. Don't underestimate the challenge created by not moving forward together and don't underestimate the power of moving forward together with a shared goal.' In those few words, Steve laid down the challenge to all of conservation in the UK and Ireland.

A shared goal, however, does not guarantee a shared route to obtaining it. The only time in the day when there was a shift in the mood of the room was when Geoff Hilton from the Wildfowl & Wetlands Trust suggested that the high numbers of foxes throughout the lowlands could be related to the release of 35 million pheasants into the countryside each year by the shooting industry. This must, he proffered, be keeping more foxes alive to eat more ground-nesting birds like curlews in the spring, making predator control a necessity in some areas. The research on this has yet to be done, but if the conversation had developed, I am sure there would have been tension.

'People come to these issues with different understanding, experiences and values,' said Steve. 'Some would wish to concentrate on habitat management and feel uncomfortable about killing predators. Others recognise the value of killing predators, especially for ground-nesting species such as curlews. These positions are often very strongly held and, it seems, difficult to reconcile. We live in a polarised and adversarial world, where people often seek to impose their world view onto others ... But if you all want to get curlews back, then you need to take ownership and work in partnership with those you disagree with.' It is a tall order, not just for curlew conservation, but for many other species too.

The afternoon was dedicated to discussions in groups on the practicalities of saving Welsh curlews, and five main measures were identified: to establish an All-Wales Curlew Working Group, to implement immediate monitoring of key curlew populations, develop curlew-specific agri-environment schemes, engage farmers and landowners in the whole process, and raise public awareness of the decline of curlews. At the time of writing, these action points were being incorporated into an action plan drawn up by NRW, and the Welsh Ornithological Society had offered to drive it forward. The challenge now is to make this happen as quickly as possible, as the loss of each breeding season is a step closer to regional extinction.

The Welsh Curlew Workshop was an energising and inspiring day. Different organisations and their supporters came together for the sake of curlews and if that spirit continues then there is hope that Wales will turn the tide for the new moon bird. Steve Redpath summed up the challenges that lie ahead. 'I would argue that the most fruitful way forward is likely to be through investing in

building collaborative partnerships where you can deliber-
ate and debate with those you disagree with and decide
what the priorities and actions should be. Such approaches
are not easy – they require energy, time, trust, a willingness
to engage, to listen and to empathise. They also require
humility.' Humility and empathy are rare words in conservation circles, they stood out amongst the usual conservation terminology and were refreshing to hear. They seemed
to strike a chord with the audience. Steve went on to say
that partnerships on their own must be combined with
good science. Without the scientific basis for action the
divisions simply form again as people take an emotional
rather than objective view. Balancing all of this is the fine
art of good conservation. It is not always achieved, but it
felt like the agenda had shifted that day. I hope the same
desire to work across boundaries will be manifest in the
4th Curlew Workshop, to be held in Scotland at the end of
2018.

When I set out on the Curlew Walk in April 2016 I
thought I would simply be on a fact-finding mission,
coupled with an exploration of the rich contribution that
curlews have made to our lives. I imagined that the solution to their decline would be raising awareness of their
plight and restoring their habitat. If this could be achieved,
all would be well. That proved to be naïve. I was, in fact,
heading straight into some of the most complex and difficult conservation issues of our time, issues involving
culture, class, politics and economics. What emerged from
all the subsequent talks and debates was that the most
pressing issues that bear down on wading birds like curlews

are the leviathans of climate change, how we feed ourselves, and how we will deal with the predator imbalance we have created across the land. The protection of wildlife like curlews draws us into ontological arguments about how we see our place on Earth alongside other species, and the rights we assume for ourselves over the natural world.

They also challenge us to think outside political and national boundaries – on the scale of landscapes. Curlews bind the coast to inland mountain slopes, and pretty much everything in between. They link county to county, country to country and the UK to Europe. They reinforce our global responsibility for life on an interconnected planet, yet this is not always a concept that is easy to accommodate.

The workshops have also suggested that we cannot for much longer avoid the issue of predator control. This nettle often proves too painful to grasp. Most wildlife organisations are reluctant to talk about it publicly for fear of alienating their memberships. The evidence, however, clearly shows that without reducing the number of, usually, foxes and crows in the breeding season, ground-nesting birds like curlews will not survive even the first half of the twenty-first century. It is an uncomfortable fact, but it is the reality of the situation we have created. Our fragmented landscapes, warming climate and the spread of urbanisation have increased the numbers of those animals that are good at exploiting our intense and peopled landscapes. The same process has decreased the niches available for more specialist creatures that need diversity. There is no easy way for us to put this right. Shooting foxes or trapping crows is distasteful for many people who love wildlife, myself included, but I cannot see an alternative in the short term in the areas where ground-nesting birds like curlews still breed. Any control has to be what I term LTP: Local to the nesting area; Targeted to the predatory species known to be a problem (which varies from place to place); and Proportionate (not overkill, if you will forgive the pun). Releasing Armageddon on generalist predators would be utterly wrong; our response has to be sensitive and balanced, and only employed until the numbers of birds builds up again and they can fend off predators themselves. But this is a message that not everyone wants to hear.

The series of Curlew Workshops helped bring into focus all of this complexity and controversy, but it also brought together people who are passionate about creating a future for these birds. They revealed the immense difficulties that curlews face, but also the real love that exists for them. I have no idea whether the initiatives that have emerged are enough to secure their future, but at least we will have tried to help one species of curlew in one part of the Earth.

Out of the eight curlew species around the world, two have already most likely gone extinct. The last reliable sightings of the Eskimo curlew, a migrant species between Patagonia and the Arctic, were recorded in the early 1960s. They were once one of the most numerous water-birds in the world, until changes to the North American feeding grounds, and the greed of hunters that shot two million birds a year, ended the spectacle of their massed flights across the Americas. The last confirmed record of a single slender-billed curlew, another long-distance migrant whose peregrinations took it from Siberia to the Mediterranean, was in the late 1990s. After extensive searches, they too seem to have slipped away. Three out of the remaining six species are in various degrees of peril, including the Eurasian Curlew, and appear under the headings of Endangered, Vulnerable and Near-Threatened, titles no creature wants to inherit.

The cry of curlews is telling us about the state of wild, wet places, and reminding us of what we may lose. The unbearably sad, yet beautiful, *Last of the Curlews*, by Fred Bodsworth, imagines the final migratory flight of the last two Eskimo curlews on Earth. The female is shot by a hunter over North America, before they can reach their destination, leaving the male to arrive alone in the Arctic. He calls his haunting mating song to his lifelong partner in vain, but her body lies in the mud many miles to the south:

> The snow-water ponds and the cobblestone bar and the dwarfed willows that stood beside the S twist of the tundra river were unchanged. The curlew was tired from the long flight. But when a golden plover flew too close to the territory's boundary he darted madly to the attack. The Arctic summer would be short. The territory must be held in readiness for the female his instinct told him soon would come.

It is a painful read. In the afterword, Nobel physicist Murray Gell-Mann wonders if we have learned the lessons from their demise, from our careless and casual assumption that they will always be there. He writes that, 'Seeking greater wisdom includes learning how to be a good ancestor as well as a caring relation.'

Being an ancestor of whom future generations will be proud is a daunting task. It will require a lot of us. The last forty years has seen a 50 per cent decline in the mass of wildlife on planet Earth. In the UK, half the number of birds sing and bees buzz, there are fewer flowers in the meadows, and fish in the sea. Overall natural sound, colour and vibrancy in our lives have diminished. Starkly, the 2016 State of Nature Report described the UK as one of the 'most nature-depleted' countries on Earth. The memory of a land alive with wildlife is fading away and a threadbare landscape is becoming the norm. E.O. Wilson's predicted Age of Loneliness is dawning. The challenge is to transform the twenty-first century into the Age of Abundance.

Perhaps curlews have a part to play in making this happen. Recounting their myriad myths and legends about life, death, joy and hope reminds us that the natural world is an endless repository of wonder and creativity. Their haunting calls have the ability to coalesce emotions, and they have inspired stories so rich that they expose our psyche, allowing us to express what is so often difficult to articulate. They touch the spiritual as well as excite the scientific, they are both known and mysterious, making them binders of different worlds. Birds like curlews have contributed so much to our cultural, scientific, aesthetic and spiritual lives, and inspire so much of what makes us human. To lose them would be to diminish ourselves, and to diminish our ability to express what we feel so deeply.

We are fortunate that they are still with us, and we have time to do the right thing – to allow them to live wild lives on a whirling, blue, sparkling planet that we all call home. Astronauts who first looked back on planet Earth from the early space missions were moved by the sight of this iconic blue marble wrapped in lace, unique and full of life. Space Shuttle astronaut Loren Acton wrote:

> Looking outward to the blackness of space, sprinkled with the glory of a universe of lights, I saw majesty – but no welcome. Below was a welcoming planet. There, contained in the thin, moving, incredibly fragile shell of the biosphere is everything that is dear to you.

He was deeply moved by what he saw, and if he could have heard the Earth, too, he could somehow have listened in to our singing planet, he would have heard wind, rain, oceans, thunder, the songs of whales and the howling of monkeys. He would have heard the rich and varied music of birds and would have caught the haunting sound of *hiraeth*, of love, loss, joy and sorrow that is the call of the curlew. It would be a tragedy if, on our watch, we let that cry fade away from the song of the Earth.

Notes

Chapter 1 – WHAT IS A CURLEW?

1. Alan McClure, 'Schrödinger's Curlew' (2011)
2. Norman MacCaig, 'Curlew' (1987) © The Estate of Norman MacCaig. Reproduced with permission of the Licensor through PLSclear
3. Alan McClure, 'Schrödinger's Curlew' (2011)
4. C.S. Lewis, *Surprised by Joy: The Shape of My Early Life* (1955)
5. Ted Hughes, 'Curlews Lift'
6. Lord Edward Grey, 'The Charm of Birds' (1927)

Chapter 2 – BEGINNING AT THE END

1. *Scottish Birds*, vol 31, 'Satellite Tracking of a Curlew migrating between Scotland and Finland', R.H. Dennis, B. Etheridge, S. Foster, J. Heaton & R.L. Swann (2011)
2. 'The Great Rush of Birds on the Night of 29–30 March', as observed in Ireland by R.M. Barrington, M.A. Published in the *Irish Naturalist*, Vol. XX, June 1911

Chapter 3 – ARRIVING IN IRELAND

1. Jeremy Hooker, *The Cut of the Light: Collected Poems 1965–2005* (2006)
2. 'The Seafarer', Anglo-Saxon poem
3. Parish of Glenwherry, Co. Antrim Statistical Account (1836)
4. James McKowen, *The Harp of Erin* (1869)
5. Desmond Nethersole-Thompson, *Waders: Their Breeding, Haunts and Watchers* (2010)
6. Ted Hughes, *The Hawk in the Rain* (1957)
7. Austin Clarke, *The Singing Men at Cashel* (1936)
8. *The Collected Works in Verse and Prose of William Butler Yeats*, Vol. 8 (of 8)

Chapter 4 – THE LAND OF LAKES

1. John Clare (1793–1864), 'Landrail'
2. RSPB Lough Beg Management Plan (2010)
3. T.P. Flanagan, 'On Arney Bridge' (1945) © The Estate of T.P. Flanagan
4. Moira O'Neill, 'The Fairy Lough' (1901)

Chapter 5 – ENTERING EIRE

1. John Wesley (1703–1791), *The Journal of the Rev. John Wesley, A.M.*, edited by Curnock, Nehemiah; Telford, John (1851–1936)
2. W.B. Yeats, *Four Years: 1887–1891* (1921)

Chapter 6 – INTO THE BOGS

1. John Moriarty, *What the Curlew Said* (The Lilliput Press, 2007)
2. A report on bog development, *London News*, 28 September 1850
3. Bord na Móna website: https://www.bordnamonaliving history.ie/, A history of peat extraction in Ireland
4. Founding Father Dr. C.S. 'Todd' Andrews (1901–1985), Scéal na Móna, Vol. 13, no. 41, April 2002, pp18–21
5. W.B. Yeats, 'The Countess Cathleen' (1892)
6. James Jennings, *Ornithologia; Or, The Birds: A Poem in Two Parts* (1828)

Chapter 7 – INTO WALES

1. Roger Lovegrove, Graham Williams, Iolo Williams, *Birds in Wales* (1994)
2. Robert Burns, 'Letter to Mrs Anna Dunlop' (1789)
3. Alice Gillington, 'The Seven Whistlers', Edmund Clarence Stedman, ed. (1833–1908). *A Victorian Anthology* (1837–1895)
4. Pearce-Higgins, J.W., Stephen, L., Langston, R.W., Bainbridge, I.P. and Bullman, R., 'The distribution of breeding birds around upland wind farms', *Journal of Applied Ecology*, 46: 1323–1331 (2009)
5. National Assembly for Wales Renewable Energy (August 2013)

Chapter 8 – SOUTHERN ENGLAND CURLEWS

1. Richard Murchison, 'On the Silurian System founded on the geological researches in the counties of Salop, Hereford, Radnor, Caermarthen, Brecon, Pembroke, Monmouth, Gloucester, Worcester, and Stafford; with descriptions of coal fields and overlying formations' (1839)
2. Walter White, *All Around the Wrekin* (1860)
3. Magdalene Weale, *Through the Highlands of Shropshire on Horseback* (1935)
4. H.W. Timperley, *Shropshire Hills* (1947)

Chapter 9 – CURLEW MOORS

1. R.S. Thomas, 'The Minister' (1953)
2. Dallimer M., Tinch D., Acs S., Hanley N., Southall H.R., Gaston K.J. & Armsworth P.R., '100 years of change: examining agricultural trends, habitat change and stakeholder perceptions through the 20th century', *Journal of Applied Ecology*, 46 (2), pages 334–343 (2009)

Chapter 10 – CURLEWS AND CONTROVERSY

1. John Muir, *My First Summer in Sierra* (1869)
2. David Hey, *A History of the Peak District Moors* (2014)
3. Whitfield, D.P. & Fielding, A.H., 'Analyses of the fates of satellite tracked golden eagles in Scotland', *Scottish Natural Heritage Commissioned Report No. 982* (2017)
4. https://news.gov.scot/news/golden-eagle-deaths

5. www.langholmproject.com
6. http://jncc.defra.gov.uk/pdf/jncc441.pdf
7. https://www.gov.uk/government/uploads/system/uploads/attachment_data/file/491818/hen-harrier-action-plan-england-2016.pdf
8. https://ww2.rspb.org.uk/community/ourwork/b/martinharper/archive/2017/09/04/the-conservationist-39-s-dilemma-an-update-on-the-science-policy-and-practice-of-the-impact-of-predators-on-wild-birds-4.aspx1
9. G. Matt Davies, Nicholas Kettridge, Cathelijne R. Stoof, Alan Gray, Davide Ascoli, Paulo M. Fernandes, Rob Marrs, Katherine A. Allen, Stefan H. Doerr, Gareth D. Clay, Julia McMorrow, Vigdis Vandvik, 'The role of fire in UK peatland and moorland management: the need for informed debate' (2016)
10. http://ec.europa.eu/eurostat/statistics-explained/index.php/Agriculture_-_greenhouse_gas_emission_statistics

Chapter 11 — SEEING THE LAST CURLEW

1. https://www.rspb.org.uk/Images/naturalthinking_tcm9-161856.pdf
2. W.S. Graham, *Two Love Poems in New Collected Poems* (2015)
3. David Rothenberg, Tina C. Roeske, Henning U. Voss, Marc Naguib, Ofer Tchernichovski, 'Investigation of musicality in birdsong', *Hearing Research*, Vol. 308 (2013)
4. John Coulter, 'A Rhyme of Two Worlds' (1946), in *Irish Writing in the Twentieth Century: A Reader*, edited by David Pierce (2000)
5. John Fowles, *Wormholes* (2010)
6. Langston Hughes, 'Dreams', from *The Collected Poems of Langston Hughes* published by Alfred A. Knopf/Vintage. Copyright © 1994 by the Estate of Langston Hughes.

Chapter 12 — REFLECTIONS

1. Dallimer M., Tinch D., Acs S., Hanley N., Southall H.R., Gaston K.J. & Armsworth P.R., '100 years of change: examining agricultural trends, habitat change and stakeholder perceptions through the 20th century', *Journal of Applied Ecology*, 46 (2), pages 334–343 (2009)

Acknowledgements

Deep gratitude to Professor Tim Birkhead, Brian Clarke and Kate Copestake for their invaluable comments on every chapter. Huge thanks to everyone who donated to my crowdfunding – you made the walk a reality. Also to those who supported me with their art (Adam Entwistle, Jessica Holm, Anne Harrington Rees, Elkie Hector and Philip Snow) and sculptures (Fiona Smith Darragh), and Baron Brady for composing the lovely 'St Beuno and the Curlew' song which can be heard on my website. Also thank you to the following for helping with publicity: wildlife sound recordist, Geoff Sample, for allowing me to use some of his curlew calls, *The Proclaimers* for letting me use their famous '500 Miles' song and Richard Steele for his photographs. Also huge thanks to Alison Hull for knitting me two incredible curlew-jumpers and Ilse Laddemann for making a pair of trousers. Thank you to Martin

Balacombe for taking on the daunting task of helping me get fit enough to do the walk and grateful hugs to my Irish aunts and friends who gave me such a good send-off from Enniskillen – Ursula Nugent, Elaine Duffy, Marian Kenny, Peggy Lowry, and also to Grainne Nugent and Pat Carlin, who were there in spirit.

Once on the walk, so much heartfelt thanks go to everyone who put me up, gave me lifts, fed me, sent me messages of support and kept me going. Only some of you are mentioned in the text, but every one of you is woven into the spirit of the book and I can't thank you enough for your kindness: Tommy Earley, Martina Fox, Nathy Gilligan and Thora Crooks, Noel Kiernan, Sean McDonagh, Brian Caffrey and Kathryn Finney, Jean McMahon, Monica Foran, Fiona Smith Darragh, Liam Moore, Ursula Nugent, Angie Davies, Mary Stevenson and Adrian Drake-Lee, Tim and Pat Higgins, Rachel Taylor and Steve Dodd, Nettie and Rob Collister, Nick and Celia Jenkins, Alyson and Richard Small, Randal and Sarah Sparrow, Maggie and Mark Turner, Denis at High Ash Farm Outdoor Centre, Jean Gollner, Tim and Miriam Birkhead, Karen and Nigel Lowthrop.

Thanks to Paddy Sheridan and Tom McCormack who organised fellow walkers and arranged a successful talk in Clane in Ireland. Also to Sheila Frazer, Mark Dowd and Martin Poulsom for walking companionship. Once back home, huge gratitude to Alison Steele and Martin White for providing a light-filled and quiet space to write in, and likewise to Mary Stevenson and Adrian Drake-Lee for their bolt hole in Bedford. To Mike Smart, Geoff Hilton, Phil Sheldrake, Tom Orde-Powlett, Amanda Perkins and Barry

O'Donoghue for being such great curlew-mates, and to Graham Appleton who is ever-ready with the right information when called upon. Love and thanks to all those friends who are always there, whether I'm down in the dumps or flying high. I'd also like to thank my editor, Myles Archibald, for having faith in me to write this book. And finally, the person who did more than anyone, thank you Julian, my husband, who is always with me every step of the way.

Index

Index